Dancing
on the Earth

Women's Stories of
Healing through Dance

To Roberta:
Dance, dance
wherever you may be:
And find your true rhythm.

as you walk the
earth may you
feel her rhythm
+ find your
own - true
dance
Wendy

FINDHORN PRESS

Dancing on the Earth

Women's Stories of Healing through Dance

Edited by
Johanna Leseho, Ph.D. &
Sandra McMaster, M.Ed.

FINDHORN PRESS

Published in 2010 by Findhorn Press, Scotland

ISBN 978-1-84409-545-2

Edited by Shari Mueller
Cover & Interior design by Damian Keenan
Drawings by Sandra McMaster
Printed and bound in the European Union

1 2 3 4 5 6 7 8 9 17 16 15 14 13 12 11

Published by
Findhorn Press
117-121 High Street,
Forres IV36 1AB,
Scotland, UK

t +44 (0)1309 690582
f +44 (0)131 777 2711
e info@findhornpress.com
www.findhornpress.com

Contents

DEDICATION

To the dancer in us all.
May you connect to the rhythm
of your own sweet wisdom.

ACKNOWLEDGEMENTS

This book has been a collaborative effort, from the time of its birthing to publication. We would like first to thank the women who joined us in this project, offering their stories, time and patience. Acknowledgement for patience also goes to our editor, Sabine Weekes and her team as we maneuvered through this process for the first time. We are grateful she and the folks at Findhorn Press helped this book to find its voice. A special thanks to Di Brandt for her editing support at the conception of this project and to Laurie Block who was invaluable as we brought it to completion. And finally we express our heartfelt gratitude to our partners, Laurie Block and George McMaster, who provided support, encouragement and belief in our abilities to bring these stories forth.

Blessings, J. L. and S. M.
January, 2011

I am happy even before I have a reason.

I am full of Light even before the sky
Can greet the sun or the moon.

Dear companions,
We have been in love with the Divine
For so very, very long.

What can we now do but
Forever Dance!

—HAFIZ

Dancing on the Earth

————

THIS BOOK IS ABOUT HEALING through connection and reconnection with our bodies. It is about the power of dance. The title, *Dancing on the Earth,* speaks to the desire and need to connect with our bodies by finding that which grounds us and brings us to our center. Contributors to this book come from around the globe, bringing with them different languages, experiences, training, and worldviews. Each of the authors offers both a different form of dance as well as a different perspective on movement and its relationship to healing.

The word "healing" is defined in numerous ways. For some it could entail a new way of viewing a situation, for others an ability to deal with life's circumstances, and for still others it would embody a full and unequivocal cure from dis-ease. As therapists, we see healing as a process or journey towards awareness, growth, and a new way of being in the world. The purpose of this book is to share the impact of dance on the lives of women and to offer it also as a tool that therapists can suggest to their clients. Expressive therapies enhance talk therapy and dance can be a powerful path to healing for some. We can, whether through dance or some other form of expression, discover a connection to something larger than ourselves that has the power to carry us forward.

Each of us was called to this book from different paths in which dance has influenced and inspired our lives. In the coming together of these stories is the story of all women who have felt silenced, depressed, or who have yearned to "be at home" in their skin, to find happiness and to connect with that which is Spirit. In her chapter, "Liturgical Dance as an Avenue to God," Kathryn Mihelick shares the following insight, "The non-verbal, visceral, experiential nature of movement makes it a language of the heart, a language that cannot be put entirely into words." This is the power of dance—the power to connect us to our hearts, to teach us to "listen" beyond the words to that which we feel, to "listen" to our emotional world and the sensations of our body in motion.

In the pages that follow, the "voice" of dance will take the reader on a journey of rhythmic movement, personal insight, and deep connection. Rhavina Schertenleib shares in "Dancing for Peace" that, "The intention of the dance is to give us back the meaning of human, planetary, and cosmic unity, celebrating this revolution through singing, meditation, and strong, vibrant dance." Here, dance is the vehicle for peace and the pathway for creating connection to oneself, one's community, and a larger universal vision.

All too often women are left to define their experience in silence and tend to minimize their own journey. In "God Loves Us When We Dance: Creative Movement as an Agent for Transformation," Johanna Leseho observes that "Dance offers transformation from a feeling of insignificance to knowing your own worth and being willing to (finally) inhabit the space you deserve."

This book is meant to celebrate, to uplift, and to beckon you to take your place in the world. As dancers and healers, we invite you, the reader, to take your place in the circle with us and allow our experiences to inspire you, to help you discover one more path to yourself, one more path to your passionate being.

Although this book is about dance as an avenue to wholeness and a means of expansion, not everyone will find their healing through dance. Perhaps it is your quiet time in the garden that provides you with a deep sense of peace and fulfillment. Perhaps it is singing in a choir when your voice, body, and soul resonate perfectly with the music and voices of others. Whatever your path, allow yourself to step firmly upon it and surrender to the healing power it offers. You will never regret it.

Go in peace,
Johanna and Sandra

CHAPTER ONE

God Loves Us When We Dance: Creative Movement as an Agent for Transformation

Johanna Leseho

Been Dancing All My Life

I'M FIVE YEARS OLD at summer camp in Ontario, Canada: pine trees, wooden docks, wide open playing fields, singing at mealtimes. Every Friday evening and Saturday morning the dining hall becomes a dance floor swirling with Jewish folk dances. Perhaps 150 or more campers and counselors, from five to fifty years old, holding hands, joined in circles, arms stretched upward as we move as one into the center in praise of life. Singing "Hava Nagila" (Let us Rejoice), we dance the Horah and other Israeli dances; spinning, skipping, laughing, feeling free and yet so much a part of the whole, connected to each other, to our history and tradition. I love camp so much I refuse to go home. They have to put another bunk bed in the cabin to make room for me to stay the second month.

Ballroom dance classes begin when I am seven or eight. Saturday afternoons my brother, sister, and I walk the eight blocks to the Latin American Dance Studio in Toronto. I'm excited as we climb the stairs. I love the music, love learning and practicing new steps each week, love showing off with my siblings at weddings and bar mitzvahs. The freedom I feel in allowing my hips to sway from side to side. Feeling the music move my body without any effort. Dancing with a partner, knowing that together we create a sparkling, glowing energy that everyone can appreciate and enjoy.

At eleven, I begin lessons in jazz and modern dance. The sense of freedom expands beyond my dreams. I'm leaping across the floor, filling the space of the studio, and my living room. The music draws out the movements, leading me into the next step, and then the next and the next. My body stretches and strengthens, becoming lithe and powerful. I'm beginning to live in my own skin, to control my own body and movement. I feel free, exhilarated, alive.

And then it stopped, the lessons, the encouragement. My father withdrew his payment for classes. He said he was afraid I'd want to become a professional dancer and that "all entertainers have a very sad life." He was saving me from myself. Maybe. Or maybe he was perpetuating his own life's tragedy. He'd given up his own dreams of becoming a concert pianist to make money for his family—first his parents, then his wife and children. It was the late 1930s when my parents' first child was born in Toronto. It wasn't a time when you could afford to be frivolous. Better to work at something you could rely on—first creating a printing business, then an electrical company—than to try to make a living in the arts.

But does it need to be all or nothing? Did he have to deny his love of music all together? We had a grand piano in our home that I never once heard him play. He never even turned on the stereo. I know he had accepted his role as breadwinner and acted out of his sense of responsibility. But I saw what denying his passion did to him, as he lay in bed for most of the last twenty-odd years of his life, staring at the ceiling, waiting to die. I wonder if seeing my light shine when dancing was so painful to him that he—unconsciously—needed to dull it. It certainly had that effect.

I followed my father's pattern in allowing my life to take a few other turns during my adolescence and young adulthood (it was, after all, the time of drugs, sex, and rock 'n roll) and denied the importance that dance held for me. I relegated it to the very back burner, something to be done at parties and very occasionally at home alone. This was during the years I most needed something to hold me grounded as I tried to navigate the tremulous years of adolescence. I didn't know I could have used dance to draw me out of the mild depressions and days of deep loneliness that I experienced all too often back then.

As I grew older and left home to find my way in the world, I still didn't know that I could dance to help me through the pain of separations and betrayal from girlfriends and lovers, or to create a center for myself from which to determine the appropriate professional and spiritual path to follow. Unsure of who I was, what I wanted, and how to honor both of these, I would allow myself to be swayed by the wants and needs of others. I didn't know I could dance my way through anxiety and fear or use it to expand my joy.

I spent years searching for a connection to the Divine in various spiritual paths, including Judaism, Buddhism, Sufism, Goddess Spirituality, and The Diamond Approach (a spiritual path that incorporates psychological processing). I attended countless personal development workshops to examine my own nature and how to open more to myself, to others, and to Spirit. I kept trying to improve, to become a better person, to learn more. It didn't really occur to me that I had the key within me. And though I learned a great deal from walking down these paths, if I had paid attention to what made my heart and soul sing, if I had listened, I could have danced my way to The Beloved and perhaps suffered less along the way.

I know that now. I've had some remarkable experiences that connected dance, spirituality, growth, and healing. After a sitting meditation early one morning at a retreat in Colorado, we went outside to be present for the sunrise. As the golden orb rose above the mountains, I felt my body connect with the sun and experienced it being filled with Spirit. My body was being danced up the road. I simply allowed the movement to flow through me, allowed my body to be moved by Spirit. There was an incredible rush of energy—a burst of joy that radiated from me—an inner glow deeply resonating with the warmth and strength of the sun's rays.

During a meditation and dance workshop, near the end of two hours of dancing with my eyes closed while my body was still moving rhythmically to the beat of the music, I experienced a deep stillness within. I touched the core of my being, the still center point of my essence. A channel opened inside me, from my head to my feet, that connected me deeply with God, Spirit, the Universe. Divine energy flowed between me and the heavens, connecting my essence with All-That-Is. As I continued to move and sway, tears streamed down my cheeks.

I've felt physically showered with grace while dancing the 21 Praises to Green Tara (Buddhist goddess of compassion) and witnessed the radiance of the divine feminine shining through me. And I wanted to know if other women felt the same. So I designed a research project to find out if other women also experience dance as a connection to the Divine, as an avenue for psychic transformation. I wanted to know how women use dance to move through the general stresses of life, and even to work through trauma, dancing to heal. And as a counselor, educator, I wondered if a counselor might support women in integrating dance into their lives in order to find creativity, strength, and healing.

My research led me to speak with twenty-nine women of numerous ethnic, cultural, and spiritual backgrounds in twelve countries (Canada, U.S., England, Australia, New Zealand, Persia, Brazil, India, Palestine, South Africa, Germany, and Japan), engaged in a variety of forms of movement. The women ranged in age from twenty-eight to sixty-seven, and worked in such diverse areas as education, counseling, management, leadership, health care, art, and dance.

Johanna as Tara: I am in my own Divinity

I asked each woman I talked with to tell me a story of how participating in creative movement has helped her survive life's challenges and experience spiritual growth. What follows is their response to this exploration. I've looked for themes that unite the women, suggesting their experiences might be relevant for many of us. Their stories are presented in their own words (using pseudonyms to protect their anonymity) so that they may speak for themselves. I've found that I am not the only one who finds her way to the Divine through dance. I've also discovered it is common for women to take refuge in movement to support them through the traumas and trials of life. In the words of one of the Dances of Universal Peace (as taught by Anahata Iradah during a Tara dance camp):

I sing,
I dance,
The eternal ecstasy of Being.
I call forth my Spirit into joy.
My suffering and fears have departed,
My body is filled with light! [1]

What the Stories Say

Universally, the women I spoke with describe dance as a natural healing for body, mind, and spirit. A few of them expressed with enthusiasm how, without thought or planning, their bodies knew instinctively that dance was their avenue to healing. As Anna put it:

> *"Whether I was in ecstasy or in despair, my body would naturally move when there was something to express."*

Some of the women I spoke with, however, lost their relationship to dance when life presented them with severe challenges or traumas, or it dropped away for lack of support. However, once dance became part of their lives, the process of healing began.

> *"I was frozen in fear and grief. Then one day I turned the music on and my body started dancing again, and it was like I forgot about everything and just embraced the joy of moving. And that was sort of the turning point of where I thought that it is definitely a healing thing, in that I had abandoned it but it found me again."*

Sophia described a time when she felt that she might die from all that she was forced to manage in her life as a young mother of two small children, negotiating a divorce. She developed "a sickness that could have been very serious… And then [I] started to dance and to just feel this overwhelming energy that started to come up from inside me… I felt my inner light start to get bigger again." By connecting to her authentic self, Sophia found that dance led her through a bigger healing journey. Once she identified what was important to her, other aspects of her life, as well as problems within her body, began to show themselves and so, could be engaged and healed. "It's like the doorways started to open beautifully to… bring a whole bunch of things together that integrated mind, body and soul back to a healthy, balanced place."

John Grinder, one of the founders of Neurolinguistic Programming, often said that if something's really stuck in your psyche, your life, or your spirit, you just move your body. Dance therapist Gabrielle Roth agrees that psychological healing will be achieved through movement of the body.[2] This was precisely the experience of the participants in this study. Ingrid, who had been trained in somatic psychology, stated that,

> "... it was invaluable for me to learn how, through breathing and movement, we can unblock ourselves. There is just so much blockage that happens because we don't move. So I think it is crucial, especially for women because we tend to be worriers... we take care of so many things."

The relationship between body and mind has become more widely accepted in Western mainstream culture in the recent past. We understand that chronically holding in strong emotions can lead to both psychological distress and physical illness. In her book, *Healing Through the Dark Emotions*, Miriam Greenspan argues that it is the inability or resistance to feeling our "negative" emotions that restricts true emotional wisdom and healing. Specifically, "aborted grief, fear, and despair are at the root of the characteristic psychological 'disorders' of our time—depression, anxiety, addiction, irrational violence, and psychic numbing." [3] Rather than trying to control these painful feelings, we might "use these energies for emotional, spiritual, and social transformation." [4]

But for many, the verbal expression of feelings remains unfamiliar, unsafe, or uncomfortable. As Claire, a teacher of belly dance, suggested, "Dance gives us a vehicle of expressing things that we have inside of us that we normally wouldn't express, and that is a wonderful healing." This message was repeated many times by many of the participants in the study, as the following statement expresses:

> "I think, too, when I dance, sometimes it's a huge release of the emotions and I end up bawling. But other times it's the most incredible joy that I can feel. Or it's like everything is in sync with you. Like my body and my brain and my emotions are all split off and jagged but then when I dance it all lines up."

Events often happen when we are too young to be able to process their meaning. The psyche will suppress thoughts, memories, feelings that create anxiety and disable the child from existing in the world. While we may grow into intelligent, competent, and responsible adults, these memories may remain unconscious. According to various therapeutic approaches, as long as something is hidden, it cannot be transformed. For true healing to occur, suppressed feelings must be brought into our awareness, examined, and moved through.

Not only does dance provide a release of emotions, it also draws negative experiences and memories from within the psyche and exposes them to the light of consciousness so that the individual may have an opportunity to heal at a deeper level. After being taught a particular sacred dance in a workshop, Miranda recalled how all of the women in the group were "hit with a ton of bricks that evening. Like all their pain, all their life experiences had hit them."

In other classes, dancers might cry or suddenly shiver or look like things are releasing in their bodies. A channel opens to the deepest parts of ourselves and we are supported in both healing and integration. So the dance has been a part of that process of opening physically, psychologically, spiritually, allowing these other pieces to come in.

A few of the women spoke of the sensation of becoming a more whole person. As Selingi stated, "When I dance I can feel something else inside of me comes alive." Some were more relaxed in themselves, so much happier and vibrant. Life became easier and soft and light. Julia realized, after a few years of engaging in different forms of dance, "There was a sadness or heaviness and shyness and a whole lot of different things that I've completely shifted; they're just gone."

One very important transformative aspect of dance for women is becoming more accepting of themselves, particularly their bodies. Many of the women in my study gained a connection to their feminine wisdom, energy, and beauty. In a culture that reveres a very narrow view of what a woman should look like, dance allows women to make peace with and be comfortable in their bodies regardless of their shape or size. For some, the healing was profound.

> "It taught me to stay in my body and embrace that part of me that I wanted nothing to do with because somehow it got all messed up and if you moved your hips or had a body that looked female then you deserved what had happened to you. So just to see women move their hips with control it was like power that I wanted, that my body could actually be powerful."

Denying our bodies and wishing to fade from the view of others is a natural response to physical and sexual abuse and often leads to anorexia.[5] However, through dance, Sarala learned to enlarge

> "... the tiny bit of space that I've taken up for so long. When I dance I take a whole block of space and my moves are usually really big and I can take up the entire park and it's... been an okay thing. Because, I mean, I spent my life curled up and hiding for fear of being found and hurt or just curled up on the inside because I was afraid of the world. And this is the first time that I take up space and I don't feel guilty about taking up the space."

It is easy to let the stressors and pressures of life wear us down, turn us away from our spiritual paths, and minimize our self-worth. Many of us forget who we are and what matters to us. We allow ourselves to be controlled and manipulated by others or by events. We cease to respond to situations and instead believe we can only react—automatically, defensively—without thought or intention. However, through dance we learn to grow into ourselves again and re-establish our true nature.

> *"Through my grief and loss, I had become very small... so when I started [dancing] again I realized that there's so much bigness in me... energy and light... it reminded me of who I was, because I had forgotten."*

For women in this study, dance is a way back to themselves. It is a way to let go of stress and release tensions out of the body. It is a healing of the heart, a way to move beyond anger and increase the ability to trust others and themselves. It can be a tool for survival. As Ellie declared, "The connection of body and mind kept me from going into depression." Dance offers transformation from a feeling of insignificance to knowing your own worth and being willing to (finally) inhabit the space that you deserve.

Not Just When We Are Dancing

Although we tend to compartmentalize our lives—this is work, this is family, this is entertainment—it doesn't actually work that way. Everything we think and do and feel is interconnected, and what occurs in one realm of our lives affects all the others. Having the experience of feeling freedom and connectivity inside of the class, you know how to have that outside of class. The women in this study were very aware of how their experiences of dance altered who they are, not just while dancing, but in other dimensions of their lives.

> *"And the better that I've danced the more that I've healed, the more I've understood that to dance tango you have to be on your axis, on your own center, and grounded... [And it] just kind of expands to the rest of your life so that the rest of your life goes back to that sense of being grounded, of being centered, of being on your own axis, so that as things come at you and hit you, you know where your emotional center is."*

Growth, transformation, and empowerment were all terms repeatedly used. Bonney (real name) taught belly dancing to teenage girls over a ten-year period. She said they learned to "honor their bodies as temples... [as] sacred vehicles for our souls. [Because of this] none of them had drug problems, none of them had drinking problems, none of them got into sexuality until they were, like, nineteen, twenty years old."

Dance teachers witness many experiences of growth and healing in their students. One group of women prepared for a dance performance over a two-year period. It was their teachers' belief that dance was able "to take their pain from the dying of the cancerous husband and from the dying mother and put it into grace... to see dance as a tool of transformation that you can go beyond. And it's not about getting [the pain] out of the way, it's about getting through it and digesting it and transforming it."

The benefits of participating in creative movement spread into many other areas of these women's lives. There were transformations in identifying and expressing "harder" emotions like anger, fear, or sadness; insights into themselves; changes in levels of trust; and openness to simply experiencing life as well as in meeting the demands of their lives. "When I come home I'm just all energized... dance feeds me to do all this other big responsible work that I have to do." Through dance, these women naturally developed healthier lifestyles. As one woman put it,

"I have been able to grow in a way that supports my health at a biological level (as opposed to rational or moral level). I am more of a 'type A.' In the past it was sometimes difficult for me to slow down, to the fate of my own destruction, like getting into accidents. Now I am able to harmonize better, to organically shift my speed."

We all contain both masculine (yang) and feminine (yin) characteristics. Masculine qualities include such things as muscular strength, analytical and rational thinking, active, assertive, and aggressive energy, as well as self-reliance and independence. Feminine qualities include passivity/receptivity, softness, compassion, nurturing as well as intuitive thinking, cooperation, and responsiveness.[6] For people to be fully balanced, they must have access to both their masculine and feminine natures and be able to draw from both yin and yang energies. Regardless of the form of creative movement the women in my study explored, there were numerous experiences of expanding their sense of themselves and their ways of being in the world. They came to recognize qualities and characteristics within themselves that were previously hidden from their consciousness. As Sherrill observed, the dance "brought forth strength of my body and expression, and that gave me an aspect of myself that I hadn't explored previously."

One of the dances I encountered in this study was the The Mandala Dance of the 21 Praises of Tara, created by Prema Dasara (real name) of Hawaii, as a means of embodying a particular Tibetan Buddhist meditation practice. Tara is considered the feminine aspect of the Buddha and the mother of all Buddhas. The 21 Praises address the qualities of Tara, qualities that we may each embrace and develop within ourselves. In the Mandala Dance, women move through a spiral formation until each reaches the center from which she is born as Goddess Tara. As Prema explains, women "go into psyche, relinquish inadequacy, and relate to being the Divine." Janet, another Tara dancer, described this sacred dance experience as "personally transforming for me. I love to present myself to the world as a goddess, that I am in my own divinity." Mona speaks of what she perceives to be the experience of all of those who participate in the Tara dance, "And by the end of the night, everybody who has come, we speak softer, we feel lighter, problems have dissolved."

Two of the women in the study live in Brazil. They described how difficult it can be for many living in the slums to hold onto that sense of the sacred, or of one's own power. Violence and drug abuse are rampant, growing out of poverty and homelessness. With the support of financial sponsors, a small group of young people are training to become leaders of Dances of Universal Peace, for they have found that doing these dances is bringing a change for the positive within their home communities.

Dances of Universal Peace, formulated by Samuel L. Lewis in the 1960s, are a form of spiritual meditative dance, where the dancers move in a circle while chanting sacred phrases that have been put to traditional or contemporary melodies in a wide range of languages, including Arabic, Persian, English, Hebrew, Hawaiian, and Sanskrit. Many believe that peace can be promoted through the experience of unity as the dancers come to understand that the same truth lies at the heart of all religions. At the same time, the practice is purported to develop the participants' spiritual awareness, awareness of their own body, and the awareness of the presence of others.[7] A few of the female trainees described their experiences of how these dances have helped them to move beyond their problems:

> *"I like the feeling that the dances bring to us. When I feel anguish, I sing and dance and so it dissolves, this feeling goes away and I feel light. I don't want to 'stay small,' I want to go out and interact." (16-year-old)*

> *"The Dances of Universal Peace make me feel peace inside. They help to dilute all the bad things I have inside of me." (20-year-old)*

> *"When I have a problem and I dance, at the end the problem is gone! These dances help to transform my life." (24-year-old)*

Dancing and Spirituality

Ultimately, I am convinced that it is the connection to one's sense of the spiritual that infuses dance with the power to heal and transform. Spirituality means many different things to different people. For some it is a connection to the mystery of life[8] or a willingness to trust.[9] Others might define spirituality in relation to a transcendental dimension,[10] and living a life that is consistent with knowing that Spirit dwells within each of us.[11]

Throughout the psychological literature, words like transcendence, wholeness, connectedness, and meaning appear repeatedly in relation to spirituality. Carl Jung believed that images of wholeness exist within the unconscious mind and come unbidden into our consciousness.[12]

They can support us in meeting our life challenges, and in the case of dance, can help us move through dark times with grace and greater ease.

> *"It was kind of like the dark night of the soul. A moment when I was 44 or 45, where I had a kind of betrayal in my relationship with my husband and a betrayal with a sister… And through the practice of these forms of sacred dance… one of the ways that I was able to traverse it was through the empowerment that happens when I allow my sacred nature, you know, my true sacred nature to step forward even in the midst of a human personality that was very devastated."*

For the women I spoke with, dance was at least one means of connecting to the sacred. Some talked about how they didn't get the whole God thing the way other people did. Those who left the church of their childhood said they missed the worship, the connecting to One but found that connection through the dance. "That pure release when you're dancing… is so close to worship. It's so close to that pure release of your spirit when you're worshipping. I can feel it like lightness inside." Dance brought many of the women I talked with back to their spirituality:

> *"Dancing has always brought me joy—it's a joyful thing. I found it as a way of communing in a spiritual way. I guess in a way I was forgoing my spirituality, and I kind of got back to it and that for me was through dancing."*

Dance also brought them back to a sense of themselves that they had lost, as one woman described:

> *"It's the thing that connects me to who I am or helps me figure it out. And when I dance in the park it feels like I connect to the sky and the stars and*

*everything else that's around there… I never knew that there would still be
that part of me that could have the joy that I hear everyone else talk about,
that I feel so sad I missed out on. When I dance, I feel what they talk about."*

For Laura, dance is an expression of joyous spirituality while Berte describes it as an
experience of pure bliss. Danielle claims,

*"It's a visceral thing. I think it actually is coming from my spirit and then
it comes through my body… There's an essence of being that is always
brought to my attention when I dance, so in a way it's very much like
meditating, it reminds you of your true spirit."*

There is a sense of embodying one's own essence. Many women use dance as their
spiritual practice. "I do it as something that helps my mood. It helps my spirit. It up-
lifts me… Even when we are alone, we are in company of a greater spirit. And when
we dance, we embody that greater spirit inside ourselves."

There is an old Sufi saying that states, "God respects us when we work, but loves us
when we dance." It appears that our own divine nature feels the same way.

• • • •

JOHANNA LESEHO is an associate professor in the Faculty of Education at Brandon University in Manitoba, Canada, as well as a certified Laughter Yoga instruc-
tor. Her introduction to dance started at age six and since then she has taken classes
in ballroom, jazz, modern, Indian, and African dance as well as Dances of Universal
Peace, Five Rhythms, Biodanza, Contact Improvisation, Authentic Movement, Ecstatic Dance, and Belly Dancing. She is also a student-teacher of the Mandala Dance
of the 21 Praises of Tara (Tibetan Buddhist Goddess of Compassion). Her most recent research project, "Coming alive: creative movement as a personal coping strategy
on the path to healing and growth," was the impetus for this book.

CHAPTER TWO

Contact Improvisation as Metaphor for Relationship to Self and Other

Jolie Pate

Discovering Creative Movement

D ANCING WAS FORBIDDEN in my family. My parents were both brought up in fundamentalist Christian homes where they were taught that dancing was sinful. This prohibition was passed on to me by the Church of the Nazarene and my family. As a child, I did not even suspect I had an interest in or a talent for dancing. Instead my love of movement revealed itself by being an active child. I was rather tomboyish in my outdoor games of cowboys and Indians, cops and robbers, and tree climbing. In young adulthood, I was active in aerobics and ice-skating, but it never occurred to me to explore dance, even though many times people pointed out that I seemed to enjoy movement. Dance was simply not an option in my awareness. Today, ten years after my first dance experience, I remain grateful to my friend Marilyn, who stretched my awareness into the world of dance by convincing me to attend one of the local dances with her. In that dance world, I discovered Contact Improvisation, which has influenced my way of being in the world.

Contact Improvisation owes its existence to the vision of its founder, Steve Paxton. Growing out of a series of experiments in the 1970s at Oberlin College in Ohio, Paxton involved many other dancers in its development, many of whom are still involved in its teaching. Paxton began by exploring commonplace movements like walking and standing. He then moved on to the specific movements arising from the pairing of bodies in the extremes of motion. The video *Magnesium*[13] documents these early beginnings, in which eleven men repeatedly fling themselves at each other, colliding, sliding, and falling onto cushioned mats. Contact Improvisation as a dance form grew out of these early experiments. Contact dancers find ways to pivot, roll, balance, and fall following sensation and the momentum of their moving bodies, without a predetermined plan or musical accompaniment. Nancy Stark Smith was a student watching these aikido-like moves and convinced Steve Paxton to expand this exploration to include women as well. Her sports background was instrumental in adding balance and recognition of the floor as a partner. Smith and Paxton continue to dance and teach. They founded *Contact Quarterly,* a journal that offers articles on the form as it exists today and connects this far-flung community.

The form has grown into a worldwide community practice, performed at local dances called jams. Jams occur weekly in many major cities in North and South America, Europe, Asia, Israel, Australia, and Africa. Groups of dancers who love the form come to know each other in community. It is a great pleasure to visit other Contact Improvisation jams while traveling.

After gaining a few beginning skills, I attended a dance on my own. I simply sprawled on the floor. Lying on my back, I waited for the urge to move to arise from within my body. I held no preconception of how this would show up. I waited with curiosity to let my body speak its desire. Within a few minutes, my arms and legs wanted to stretch and slide across the floor. I responded by slowly moving each body part as it requested. Soon I was moving smoothly, one movement blending into the next, staying on the floor as long as my body desired. In this movement, as I rolled over to my belly, I began to cry, a sob deep from within. For the first time I can ever remember, i was fully aware of being in my body. This contact of body and floor touched a place in me that was beyond desire, beyond body. It was in my soul. It was sacred. It was home, finally home, after all this time. My very being welcomed itself home.

The paradox of this particular journey home is that it is not possible to accomplish alone. Without others interacting with me as teachers, dance partners, and witnesses, I would not have achieved the same level of awareness of my own body in relation to the floor beneath my feet, and the people around me. I would not be as conscious of the rhythms in my body that set my unique pace, or the power of touch that aids me in finding the boundary of my own skin. I would not know the importance of being in my own dance while I share a dance with another. I would not know how to trust my safety to others while taking care of my own safety first. Establishing a relationship of trust with oneself, I have found, is the foundation of a safe and enjoyable dance experience, as well as the foundation of a safe and enjoyable relationship with others.

My first task in exploring Contact Improvisation was to understand what it meant to be "home." This turned out to be a twofold experience for me. The first home was in my body and the second home was in my spirit. My awareness shifted when I learned to tune into myself first as soon as I arrived at the dance. Before this awareness, I would typically walk into the dance and notice everything around me. I would note the good dancers and wish I could dance like them. I would look around the room and eliminate many of the possible dances because I judged the dancers would not want to dance with me. I would then find some friendly faces and join in the dance. I would enjoy the movement and the connection with the others and have fun trying out new dance moves. Yet, I would often leave the dance not really knowing if I was fully in my dance. I was trying to be the best dancer I could be but sometimes I would get caught up in the fast energy of the dance and find myself in over my head. There were times I would fall or turn my ankle or pull some muscle by trying to take too much of someone's weight on my back.

In essence, I was "other focused." I began each dance wondering how I would fit in, not with whom I was and how I wanted to join in. I have since learned to walk into the dance and greet people as I pass them. But before engaging in any dances, I find a spot on the floor and lie down to arrive in my body. I breathe deeply, relaxing into the floor, letting all my weight pour into the floor with full trust that the floor will hold me. I look for the muscles that are still pulling away from the floor and relax those. I tune in to me, listen to my heartbeat, and know I am separate, but acknowledge I want connection. I feel my body's connection to the floor and its connection to me. I am grateful for the earth's gravity that lets me spring and jump, yet holds my weight completely leaving no need for tension. I remember that I am responsible for my own safety.

Physical forces are powerful teachers. I think of gravity as my friend. It keeps me tethered to this earth as I run and play. However, I must remain aware of its direction of pull in relation to my body as I change levels, land after jumping, or when I am being lifted. My hands and feet, which are my "landing gear," must be free and ready to engage at all times. This is essential for landing safely. I love the floor. It meets me where I am every time. It holds me. It is dependable. In contact with the floor, I find me. I find my small dance that expands into a full range of movement experience without ever leaving myself yet feeling the full extension of my body. I find the openings that I am willing to share with others. I can allow my spirit to soar. One of my particularly hard lessons has been learning to let my spirit soar while staying within the limits of my body. If my spirit gets ahead of my body, the floor is consistently there to remind me of my error with a bump. Then, just as in relationship bumps, I must dust myself off, survey the damage, gather myself, and proceed toward wholeness and greater awareness.

Relationship with myself requires the discovery and development of my solo dance. This dance is best found by initiating all movement from my core, my own center of gravity. With movement from my center, I find the edge of balance and imbalance, of flexibility and stiffness, of strength and weakness, of equilibrium and disequilibrium. My solo dance is where I come home when I have over-extended, or lost my way. My solo dance centers me. It teachers me how to fall softly, to follow my own desires, to expand as much or as little as I like. It shows me the full extension of me. It can take me into utter stillness and rest. It is an intimate connection with my essence. Strength, flexibility, and balance develop in the body while learning this dance. These same traits are required in an intimate relationship with another.

Coming home to my body means tuning in to myself in a physical and emotional way. It means letting my desires and limitations guide my dancing. Coming home to my spirit means honoring who I am in any given moment and dancing with that. It means abandoning the agenda of looking good, or not being good enough, but to dance from the inside out. It is about letting the dance dance me. It is body dancing body. It is dancing without sexualizing, without shame, without hidden motive. It is dancing for no other purpose but to be in the joy of dance, in creative expression, and a shared joyful experience. This is a sacred time to be in a solo dance or to be synchronized with another in movement.

Dancing with Others

It may be hard to imagine being in physical contact with another, dancing without music, and without a traditional dance frame. The feel of this dance is akin to the feel of rolling on an exercise ball. While sitting or lying on the ball, one can rock back and forth, noticing how one's core muscles must get involved to stay upright. It is easy to feel the pressure of the ball pushing back into you as you lie or sit on the ball. With a stretch of the imagination, you can feel the floor holding both you and the ball. You must listen through sensation to know where to keep your center to stay in balance. You can find the rolling point of contact as you move from side to side staying in contact with the ball. You can feel how gravity and the momentum of movement carries you along.

When dancing with a partner, rather than an exercise ball, all these concepts are still at play. The main difference is that another person is more communicative and self-propelled than an exercise ball so the dance becomes a two-way dialogue. The movement remains as the non-verbal communication builds the dance. A physical awareness of skin, muscle, bone, organs, breath, gravity, momentum, and the other dancer: these are the layers of Contact Improvisation. Just like in dancing with the ball, one must move from core to maintain balance, land safely as gravity pulls you back to earth, and enjoy the ride of giving some or all of your weight to another.

In Contact Improvisation, the dancers' centers are in physical contact and both dancers are moving from their core. Sharing core weight lines up the physical forces like a fulcrum. The weight then becomes more effortless to move because it is in full balance. This is a powerful place to be and you know intrinsically when it occurs, like hitting the sweet spot on a tennis racket. Here, one may feel in awe of the power of centeredness. It is a compelling place to be, but impossible to stay in all the time. Just as in life, we commonly fall away from our core power only to return again. This falling away and returning to core is the dance of life enacted in Contact Improvisation. The cycle of being lost then found is central to the process of being human. Contact Improvisation offers an opportunity to yield to these possibilities, to simply show up and pay close attention to the lived experience and dance it.

A physical awareness of skin, muscle, bone, organs, breath, gravity, momentum, and the other dancer

My solo dance always accompanies me as I enter a dance with another. As I give my weight to a dance partner, I decide whether to trust them with only part of my weight or all of it like the floor. Knowing how much trust and weight to give a partner is a metaphor for relationship. I must decide how much of me I can safely let the other hold. I am responsible for giving my weight in small increments as I test the water. This is true in Contact Improvisation and in relationship.

Knowing how much weight to take from another is as important as deciding how much to give. This includes knowing how much of another's weight am I capable of holding or even want to hold. I give myself permission to know my limits and my desires. Some dancers are simply too much for me to lift, others may want to get too close, even others may find me at a time when I am not ready to engage. Respect for my own boundaries, limitations and needs is paramount both in a dance with physical forces and in relationship. My spirit home resides here too. This is respecting my true yesses and true nos as I interact with another dancer. Honoring who I am in each moment keeps my body and spirit safe and playful.

In Contact Improvisation, many dances are danced in duets. The method of entering a duet is usually done without any spoken word. One person may be in a solo dance that looks compelling for another dancer to join. The potential joiner will dance near the first, offering an invitation to make the dance a duet. The first dancer may accept the invitation or not. The potential joiner learns not to take the acceptance or rejection personally. The original dancer may not be ready to leave his or her solo dance, and that is fine. If however, the offer is accepted, the dancers form a duet. The movement that ensues is initiated from the point of contact between the two dancers, where their centers of balance are in contact. It is not uncommon to see contact duets danced with eyes closed or with a soft gaze, noticing only large shapes and the orientation of the room, but not one's partner. This serves to avoid collisions with other dancers and to keep one's balance.

A common move is called a "rolling point of contact." The dancers lean into each other, "listening" carefully to how much weight each one trusts giving to the partner. As trust develops, the dance takes on more risks, transitioning to different levels, giving each other more weight or playing with speed and momentum of the movement. The contact between the dancers takes on an air of exploration and curiosity. Because the dance is not choreographed, the course of the dance unfolds from "actively listening" at the point of contact, where the two bodies meet. Sometimes the dance develops into a playful and rowdy dance or sometimes into slow, soft, sensuous movement taking time to find stillness and breath. When the movement is at its best, the dancers are looking for the path the dance wants to go, not forcing the direction. This is accomplished by listening simultaneously to oneself and to one's partner at the point of contact.

Centers of balance in contact

True conversation is not scripted. It is not planned ahead of time. It is a dialogue built on listening and responding. The improvisational nature of dancing with a partner is like a verbal conversation in this way. Contact Improvisation necessitates listening with all the senses. True conversation depends on both people wanting to make contact. It means cooperating and resisting. It depends upon being able to leave and to return. One must not take everything personally. Sometimes you must let the other person go even before you are ready, or to leave when you are ready. It requires being able to take the risk of offering something that may be rejected. It lets you know how it feels to be left out or included. It takes being respectful of the other without taking responsibility for him or her. It obliges one to set boundaries both physical and emotional. It insists upon sharing your solo dance with another, yet never losing sight of who you are, even as the dance becomes bigger than the two dancers and merges into oneness. The dance taps into spirit, but lands swiftly in the body if one dancer forgets to honor the physical forces. Landing gear must always be ready to engage. Each dancer is completely responsible for his or her own safety. All these things are true in relationships as well.

In Contact Improvisation, as well as in relationship, it is important to know where you stand with your partner. Ironically, the safety of the dancers increases when they are in close contact. It is easy to lose safety during movement when there is a gap between the two people. If one pulls away without warning or is ambivalent about giving weight, it is then hard to know where you stand with this partner. If you have given too much of your center of gravity to the partner who moves away, you must either find contact again or find your own center and flexibility to land safely on the floor.

In partner dance, communication is in the body, not in verbal communication, so the "listening" must occur at the point of contact. In order to follow the flow of the conversation, the dancer must be ready to change levels, and transition direction or speed while staying in contact with their partner. The safety of the conversation is built by keeping as much surface as possible in contact with one's partner. This is counterintuitive. One may think that distance is the key to safety but it is much easier to know where you and your partner are in relation to each other by remaining in contact. I must constantly listen to my body and my partner's body at the point of contact to decide if my partner can hold my center of gravity or if I should hold on to it. I decide this not by throwing my whole weight onto my partner at once but by giving my weight in increments. I am responsible for making the adjustment if my arm is being stretched uncomfortably or if I am off balance. My partner is there for support, but I must know how to slide safely to the floor or disengage if I find myself in a precarious position. I must feel a firm foundation before I trust my physical safety to another. I must make the necessary adjustments based on my limits and desires. It is much better to give my weight to what *is* rather than what I *want* there to be. Communication around all these nuances must be equally shared. All this feels very true in relationship as well.

In traditional dance frames, there is a designated leader and follower. Usually the man is the leader and the woman is the follower. In Contact Improvisation, leading and following is egalitarian. The lead switches by way of nonverbal communication when one person takes the lead away from the other, or when one gives over the lead to the other. The fact that these roles switch back and forth requires that communication channels be open always. There is no given way the dance will always unfold. It is truly improvisational. Aligning the lead function with the flow of the dance rather than with gender roles is true dialogue.

Dance in Community

One's solo dance becomes enriched when shared with or witnessed by another. Contact Improvisation is typically not a performance, it is an experience. It is a community bonded on the love of the dance form with a commitment to respecting each other and to exploring creativity, movement, and connection to each other within the container of community. The intention is to dance each dance within the context of all others, not just with individual dance partners.

Keeping a soft focus of vision while dancing allows each dancer to keep an awareness of where one is in space and in relation to others. Each dance is a part of the greater whole of the community. Dancers keep an awareness of other dancers in the room not simply for the sake of physical safety, but also emotional safety, and acknowledgement of others. As in any community, many types of relationships form on and off the dance floor, so each dancer must respect the fact that one's dance partner may be in a committed relationship, and dance with the appropriate boundaries to respect that. Just as it takes a village to raise a child, it takes a community to support relationships that are created. Honoring individual differences is key to keeping creative exploration open.

A round robin is a common practice at a Contact Improvisation community jam. The group creates an open space in the center of the room by sitting in a large circle on the floor to act as witnesses to the dancers who will dance in pairs and transitional trios. Any dancer may come into the circle and dance a solo dance until someone follows a desire to join the dance and forms a duet. When a third person arrives the three will dance for a short time of transition until the first dancer leaves and joins the circle to become a witness. The newly formed duet continues until another dancer enters and the transition phase repeats. This is a beautiful experience both for the dancers and the witnesses. The round robin is typically done in silence and without music, so it can become a meditative experience of witnessing and experiencing, of entering and leaving, of seeing and being seen, of surrendering and receiving. It gives dancers the opportunity to overcome shyness and return to the animal body in which they live, allowing body to be body, allowing it to show its own intentions. In a safe container such as this, it is beautiful to experience the process of seeing and being seen. Sometimes magnificent, sometimes comical, sometimes mundane shapes are made by these moving sculptures that are human animal bodies experiencing the joy of movement and connection with another, like puppies rolling over each other. Animals can do this quite naturally. Humans can as well; however, it takes being with oneself and forgetting oneself simultaneously.

Belonging to the Contact Improvisation community has helped me accept my right and need to belong. I belong in my body. I belong in this time and place. I belong with people who share the call of the dance. In essence, I belong because I am here and feel the call to be here. With the community offering full respect and acknowledgment of physical and emotional forces that are present, I can accept the invitation to explore who I am with the knowledge that I need contact with others to know where I am. I belong in this community, on the floor, in my body, being myself, seeing and being seen.

Contact Improvisation as a Metaphor for Life

There are a number of metaphors that Contact Improvisation represents in my life; accepting my weight in the world and knowing that the world can hold it. It is finding the density of my body and feeling the felt sense of moving that density. It is finding mindfulness. It is becoming aware that my body is connected to something greater than itself. It is receiving and giving support. Contact with another gives me feedback about my existence in space. I am here now in this body, in this moment, in time and space. The proof is in the point of contact I feel with the floor or my partner. I trust that gravity will hold me in my place. Life force pushes up and away from gravity and it gives into gravity for rest, trusting that life force will arise again from stillness, knowing all beginnings come from endings. Living in unforced momentum, this is truly a dance with life.

Contact Improvisation accompanies my soul's journey as I dance my bodily-held spirit dance. I have learned that being *with* myself is very different from being *by* myself. My discoveries have truly enriched my already good life. They have helped me explore the meaning of my existence, which is no more and no less than connection to what is and choosing how fully I want to embrace it.

I want to acknowledge my friends and teachers in the Contact Improvisation community who have danced with me and taught me so much. I feel honored to have crossed their paths ten years ago and want to continue learning, growing, and experiencing life through dance, even as my body ages. I have been told there was a conversation at the Contact Improvisation thirty-sixth Anniversary Celebration held at Juniata College in central Pennsylvania, about aging and dance. The lively discussion led to a folk wisdom conclusion: "Dance with the body you have."

• • • •

JOLIE PATE works as a licensed psychiatric emergency services clinician in a Boston area hospital. She answered her "call to the dance" 10 years ago when a friend persuaded her to experience a "barefoot boogie," by attending a continuation of Boston's "Dance Free" founded in 1969. Since she had grown up in a family whose religion forbade dancing, she had never learned to dance. Furthermore, she had the cultural idea that social dancing was about standing by the wall with humiliation and fear waiting to be chosen. However, she took the risk. Upon arrival at the boogie, she was informed that the only rule was that one could move in any way he or she wanted as long as no-one got hurt. Lying on the floor in the midst of dancers moving to world music in pairs, solos, or groups, she realized she had come Home, and cried. Jolie now dances for seven hours or more each week, attends workshops and dance events, and performs in a variety of venues.

CHAPTER THREE

Dance, Destiny, and Love

────

Bonney Meyer

Destiny

A T THE AGE OF TWENTY-NINE I was looking for direction in my life and decided to have a psychic reading. The woman was straightforward, factual, and simple in her delivery of my future... and I resonated with most of it. But there was one thing she said that twanged like an out-of-tune piano string: "You're going to be working with children—young girls—and there's lots of love." In my head I was thinking, "Whoa! Train off the track! I don't have children. I don't want children. I don't want to work with children." And I didn't give it much thought from then on... until my life transitioned again.

I had just had my forty-second birthday, moved from Berkeley to Sebastopol, California and life was full of new and exciting things. I had been invited to do one of my signature sacred dances known as "Blessings from the Moon Goddess" at an event in Marin County. It was a magical evening, which continued on the hour-long ride back home. After the event, I was approached by a lovely woman with a German accent and twinkly eyes. Her name was Margita and she was telling me how happy she was to have made the extra effort to attend the dance concert by bus. So of course, I said, "Where do you live?" "Sebastopol" she responded. "I just moved there! Would you like a ride home?"

We hopped in my car and floated northbound, as if on a flying carpet that was on autopilot.

Margita and I immediately locked into an intense discussion about ourselves, dance, and life. When I dropped her off at her home, she asked if I taught dance to children. My response came much too quickly, "No, no, no, no, no! I only work with adults and mostly women." "Hmmmm," she said in a slow dreamy way, "I bet you'd be great with kids." "No, I doubt it," I said. "I don't have the patience for kids. I'm the oldest of six siblings and the eldest of thirty-six grandchildren. I was surrounded by them for half my life, escaped and have no desire to be with them again." She smiled sweetly and once again said, "Hmmm… I just think you would be wonderful with little girls. You have so much to share. I have a nine-year-old girl. If I set up a class with my daughter and some of her friends, would you try it?"

Well at this juncture in the story, I can tell you Margita was not going to take "no" for an answer. We exchanged numbers and promised to talk in the future. A month or so passed and I got a call from her. "Hi! We are all set. The girls are very excited to dance, the moms are looking forward to meeting you, I have rented a space for a month…" "Margita!" I gasped. "Stop. Wait. You rented a dance space for a month?!"

She pleaded in a voice sweet as honey, "Bonney, pleeease? It is just four weeks. And if you don't like it, we won't schedule any more classes."

As a retired ICU nurse, I'm used to thinking fast and furious on my feet using a process referred to as SOAP:

SUBJECTIVE: *Silent Scream, "NOOOOOOoooooo! I don't want to do this!"*
OBJECTIVE: *I'm certainly qualified to teach dance and many other things. I want to meet more people in the community and it would be an opportunity for personal growth. I learned long ago that those things I feared or protested against strongly were the very things I needed to DO next.*
ASSESSMENT: *I'm here. Margita is here. The class has been organized, the space secured, the money collected. All I have to do is… Show Up! Could this be the answer to my sincere and heartfelt prayer, "Goddess, please show me my next step?" I check my vital signs. Temperature: skin warm and flushed petunia pink. Pulse: galloping along at a steady, somewhat increased rate. Respiration: faster than usual and shallow as a one inch deep birdbath.*
PLAN: *"OK Margita. I'll be there. But I can't promise you anything beyond the four weeks. I'll try and then we'll see what happens." Dear Goddess, this is not what I had in mind!*

Dance, Life, and What I Have Learned

Before meeting with these little girls, I couldn't help but ask myself, what will I teach them? And how will I teach them? I started this exploration by contemplating what dance means to me. The beginning of this query can be traced back to my experience with a health practitioner who used Applied Kinesiology as a method of testing and monitoring her clients. Simply put, Applied Kinesiology (AK) is a form of diagnosis using muscle testing as a primary feedback mechanism to examine how a person's body is functioning. When properly applied, the outcome of an AK diagnosis will determine the best form of therapy for the patient.

One day someone was doing muscle testing with me and asked, "What are your favorite things to do?" Scanning the inner regions of my brain I responded, "reading, hikes in nature, cooking and eating, dancing, laughing, meditation, visiting with friends, sex, and travel, not necessarily in that order." Then she said a peculiar thing, "I would like to test what percent of Spirit manifests in your body when you do each of these activities." I held out my arm and she asked, "What percent of Spirit manifests in Bonney's body when she (fill in the blank)?" Most of the activities registered somewhere between 40 and 70 percent. Dance registered 100 percent!

This immediately resonated with me. I feel most alive when I am dancing. My mind stops and my body moves effortlessly, as graceful currents of energy create moving sculptures with my earthen form and I feel blissfully happy. It's nothing short of transcendent. Dancing has become sacred to me and I embrace it as a moving meditation, as one of my spiritual practices.

I certainly didn't grow up with the notion that either the body or dancing was sacred. Instead, my childhood upbringing and religion taught me to deny my body and femininity. And dancing… well, that was considered frivolous and unimportant. Ultimately, I was attracted to belly dancing as the vehicle for healing the separation between head, heart, and body and for learning how to love my female form.

Before I started belly dancing, I wore baggy clothes to hide my voluptuous curves, resented my big breasts for getting in the way of playing sports, cursed my monthly period, wore my hair as short as a pixie's, spent most of my waking hours in my head (Thoughts! Too many thoughts!), and preferred the company of men. I just didn't understand women, and here I was in this female body! In my mid-twenties, I was at a party where the evening's entertainment was a belly dancer. "Mesmerized" is a good word to describe my experience watching her. My heart and body vibrated with excitement and my mind went into judgment and criticism of how dancing that way was demeaning. Didn't this woman know about women's liberation? I was to discover that she did. The secrets of the dance would eventually liberate me from the realm of too many thoughts and allow me to access my senses, my sensuality, and sexuality. This in turn began to melt the fortress around my heart to feel again. It took many years of dancing and a few years of therapy, but I eventually regained my whole rainbow of emotional expression and came to realize that the judgment and criticism of the dance was simply my fear of knowing more about myself and life.

Reflecting further about what dancing has taught me I found: discipline, practice, commitment, surrender, present moment awareness, limitations, emotional expression, storytelling, and creativity (I could be anything I wanted to be—from a dragon fly to a goddess!). It also gave me the opportunity to connect with others, dancing through time and the space that was provided. I was transitioning from being a lone wolf to learning how to be and work with others. I learned patience, assertiveness, flexibility, timing, boundaries, respect, sharing, group cohesiveness, and how to give, and began to accept and work with all of it. Finally, dancing introduced me to all kinds of amazing people, new music, exotic cultures, and costume design. It showed me how a world of such rich diversity as ours can be bridged into human oneness via music and dance. Through this, I learned compassion and good will.

I've often thought that Life is a Dance and that Dance is Life. The following are my top ten (plus one) from my treasure chest of wisdom teachings that are applicable to both:

- A flexible mind renders a flexible body (and vice-versa).
- Timing is important and transitions happen…
  in dance routines and in life.
- If you practice (choreography), you can master it (improvisation).
- We dance (live) better when we're grounded and centered.
- Keep smiling even if you make a mistake.
- Listen to and trust your body. Dance from your heart.
- If you fall, pick yourself up and keep on moving.
- Be aware of other people so you don't bump into them.
- Every step is significant and you don't always need to know what the next step is.
- Be aware of your limitations and work with them. They teach you.
- If you're stuck, move your body. If you are tired, stop.

It was through these revelations that my true purpose for being with the girls crystallized. It was two-fold. I was to teach them to love every inch of their intelligent, magical, beautiful bodies as the vehicle for a Soul that is free, joyful, creative, and wise. Could I create an experience that allowed them to know they were multi-dimensional beings? Could I support them to integrate these dimensions: head, heart, and body? For this would lead to the second objective: Embodiment of Spirit through dance. I further wondered, if love of body, self, and spirit would protect them from some of the challenges of a teenager's life? No small task! My pondering continued, how in the world am I going to teach all these things to children? And did I mention how the idea of being with children just stresses me out?

Who's Teaching Who

I usually have more questions than I do answers but I had to start somewhere. I decided to call the class "World Dance for Children" and start by teaching them about their bodies via belly dancing. This dance genre was created by women for women and has been passed down from mothers to daughters for thousands of years. The muscular isolation technique from belly dance would help them in any other kind of dance they wanted to explore later.

It was Friday afternoon on a warm, beautiful, fall day. I had over-prepared as usual for the class I was about to teach to these six little girls. Margita was waiting for me outside the studio door, "Hi Bonney! Everyone is here." She gently touched my hand saying, "There are a few more girls who wanted to take the class." I had no idea at the time how crossing the threshold of that studio door was going to change my life forever. I followed Margita into the room and froze in my tracks, a mere step beyond the door jam. Honestly, I really don't remember how long I stood there taking in the scene before me, counting to myself, "one, two, three... sixteen, seventeen, eighteen." She must have seen the lack of animation in my body and the terror in my eyes because she offered reassurance and tenderness, "They're just little girls. You'll do fine. I'll be back in an hour. Have fun! Bye-bye!"

I tried to make sense of the chaos. Eighteen half-pints between the ages of seven and ten bouncing off each other and the walls like atoms in a steel box. They were tossing multi-colored balls, doing cartwheels, running up the wall and jumping off, singing, whirling, screaming, laughing. Being half hermit and preferring the company of quiet cats, this was clearly sensory overload. I wondered if I could be thrown in jail for abandoning a dance class.

As the shock wore off and I regained my senses, I moved into the center of the room. My efforts to bring order to the chaos were feeble and slow. Somehow, after thirty minutes they were all sitting, or more accurately, squirming, in a circle on the floor. I introduced myself, "Hi! My name is Bonney and I really like to dance. Please tell me your name and one thing you like to do." Like a cacophony of Amazon jungle birds they all answered at once. OK, my mistake. Be more specific. "One at a time!" I begged. In between trips to the bathroom, sips of water, and spontaneous outbursts of conversation by these jungle birds, I was able to learn their names. That concluded our first meeting.

I suppose I could say the next two classes were uneventful, as they were very much like the first. I did manage to teach them three or four basic belly dance moves: basic stance, hip bumps, hip twists, and up and down hip technique. I continued to be absolutely baffled at how to get their attention and keep it. At the beginning of the fourth class I stood in the middle of the room and said softly and ever so kindly, "Girls, please form a circle. Girls, girls… Pleazzzzzeee form a circle." No response. The chaos continued around me. When did I become invisible? My efforts defeated, I sat down feeling frustrated and thinking if a parent walked in now, they would know I was an imposter, a phony, that I didn't know what I was doing (which was true). I could feel energy rising in my body. I identified this energy as anger. I explored what was beneath the anger. I knew the girls were simply being normal, healthy kids. I didn't want to yell. And then insight struck with the speed and surge of a racehorse out of the gate. I had given my power away to these adorable creatures and they were happy to take it!

Rising to my feet, breathing into my belly with the intention to take back my power, I released an ear-piercing vocal call I had learned in African dance. It must have been loud because many of them covered their ears with their hands and all of them froze in place as if playing the game "Statue." Thirty-six eyeballs stared at me, waiting for me to say something. I said nothing. One by one I pointed at each girl and directed her where to sit. When the last girl sat down and the circle was complete, I joined the formation and sat among them with the straight back of a Queen. No one said a word. Their eyes were orbs of wonder, curiosity, and maybe some fear. I wasn't sure. They wiggled and squirmed and shot each other furtive glances, but not a single one spoke. For the next five minutes, I breathed and leisurely stared at them, fixing my gaze on each girl until I knew somewhere in my heart that she saw me and acknowledged my presence. Calmly I asked, "What do I have to do to get your attention?" There was a pause filled with the electric current of synapses hissing. To this day, I wish I had a camera to capture the silent expressions on their faces, which seemed to convey thoughts of "Huh?" "I don't know." "I'm puzzled." "Are we done yet?" "I'm thinking, I'm thinking!" The silence was broken when Chelsea, with big brown eyes and a smile that radiated the playfulness of a woodland elf said, "Well… what you did worked pretty good." Others murmured and nodded in agreement. I was laughing on the inside but maintained the inscrutable affect of the Queen.

The tension in the room evaporated like mist in sunshine. I decided to speak from my heart, offer my truth and let them decide what they wanted to do for themselves. "I love to dance. I love to teach dance. There are a lot of cool things I can show you and help you with. I want you to have fun being here and enjoy dancing as much as I do. And I want to have fun too, because if I'm not having fun, I don't want to be here. The last few weeks have not been fun for me. So I'm wondering if we can figure out a way for all of us to have fun and keep this dance class going… if that's what you want. So let's talk about how we can make this work for all of us and make some agreements with each other."

Heads started nodding "yes" and verbal bubbles of "OK" started floating up from the group. I continued, "I want to hear your suggestions. Raise your hand to speak and everyone else please focus your full attention on whoever is talking. Who would like to go first?" Clearly this was a chatty group. Many hands shot into the air and the wisdom of children poured fourth.

"Well, we have to sit so much in school. I think we just need to go crazy for awhile."

"I'm tired. I just want to lie down first."

"I get hungry after school."

"Can we play some games?"

"I don't want homework."

"Maybe we could dance outside sometime."

I truly appreciated hearing all of their offerings and thanked them. I also told them I could work with most of their wants and desires but not all of them.

Noticing that there were a few girls who did not offer a "peep" during the discussion, I was compelled to say, "Now I'm going to ask you another question. Take a moment to think about it and please be very honest when you answer. Whatever your answer is, it's OK and I'll understand and support it. So my next question is… how many of you are here because your mom or dad wanted you to be here, but you really don't want to be here yourself?" Tentatively, a few hands went up. I thanked them for their honesty and said, "It's OK. I do understand that this may not be a class you want to take. Please go home and tell your parents that you do not want to be in the class and that it's OK with the teacher. And if they have a problem with that, tell them to call Bonney." I think they were surprised and relieved. Then I asked, "How many of you want to take more dance classes?" Hands went up. "OK then, I'll see you next week." Something was moving me deeper into this journey with the girls while at the same time a very loud voice in my head still protested, "What are you doing?"

The Journey

I was rapidly awakening the fixed ideas I had about what and how to teach the girls. You see, I'm the quintessential perfectionist: organized, structured, methodical, goal-oriented, thorough. OK, you could also say obsessive, nit-picky, workaholic, critical, and lacking in playfulness. My egoic m.o. collided with the nature of this group. Their verbal virtuosity astounded me. In a most articulate manner, they expressed what they liked and did not like and they had no reservations about telling me so.

What do you do with a headstrong teacher and a group of headstrong girls? I really had to think about this. A power struggle with munchkins was esthetically displeasing to me. I was the adult and clearly I needed to take the lead here. Slogans from previous teachers wafted across the screen of my mind:

- What you resist persists.
- Cultivate skillfulness.
- The person with the most behavioral flexibility will control (I like to say guide) any given situation.
- Drive all blame into one's self.
- Fear is the beginning of wisdom.
- What you think is coming towards you, is really coming from you.
- What is your intention? And on and on.

Intention. That's always a good place to start. My intention at first was to teach the girls how to dance. That shifted into accepting them for who they were at any given moment and loving them. Dance became a secondary thing. My intention for myself was to become less of a perfectionist and transform into being more relaxed, playful, compassionate, flexible, and skillful.

As the next year unfolded, I satisfied my inner perfectionist by preparing and planning extensively for each class and I honored my intentions for my students by letting things unfold in class, abandoning the plan if needed and doing what seemed most useful in the moment. A pleasurable routine for our class evolved. The first fifteen minutes we all went "crazy." The next twenty minutes we co-created movement games. I will confess that the games I designed were to facilitate dancing their bodies and develop life skills, like, "How does your body want to move when you are really mad, sad, happy, afraid?" During the rest of the class, these aspiring dancers were beautifully focused to learn dance steps.

About four months into the class, I got a call from one of the mothers, "What exactly are you teaching in dance class?" My heart skipped a beat. Rats, the gig is up. Now everyone will know: I'm not really teaching dance… not much anyway. I heard myself say, "Why do you ask?" The mom responded by telling me about last night's dinner discussion, "We were all at the dinner table and my husband and I were having a heated discussion. At some point my daughter said, 'Time out.' My husband and I looked at her and gasped, 'What?' My daughter explained, 'This is what Bonney does in dance class when we're upset. We take a timeout and breathe and shake our bodies, we even make sounds, but no words. We do that until we feel better or calmer.

So you two need a time out.'" The mother continued, "Anyway, we were blown away. Whatever you're doing—keep on doing it!" This was the beginning of a deepening connection and bond with the mothers of these remarkable children.

As the years went by and the girls matured, we spent less time going crazy and playing games and more time dancing. I developed a "dance movements list" and as a girl mastered a movement skill she would get a brightly colored check mark celebrating her accomplishment. The time spent one-on-one was precious, as I began to learn their strengths and weaknesses, always focusing on the process rather than the perfected isolation movement and encouraging them to accept themselves where they were in the moment and keep on practicing.

Their stories were varied, unique, and unfolded like a spring flower. Karina was a tall, slender girl who ended up crying in the corner, "I can't do it. I can't do it." Making eye contact I gently said, "Karina, look at me. I don't believe you. What if you can do it but you just don't know it yet?" She looked puzzled. "Can you pretend that you know how to do this movement?" She nodded yes. "Then in your mind's eye, your imagination, see yourself doing this movement and say 'I can do it.'" Her spirit and face brightened, she whispered "I can do it" and started moving her body to match the movement of my own. "Congratulations, you've got it." Smiling from ear to ear she exclaimed, "I *can* do it!" We continued this exchange for a few months until "I can't do it" disappeared forever.

Ellya, blue-eyed and supple, moved like she did not have bones. She often had a headache, felt sore in her joints, and tired easily. Years later, she was diagnosed with Lyme disease. I and the other students were supportive and compassionate towards her, encouraging her to sit out when she was tired or in pain. Ellya would watch and practice with us in her mind. When we performed, she radiated energy and joy. One would never know she battled a chronic illness.

Chelsea, whose face was like a cherub, loved to choreograph. She knew how to listen to the music, hear a story or theme in it, and string movements together like pearls on a necklace. In seventh grade she decided she wanted to do a solo dance for the spring concert. During a private lesson, I had her close her eyes and listen to the music and "see" the story in the music, as if she were watching a movie. She then told me what she saw. I encouraged her to "tell the story" in her dance movement. Chelsea captivated the audience and received a standing ovation.

Andraya, innocent, shy, and curious as a fawn, was transformed over the years from a quiet, background presence to a young woman who found her voice and her power. By the time she was in high school, she was chiming in with opinions, suggestions, and creative insight to all the dance routines. The other girls listened and respected her input. She modeled diplomacy for the others.

Dawn was a true gypsy with a mind that traveled to a new destination every time I spoke with her. She was two years older than the others and declared them sisters in spirit. "I have more in common with the girls than I do with people in my own class!" In fact, for her high school graduation project she invited the "sophomore" girls to do a belly dance routine with her. Despite the criticism she received from her classmates about her project, Dawn spoke eloquently about the history of belly dance and her love for her sisters in spirit. And then they danced.

Erica, palpably intense, was a girl of few words and when she did speak, she was clear and to the point. If she had difficulty doing a movement, we would work on it over and over and over again, per her request, until she knew she had it. And she was the first to say in the group, "we need more practice." Nothing was going to get in her way of mastering any dance.

Simone took to belly dancing like a duck to water. She was not learning the dance, she was *remembering* it. Comfortable in her body and in her sensuality, she moved as if she had been dancing since the beginning of time. It was fascinating to follow her through her years of exploration, which included anthropology, Middle Eastern studies, and learning how to speak Arabic.

Lihi came to our band of world dancers a few years later. She had trained very young in ballet and sustained a back injury at the age of twelve. Unable to do ballet anymore, she joined our class in eighth grade. The gentle undulating movements of the spine and the grounding movements of the pelvis offered her a new vocabulary of dance with which to work. She integrated the grace and beauty of ballet into the earthen body of belly dance. She brought elegance to all of our dance routines.

I never expected to have a long-term relationship with any of these girls. There were many things competing for their time and energy like music lessons, theater, sports, martial arts, and boys. I enjoyed my time with them, thinking it would not last. Each new school year, I was delighted and a bit surprised they wanted to study another year with me. And so the years passed and we danced.

They began performing after their first year of lessons. Before the performance, they stood backstage in a circle, holding hands and chanted, "Our minds are clear, from our hearts we dance. So Be It!" Their bodies were electric, lighting up the room with joy. The hearts of the audience had been captured and it was the first of many performances over the next seven years. To this day, as young women, they still chant, "Our minds are clear, from our hearts we dance. So Be It!" before they go on stage.

In the beginning, I would create most of the choreography for the girls' public dance recitals. I would give them small sections of music where they could "make up" their own movements. These were usually short solos or duets inside the body of the larger dance piece. These young girls proved themselves to be a creative bunch. By the time their senior year recital approached, they were capable of creating the whole piece themselves. My function was primarily to supervise, inspire, and brainstorm with them if they got stuck. "My girls," as I like to call them, became seasoned performers, dancing for school and community events, parties, festivals, and in restaurants. They ventured out and studied other dance forms such as ballroom, hip-hop, and salsa. Some of them were also members of an unusual Salsa dance troupe, which incorporated belly dance into its routines. In their junior year of high school, they traveled to New York to perform and were voted "Best Dance Troupe" in Sonoma County, California.

From the beginning of our eight-year relationship, I held my intention to teach and role model life skills during our time together. What I witnessed was a deepening in friendship, sisterhood, and the blossoming of girls into young women who were comfortable in their own skins. They developed an ease, acceptance, and celebration of their bodies. They learned how to come together in the spirit of respect and support for each other rather than the catty, competitive behavior that I had experienced in dance classes as a student. They learned how to communicate and work out their differences in a skilfull way that honored themselves and others in the group. They developed full emotional spectrums and knew dance was a powerful way to express themselves.

They began performing after their first year of classes

Each of these young women developed the ability to be a leader and a follower. They worked as such a skilfull, cohesive unit that they could all talk at once. And they understood each other! It was not unusual for me to witness this and feel at a loss because I could not understand what they were saying—all at once. They were kind, however, and periodically one of them would report to me what was being discussed and the decisions they were making. Love, awe, and wonder best explain how I felt about my girls. Often those who witnessed them dancing used words such as beautiful, joyous, radiant, and powerful to describe them: each one, truly a unique expression of energy, movement, and light.

By the time they graduated from high school, their mothers and fathers breathed more easily. This group of girls had navigated through potentially troubled waters with minimal acting out via eating disorders, smoking, drug, and alcohol abuse or teen sexuality and pregnancy. They maintained high levels of self esteem, healthy relationships with parents and peers, good grades, and curiosity about life in general.

The parents of these girls formed a group when their children were in third grade to address the "how" of raising girls into healthy young women. They knew they were headed towards turbulent waters with the pre-teen and teen years. They had a vision and, in addition to dancing, these parents supported many healthy offerings to the girls through Waldorf education, music and the arts, travel, organic food, and a Life Skills class which they contracted me to teach during the high school years. What was most obvious to me was the love the parents had for their kids.

When my girls graduated from high school, I wrote this letter and gave a copy to each one:

High School Graduation
June 5, 2005

To the Daughters of My Heart,

I would like to express the deep gratitude I have in knowing all of you. Surely, eight years ago, I thought the Goddess was playing a trick on me, having organized a dance class (through Margita) with little girls! Highly unlikely, me and little girls! It was with reservation and I'll admit, some fear, I showed up for the first class. How was I to know that by the end of the first month I would fall in love with all of you. I will also confess there have been times I was not sure who was the student and who was the teacher. I continue to be in awe of your beauty, creativity, and wisdom.

Please always remember who you are... goddesses earthing spiritual energies on the planet. Honor your bodies (especially your bellies!). Honor your hearts. Honor you minds. And if for some reason you forget who you are – call me! I know I have experienced something rare, something sacred with you. And I am forever changed. For you are the dancing Daughters of My Heart. I will love you forever.

Bonney Meyer

Reflections

It is now fourteen years since we first met. The little girls I met in 1997 have "survived" the transitions, challenges, temptations, and confusion that are usually a part of teen life. They have evolved into graceful, articulate, self-confident, and poised young women. All of them have pursued higher education. Some are in the beginning stages of careers while others are finishing school or expanding their education in life through travel. None of them are married yet. Nearly all of them continued dancing while in college, starting their own belly dance classes and developing their own troupes. They continue to dance together for special events and be a close-knit group of friends. Three of them participated in a documentary film for a college project about belly dance.

They danced and spoke eloquently... I could see they had integrated not only the dance but also the life lessons. Erica recently graduated from art school in Oakland, California. Her senior project was a multi-media art exhibit, which included a belly dance performance with her long-time friends Chelsea and Andraya. Erica made their costumes, including weaving the fabric from which the hip belts were made.

I have marvelled at the self-respect these young women have shown as they navigated the realms of relationship and sexuality, drugs and alcohol, food, exercise, and life-style choices. They are creative, happy beings who clearly love themselves. That love and beauty overflows to all who know them. They are caring, giving, and also adept at setting healthy boundaries when needed. They exhibit the skills of communication and poise in their twenties, which took me until my late thirties to manifest.

Each of them has had to embrace their own personal challenges, their own physical limitations ranging from asthma to neck and back pain to Lyme disease, weight issues, school and peer pressure, break-ups with boyfriends, the illness or divorce of parents, etc. And through this unfolding of their lives, they continue to dance. For them it is more than an activity. It is a form of self-expression and connection with others.

The blossoming of girls into young women
who were comfortable in their own skin

The following are reflections from the girls themselves taken from an interview about belly dance in 2008 and from a documentary in which Chelsea, Andraya, and Karina participated.

"Belly dance for me is a way to express my physical body and also my spiritual body. I think because we learned belly dance so young, it was a way to communicate with my friends and to learn from someone who really embodied the feminine, the woman. It was a way for me to learn through her (Bonney), how to deal with the changes that were going on in my body and to understand who I was becoming as a woman rather than a girl. It really did that for me.

And we grew as a community with a group of really good friends. That really helped. It also taught me how I feel about my body. As a girl, it can be really hard and you get lost in that field of what you should look like. Belly dance takes you out of that. It's always a beautiful thing, it's always really warm and inviting. The movements are about your body and how it feels. We are dancers that push that aspect of how it makes you feel, whether or not it hurts or makes you feel good when you do it. It makes me feel beautiful when I dance." (CHELSEA)

"In doing belly dance, I feel like I need to educate myself about the core values of the culture that belly dance comes from so I've studied the history and I've studied with Arabs and Arab-Americans dancing this form. I started belly dance because I was very insecure about my body as a teenager and my mom bought me a video and some lessons at the gym. It's so empowering to be able to control your body in this way, to be able to isolate gestures, just one shoulder, just one hip. That cancels out any nervousness I might have about showing by body. When I'm belly dancing, I feel like I need to represent myself in an honorable way first and belly dance and Middle Eastern culture dance form second and women as a whole third. When I am dancing, I am a sexual being but I am not anyone's sexual object."[14] (LYDIA)

"In fifth grade, we were going through a phase of our lives where we were self-conscious and our parents thought it would be good to help our aware-ness of our bodies and to love our bodies. And to me, that's what belly dance has always been about… about loving the body that I'm in and just dancing because it makes me happy. Belly dance is a dance form that I've done all my life, it's in my body, it's in my bones. I feel like it's the most natural way for me to move, which is really amazing, it's not forced. Sometimes I see other people do other forms and it seems so forced in the body. But I find that belly dance is different on each person's body, it's adapted on each person's body to work on your body. It creates a different experience for each person — which I love! It shouldn't be the same thing, it is going to be different, it's going to look different. It's a newer thing for me to go out and belly dance for the general public now. People are either awestruck by its beauty and how mesmerizing it is or they'll go, 'Oh, that was all skanky and slutty.' And it's sad when they do that." (ANDRAYA)

"Belly dance to me is about the community that is formed by dancers and for dancers. It happens so much in belly dancing — being with the people you are with, loving them, and loving and appreciating yourself, celebrating that with your body. It's a very personal technique thing. You spend a lot of time strengthening the core of your body, so you can do these motions so that it feels right. The dance is not for anyone else, it's for yourself. It concerns me that most people pay attention to what it looks like and not what it feels like. When we learned to dance, we were not allowed to use the mirror — for years! Because if you feel it, you're doing it right. If you get distracted by what it looks like, you're not going to do it right. If it feels right to the person doing it, to the person that's dancing, it's going to look better, it's going to look beautiful." **(KARINA)**

"I've been studying belly dancing for a long time. I wanted to learn about the culture, where this dance form I love so much comes from. In order to be a well-versed, knowledgeable dancer or teacher, you need to understand the meaning of the movement in the cultural context of the country it is from. I want to help increase cross-cultural understanding between the U.S. and the Middle East." **(SIMONE)**

More comments from my girls about dance and the body, emotion, self-expression, sisterhood, joy, happiness, and spirituality:

- *"Dance makes me happy, no matter what else is going on."*
- *"Dance challenges my brain in a different way… in an artistic way."*
- *"If I feel stuck, dancing helps me get unstuck."*
- *"I'm a better person because of dance: more in tune with and connected to self, easier to express myself. Dance can help me get through a day, I'm more grounded, more peaceful."*
- *"Dancing is an instinct now which helps me stay physically active and in shape. It doesn't feel like exercise. It's not a chore. It's more a joy and a passion."*

I asked my belly dancing beauties, "What would you tell a ten-year-old girl about dancing?" Their responses:

- *"Dancing gives you a physical way to ground and express emotions, physically move and distract yourself. It really helps you to be in touch with your body and emotions."*

- *"Dance is helpful even when you don't know what you're feeling or what's going on inside. You just move and feel better."*
- *"It is something stable to fall back on. It creates stability in life when stuff is changing."*
- *"Feel it in your body and you are able to pick things up easier when learning new things."*
- *"Above all, I learned about holding an intention and developing awareness."*

Love

As their teacher, I am just beginning to appreciate the impact we have had on each other's lives. I realize that we are part of a lineage where mothers taught their daughters about life through music and dance. We are a link in the lineage, which celebrates life's transitions, joys, and sorrows with dance.

On a more personal note, I made the decision to not have children at the age of fifteen. Today, I have many daughters. What a trick Margita and the Universe played on me, to be initiated into the role of mother through something as simple and profound as a dance class for little girls. I reluctantly said yes to the responsibility of being a teacher and role model to these children. I was afraid: afraid of growing up myself, afraid of making mistakes, afraid of being trapped. Hmmm. Perhaps I was only afraid of being present with myself and the beauty of each moment life has to offer. The girls gave me this gift… they taught me how to be present. And what I am most aware of as I reflect on our past journeys together, current conversations, and hopes and dreams for the future, is the deepening current of Love.

• • • •

BONNEY MEYER is an educator, author and life coach living in North Bay in the San Francisco Bay Area of California. After working as a medical professional for two decades, she pursued extensive training in counseling modalities which ultimately led to her career in life/spiritual coaching. She is co-author of *The Joy of Relationship Cards* (Berkeley: Leap Frog Press, 1994), a deck of 64 cards and accompanying book filled with love and relationship wisdom, as well as the book, *Becoming Soulmates* (Leap Frog, 2001). As a spiritual seeker, Bonney has spent the last 30 years studying world religions and sacred dance traditions, including temple and mask dancing in Bali. Bonney has taught Middle Eastern, Bulgarian, African, Earth, Circle Dance and also, The 21 Praises of Tara Dance Mandala. Her website address is *www.bonneymeyer.com*.

CHAPTER FOUR

Liturgical Dance as an Avenue to God

Kathryn Mihelick

B EING THE CHILD of an Irish Catholic mother and a German Lutheran father, I was raised with an appreciation for the diversity of paths on the journey
of faith, even within the Christian community. With my father's sanction, most of
my religious involvement occurred in the Roman Catholic Church. Many ritual and
spiritual experiences were imprinted on me as a child growing up in this tradition,
to be revisited and nourished throughout my lifetime. The most compelling of them
was receiving communion—the Eucharist—for the first time at the age of six. I could
hardly contain my excitement at the thought of receiving the Lord Jesus right into my
own body, to fill me and to feed me for the rest of my life! The spiritual significance of
embodied prayer and ritual was to become one of the most important ongoing revelations of my life.

I wore a beautiful, white dress, a sign that my little soul and heart were clean and
pure and, hopefully, deserving of this great gift. My heart was beating rapidly as I
approached the communion railing where I would kneel to receive the Lord. When
the host—the Eucharistic wafer—was placed on my tongue, a great feeling of warmth
welled up in my body; so great that it was difficult for me to maintain a sedate and
steady walk back to my own place in the pew. But it was the moment of leaving the
church at the end of the Mass that is even more indelibly impressed in my memory.

As the service ended, our group of First Communicants moved from the pews into a single file to proceed reverently out of the church. I took my place in the line, still experiencing the awe rendered by the whole event. As I passed through the huge entrance doors onto the top step of the long, twelve step concrete stairway leading out of the church, an overwhelming elation suddenly filled my whole being, and I felt I could fly right off the steps! Of course, in a moment I was quickly brought back to earth, as the child in front of me and the one behind me continued the recessional line down the steps. But I shall never forget that brief instant, as my eyes gazed up and out, when I literally felt that if I raised my arms I would fly right across the street! That certainly was a precious moment in a very special day.

I was also deeply affected by the beauty that surrounded me in my church and realize now that an appreciation for the power of the arts to touch the spirit was beginning to be awakened in me as a child. At that young age, I was completely taken with the breathtaking colors illuminated by the sun's rays streaming through the stained glass windows; their brilliant colors bursting forth effervescently. The graceful lines of the elegant statuary reminded me of the women and men whose lives of love, service, and devotion were models for us to try to emulate as we grew up. The walls were graced with elegant paintings, exposing me to this art form for the first time. Inspired by this beauty at such a young age, little did I realize then that it was the art of dance that would one day open so many spiritual and communal doors for me. Faith was the first of two gifts I've received that have shaped my life and formed me into the person I have become. The second is dance.

And when did dance become a part of my life? I would love to be able to tell you a beautiful story… saying something like, "as a little child I always loved to twirl about, leap through the meadows, move when music played," but I cannot. Mine is not a glamorous story. I was enrolled in dance class at the tender age of three at the suggestion of a doctor, who said I needed more exercise. From very early on, I was dealing with a sluggish excretory system; in a word, I was constipated. When he said dance might help, my mother marched right out and enrolled me in a class of "kiddie" movement. Thus the embarrassing curse of constipation became a blessing in disguise; because I loved the dance class and continued taking dance classes for the next fifteen years, at first in tap, and eventually in ballet as well. My sister and I took private tap lessons and became known in our home town as the "dancing Dengler sisters." Besides giving us an excellent weekly exercise regimen, the dance gave us many local performance opportunities at venues such as senior centers, organizational luncheon and dinner gatherings, and a live performance event sponsored weekly at a downtown movie theatre. Best of all, dance proved to be helpful not only in solving my physical condition, but also in building self-assurance into my basically shy nature.

God has given each of us a body, a mind, and a spirit that together form
a wholeness which becomes palpable in dance.

After finishing high school, I attended Ohio University, pursuing a degree in journalism. Here I was introduced to modern dance, something that was not being taught in private dance studios throughout our country at that time, and even today is not offered in the majority of commercial studios. In the 1950s and 60s, dance as a professional performance pursuit in the larger cities—New York, Los Angeles, Chicago—centered on ballet, tap, and the modern jazz style popularized by choreographers such as Bob Fosse and Gus Giordano. This style continues today as an essential element in musical theatre production. In the same era, modern dance was just beginning to be established as a professional pursuit, evolving from the work of early pioneers such as Isadora Duncan, Martha Graham, Jose Limon, and Merce Cunningham. As a result, many colleges and universities had begun to incorporate a few classes of this form into their Physical Education programs. Since a very few were offering it as a major curricular focus, I remained in journalism and kept repeating the basic class in modern dance offered three times each week during the four years of my journalism degree program. The journalism training proved to be very valuable years later, when I founded the Leaven Dance Company and was responsible for promotion, press releases, and grant writing.

Like many other dance students entering college, even today, I had to be convinced at first that modern interpretive dance really was dance. Rolling on the floor...

no turn-out of any kind required... legs parallel... flexed ankle... a rigid arm... body curled into a ball... pedestrian walk, no toe to heel ballet stride? This was certainly a contrast to the grace that I had been trained to emulate in other dance genres. Little did I realize that this introduction to modern dance would be the foundation leading me to profound spiritual growth, prayer expression, and a community ritual dance practice. The movement and body placement required in other dance forms such as ballet, folk, and social dance, are precisely codified. There are exact body positions and transitional movements dictated by each form. This codification can facilitate bodily discipline, grace, beauty, and flow and encompasses classifications ranging from recreational activity to fine art. In modern dance, however, the only limitations placed on movement are those imposed by the anatomical structure of the body. Any type of movement is valid if it portrays what the dancer or choreographer intends to communicate. This gives it the freedom for external manifestation of internal impulses, thoughts, inclinations, emotions, and attitudes, however grotesque or beautifully endearing they may be. I eventually came to realize that this characteristic provides the qualities that make modern dance an effective and meaningful form for prayer.

Dance as Spiritual Expression

The first time I was asked to dance in a church service I was slightly taken aback. Dance had always been associated with artistic performance in my mind. Never had I perceived it in any other context. Before marriage and the birth of my children, I had danced professionally with Orchesis Ensemble, Heidt Touring Company, and the Indianapolis Starlight Musicals. Some years later, I received an M.A. degree in theatre with an emphasis in dance from Kent State University, and was hired to teach in their dance major program, which trains students for professional performance. I taught modern dance technique, ballet, tap, dance composition, dance history, and dance as an art form. My tenure at Kent includes choreographing and performing in many faculty concerts. However, all this did not prepare me to know how I should respond to a request to dance in church.

This request came more than 25 years ago when a deacon clergyman in my parish, knowing that I taught dance at Kent State University, asked if I would dance in a Good Friday community interfaith service to be held at my church, Holy Family Catholic Church, in Stow, Ohio, a suburban community of 35,000. I was hesitant, unaware of dance ever having been performed as worship. How could this be? Dance as worship? Isn't dance a performance? How can anyone be prayerful and really meditate if moving all around? Isn't that distracting? You don't pray with your body. Prayer emanates from the mind—through thought and contemplation—not in twirling, leaping and gliding around in compliance with a rhythm.

I decided to seek guidance from my pastor, the head of our parish, expecting that he would advise me concerning what I should do. He was a remarkably spiritual priest for whom I had always had the greatest respect, admiration, and affection. After a rather lengthy discussion, conducted with great sensitivity on his part, I left his office and suddenly realized that he had not told me what to do. In his wisdom, he had left the decision to me. I found myself both disappointed, a little annoyed that I was still faced with my dilemma, and yet amused at how deftly he had handled his responses to my concerns. He left me with complete freedom of choice.

After more prayerful consideration, I made the choice. It was one that would forever impact my life, my spiritual journey, my husband, and my six children. Recruiting four Kent State University students to join me, I choreographed a movement interpretation of the hymn, "Were You There." In the process of interpreting our reaction to the crucifixion of Christ, a wonderful thing happened. The dance did become a prayer.

As I was developing the movement for the group, my thoughts focused on being present at the crucifixion. I imagined how I would feel watching someone I loved, someone who was willing to die for me, hanging on a cross. I even pictured my own son on the cross and the horrible anguish that must have been felt by his mother, Mary. Out of this came the responses in my body that gave outer expression and form to the inner turmoil, which, in turn led to a heightened awareness of the great significance this event had for me spiritually.

As each rehearsal progressed, the physicality of expression the dancers were experiencing transmuted into palpable feelings regarding the crucifixion. We were sensing more and more clearly that what we were doing was the physical embodiment and expression of what we were holding in our minds and hearts. This was a compelling revelation to me and the other dancers as well.

The response to our dance by those in attendance at that Good Friday evening service was immediate and positive. Many people came forward to express the ways they had been touched. Some said it brought the meaning of the Good Friday events closer to them than they had ever experienced before. The effect on one of the young men in our group of four college student dancers was even more revealing. He took me aside and shared with me that he had not been a part of a worshiping community since he was a young child, nor had he thought about anything spiritual in all those years. With that evening's experience, he was now beginning to sense that there was something more he wanted in life, and he planned to search for a church community where he could pursue further exploration of this newfound dimension. And so my journey of experiencing dance as a manifestation of my faith began.

Performance or Prayer?

Some ask, as I originally had, isn't dance an artistic performance rather than an offering to God? One is secular, the other is sacred. Can it be both at the same time? My journey has shown me that it is indeed possible for dance to be both of these things simultaneously, and that the spiritual element of dance is inevitably experienced when belief becomes the motivation for the movement. There is much discussion among sacred/liturgical dancers around this issue. Before my own Good Friday experience, I argued that dance could not be perceived and regarded as a choreographed performance if it were truly to be prayer; because performance is a secular pursuit and prayer is a spiritual pursuit. But after that initial transformational experience, these two pursuits were forever fused for me. As I became more involved, this new perspective continued to grow and take shape in my mind. I became completely convinced that performance and prayer are not mutually exclusive. Dance as an art form consists of taking the gifts given us by God and doing everything we can to make them as effective as possible in production and performance. What a joy it became to perform for my creator, helping me to bond with Him more and more.

The bottom line in distinguishing between sacred and secular dance performance, as I have come to understand it, is motivation and context. The purpose of secular stage performance is generally understood to be an act of entertainment wherein the dancer finds fulfillment in accomplishing virtuosity in skill and execution, and the audience finds enjoyment in witnessing the technical expertise and artistic talent displayed. The motivation for the sacred dancer in the context of a worshipping congregation is quite different. The focus here is to give praise and honour to God. Those who believe a liturgical dancer is merely performing, and not praying, are calling into question the dancer's motivation. Who can make that judgment but the individual dancer and God?

In dancing interpretively with spiritual intent—whether spontaneously or according to a previously choreographed work—we are executing an action in praise and honor of Our Lord and offered for His greater glory! In doing so, we are "performing" this action with our whole minds, our whole bodies, our whole hearts, and our whole spirits to the very best of our God-given ability. Our God is worthy of no less than this!

The Reverend Father Robert VerEecke is a dancer, founder of a dance company, pastor of St. Ignatius Catholic Church in Boston, Massachusetts, and artist-in-residence at Boston College. In an article in the Catholic magazine, *America*, he states, "Liturgy is by nature a dialogue between performance and prayer... Isn't it the nature of ritual leadership to 'perform'? Effective preachers, soloists, and choirs are such because they are good performers."[15] This dialogue, for me, is one which has instilled me with not only the deepened relationship I mentioned, but also with increasing trust in a God who is always there leading me where it is best for me to be.

Body and Spirit:
Body as a Vehicle for Spiritual Expression

About ten years ago, I received a grant from the Ohio Arts Council to organize and sponsor a multicultural concert of sacred dance to be performed in my church in Stow, Ohio. The concert included African American, Native American, Hindu, and Christian cultural spiritual dance. Much to my chagrin, I found that there were some Catholics who maintained that dance was inappropriate for performance in a space designated for Christian worship, also stipulating that it should not be used for worship services of any kind.

Is the body an appropriate vehicle for spiritual expression? The controversial aspect of this issue in the Christian church is no doubt rooted in the centuries-old dualism promoted by ancient philosophers such as Epictitus, Plenus, and Aristotle, in which mind and body were considered separate and antithetical to one another, with mind occupying the superior position. However, whenever I am dancing in worship, I experience a sense of wholeness and oneness; everything my body is doing is the material expression of everything my spirit is feeling… they are not separated.

The Rev. VerEecke writes of his 25 years of experience in offering movement prayer retreats and workshops. He expresses amazement at the power these experiences have in freeing up individuals to encounter God in a new way, beyond simply mental activity. Movement has its own language and way of expressing what is happening within a person. He has concluded that when one's prayer to God evolves through bodily expression in movement, a true epiphany occurs. [16]

I have found this "epiphany" of which Father VerEecke speaks applies also to the import of scripture upon us. Once I have danced to the reading of a scripture passage, I never hear it in exactly the same way again. It takes on a new meaning, a personal connection. It is transmitted into my being, creating a bodily felt sense of connectedness to self, to others, and to a holy presence. In the parable of the seed (Mt. 13:10-23), God teaches that seed, in order to bear fruit, must be planted on fertile soil. In like manner, the "planting" of my feet on God's earth as I dance buoys me up, propelling me to a leap that strives to ascend to divine heights, filling me with the breath of the Holy Spirit.

Who we are and what we become are formed by our life experiences and relationships. And these are initially processed through the body… seeing, hearing, smelling, tasting, touching, and that kinesthetic sense through which we come to know our relationship with the spaces we inhabit. If in childhood we were small rather than large, pretty rather than not so pretty, agile rather than clumsy, spoke smoothly rather than haltingly, touched gently rather than slapped, shared our ice cream rather than our spinach, we found that our relationships with others grew in accordance with how the others were affected by these qualities and actions. This body "temple"—its size, its shape, its aesthetic characteristics—all impact who we are, how we may be perceived by others, how we perceive ourselves, how we process those perceptions, and, ultimately, the person we become. This has been confirmed by other leaders in sacred dance, as well.

Dance, as a form of exercise, combined with spiritual intent, can also contribute to overall health and well-being and have a powerful impact on healing. In blending the functions of body, mind, and spirit into one rhythmic, harmonious whole, our mental and emotional health is strengthened. Dr. Herbert Benson writes that his scientific studies have astonished him by showing conclusively that our bodies are "wired to believe." He found that spiritually-laden beliefs have a considerable influence on the determination of our health, and that prayer and other exercises of belief serve to nourish and heal our bodies.[17]

Dance as Communication: Life's Rhythm

When asked why we dance in the sanctuary, through the aisles of our places of worship, at special celebrations, indoors, outdoors, and at home, we reply that we dance in joy, in thanksgiving, in praise, sometimes in sorrow, in anguish, in relation to God and each other, because movement itself is a universal language.

Movement is perhaps the oldest form of communication. It is probable that humans connected with each other through movement, gesture, and possibly dance, before the development of spoken language. Bodily expression is part of our lived reality. Movement is universally understood, for the language of the body is concrete, not abstract, as words are. Our postures, gestures, and facial expressions disclose what is going on inside. Non-verbal communication through body movement reaches to the depths of our psyches and in doing so, forms connections universally understood beyond boundaries of culture and nations.

The visual aspect of dance makes it one of the most compelling forms for communication, and especially in intercultural exchanges. The visual images linger in the mind conjuring up the inexpressible, invisible realities beyond words. Dance is our link to the cosmic rhythm of the universe, putting us in synchronization with the pulse of all creation. I dance because it is impossible *not* to respond to the rhythms that are all around us and in us all the time. Dance is a mystery that transfuses, transforms, transcends everything material about us. In a paraphrase, "To move is human; to dance is divine."

Dance is our link to the cosmic rhythm of the universe

The non-verbal, visceral, experiential nature of movement makes it a language of the heart, a language that cannot be entirely put into words. I have come to realize that it is indeed in the heart where God must be found to be truly known. Intellectually, we can know who God is, but we can only know Him in relationship, through life experiences that transcend the intellect. Retreat Master Anthony DeMello puts it simply, "Prayer is to be made less with the head than with the heart...When you pray with your body you give power and body to your prayer."[18] God has given each of us a body, a mind, and a spirit that together form a wholeness that becomes palpable in dance.

Dance puts the non-verbal language of movement into patterns of rhythmic sequenced phrases, giving it form and meaning as the most finely articulated art of movement. As the oldest art form, dance was closely allied to spiritual and religious impulses, not only in primitive cultures but throughout history as well. I believe it is a gift given to us by God, made possible through these marvelous temples we call our bodies. And so, we offer ourselves back to the Lord from whom all blessings flow. It is said that your feet may learn the steps, but only your spirit can dance. Authentic, interpretive movement has the power to focus on an inner meaning, which transcends technique alone.

These attributes make dance a uniquely appropriate form for worship. I find tremendous joy in knowing that God loves me. How better to express this joy than to let it fill my whole being, exploding in joyful bursts of movement. Conversely, I find infinite peace in knowing that my God is always present to support me in times of sorrow, pain, and discouragement. How better to experience that presence than to physically reach out to accept it, assuming a shape of gratitude throughout the whole body. Dance stretches and strives for release of the Spirit, for the extension of energy. In fact it is often described as the extension of energy into space and time. The body sculpts space using patterns of time in evolving through a meaningful dynamic flow of energy variation. I am set free, my tensions are released, my boundaries extended, and I am carried outside of myself.

The core of dance is simply rhythmic movement, which in itself is symbolic of life and creation. Because it divides time in rhythmic patterns, it nurtures the basic rhythmic impulses within us, which are implanted by our Creator. We walk in a rhythm, talk in a rhythm, our hearts beat in rhythm sending our life blood through our veins rhythmically. The oxygen that sustains us is ingested into our lungs in rhythmic cadence. The very act of human procreation is rhythmical. All this, in turn, unites us with the rhythms of all creation: the ebb and flow of the tide, the pattern of the seasons, night following day, following night, following day, the recurring full cycle of the moon each month, the seasonal migration of birds, the evolution of the planets. All living creatures move through the space of creation, through the time of creation, by means of the energy in creation. Dance incorporates, reflects, and projects this essence.

Throughout the years, I have led many movement prayer workshops at churches, senior centers, and faith-related schools and organizations, and have witnessed the effect they can have, especially on teenagers, in relation to their bodies. Part of the thrust of these events has been to help the participants view their bodies with greater respect as gifts from God, and to become aware of the sacredness of the body as the true "temple of the Holy Spirit." I have observed that often early in the sessions there is significant evidence of self-consciousness about the body among participants. I witness hesitancy about full participation in interactive movement experiences—especially those involving touch—and a reluctance to let their bodies freely move into expressive attitudes.

This is not surprising, considering the pervasive media focus relegating the body to simply a tool for self-centered sensual pleasure, cosmetically enhanced glamour, exclusively physical sexual gratification, and competitive sport earmarked principally for money-making. This is a degraded understanding of the body, perpetuated even further today by the spread of the illicit use of drugs. Using the body as an instrument for prayer has the potential for restoring it to its rightful position of dignity as a sacred vessel. By the end of the prayer workshops, I have seen the teens relating in group movement experiences—even those with a component of touch—in a much more open, comfortable manner lacking any stigma or sign of reluctance. A whole new insight on the wonder and sacredness of the body has been generated.

Dance as Transformation

Leaven Dance Company came into existence in 1989 when I was invited to bring a group of dancers to perform in a concert of sacred dance in Pennsylvania. On the trip, there we began sharing our beliefs in viewing dance as having powerful potential as an agent for change, self-discovery, and personal and international peace. That is when I envisioned the nucleus of a dance company emerging. The ensemble now dwells in the firm belief that creative, authentic movement expression reflects a universal language of communication; integrates body, mind, and spirit; and promotes unity among diverse populations. The company's name, Leaven, is taken from the scripture, "The reign of God is like leaven, which a woman took and kneaded into three measures of flour. Eventually the whole mass of dough began to rise." [19] All these images, the movement, the rising, and the dough, are symbolic of the Bread of Life, which sustains us. All are metaphors for the "reign of God." We hope, in some small way through our movement offerings, to be part of the leaven which works to help give rise to the reign of God on earth.

Leaven Dance Company is a project-oriented group whose size and meeting schedule depend upon the event for which we are preparing. There are five core members participating regularly from among Kent State University faculty and students. When needed, additional dancers are brought in for concert performances and, on occasion, worship services, from the University of Akron and the northeast Ohio dance community. The pieces in the company's repertoire are choreographed to various types of accompaniment, including hymns, orchestral music, scripture readings, and sometimes movement done in silence.

In our company's dance interpretation of one scripture reading, the percussive, direct, sharp, abrupt, and angular gestures that portray, "He shall strike the ruthless with the rod of His mouth, and with the breath of His lips He shall slay the wicked," we show the destiny of isolation that the wicked bring upon themselves. These gestures are in sharp contrast to the smooth, curved, gentle, elliptical transitions from shape to shape in the movement interpretation of the verse, "The spirit of the Lord shall rest upon him; a spirit of wisdom and understanding... of counsel and strength..." By the time the reading has reached the lines, "...the wolf shall be a guest of the lamb, and the leopard shall lie down with the kid... The baby shall play by the cobra's den...

There shall be no harm or ruin on all my holy mountain..." [20] the steady release of tension in the body is transformed into a harmonious flow of energy, moving blissfully through space in depiction of the joy and peace awaiting us as God protects us from the wicked. Whenever I hear that reading now, my body assumes the feelings wrought by having experienced them not only with my sense of hearing, but with my whole being; their meaning is intensified and personalized.

I have received great joy and fulfillment in witnessing the far-reaching impression liturgical dance can make. One of my personal treasures is a letter written by my son to the executive director of the Liturgy Office of the United States Conference of Catholic Bishops. It was among a group of letters sent by persons who wished to advocate for the official sanction of the use of dance in worship, in response to some opposition to it that was occurring at the time. In my son's letter, he related the experience of bringing sacred dance into his children's school, St. Michael's, in Findlay, Ohio, as part of a special "class mass." He had invited me to do this and with the reluctant permission of the pastor, I presented a dance of prayer which was, as stated in my son's letter, "wonderfully received by the students, faculty, and other parishioners." A few months later my son's work took him out of Ohio to a new location. His letter to the liturgy director closed with the following:

"How much impact did this sacred dance have? Well, ten years later, my brother, who has been living in Atlanta, Georgia, called to say that his job was taking him to, of all places, Findlay, Ohio. He told me that when his wife enrolled their children into St. Michael's School the secretary recognized the last name and asked if she was related to me. When my brother's wife said that indeed she was related, the secretary told her about... the class mass with the liturgical dance! Ten years after this mass, hundreds of masses and students in between, and she remembered this particular mass!"

"I have told my mother, 'Mom thank you for the impression that you had on my son and countless others in Findlay, Ohio, 10 years ago. Keep spreading the word of God.'"

Sincerely,
David Mihelick

The dance presented at that time, done to Sandi Patti's vocal, "You Are A Masterpiece," is also a precious memory for me; a duet involving my seven-year-old grandson, and depicting the message that each child born into the world is God's masterpiece.

This capacity for dances of the spirit to impact those who witness it was revealed in a recent experience of our Leaven Dance Company. It is one I shall never forget. The activity therapist of a men's prison in Ohio phoned to ask our company to be part of a program he was planning that would also include speakers who would focus on general health and HIV-Aids. Assuming he was looking for an element of entertainment for his program, I suspected he was not aware of the nature of our work. Indeed, when I asked, this suspicion was confirmed. I explained that we focused on sacred and liturgical dance, expecting him to reply, "Oh, alright. Well thank you anyway. That's not exactly what I had in mind." Instead, he responded with a quick, "Oh, that will be fine." Whoops! I wondered what I had gotten myself into.

It was with trepidation that I assembled a program of pieces, uncertain what might be most appropriate for an event about which I knew very little, and for an audience very foreign to us. We were advised not to bring any valuables—including purses or wallets—into the prison with us, but to lock them in our cars. Upon arrival, we were taken through a security check before entering the prison compound. Aware that we were bringing performance attire in our traveling bags, the security personnel asked if we would be wearing any fishnet hose. I assured them that our legs were covered with opaque dance tights and the dresses we were wearing came up to our necks and nearly down to our ankles. I was made aware of their concern in this regard when a story was relayed that one of the female rehabilitation speakers had been advised that "her skirt was too short," and she had been given one of the loose fitting cotton pant suits worn by the prison medical staff to replace her own outfit when she spoke to the inmates.

Our performance took place in a section of the main facility building, where inmates who were listed on the good behavior roster were allowed to come for special activities. We were to dress in a crafts room immediately across a hall from the main room. As we dressed, we could hear the guards filing the men into the room. The two guest speakers were already seated on the platform and were waiting to be introduced. Our section of the program was a forty minute presentation of dances including: a movement interpretation of a psalm set to music; a trio, Touch of the Spirit, set to scripture readings interspersed with music; a dance depicting a poetic essay;[21] and Helen Tamiris' historic suite of dances, Negro Spirituals. These had been given to us by a representative of the Dance Notation Bureau via a grant we received for an earlier project designed to celebrate Black History month. They contained a nice blend of several songs, ranging from "Nobody Knows the Trouble I've Seen" to "When the Saints Go Marching In."

The door of our dressing room was located immediately across the hall from the entrance to the main room. When the program began with the introduction of the first speaker, I stepped out of our dressing room into the hall. The main door had been left slightly ajar and I realized I would be able to stand in the hall, unobtrusively peer through the doorway, and survey the faces of the inmates while the guest speakers gave their presentations. Yes, indeed, these were a bunch of tough-looking characters. (I immediately scolded myself for being so judgmental!) As the two speakers delivered their talks, I noted a few faces showing an expression of interest. But many stared blankly ahead, and some yawned and shifted listlessly in their seats.

The time for Leaven Dance Company's entrance arrived. The first piece was a solo by Andrea Shearer, our associate director. She stepped out to dance an interpretation of a song written by her cousin, Tom Kendzia, "Let Your Face Shine Upon Us, Lord" with lyrics taken from Psalm 80. The music was gentle and flowing. Immediately all eyes were on her and a loud catcall and a whistle erupted from the audience. Guffaws and chatter could be heard, and a boisterous atmosphere gripped the room. My heart sank. I realized this was the kind of reception I had subconsciously feared. I waited with bated breath as she began, and noticed that very slowly the noise began to subside a bit.

As the program continued, whenever I wasn't dancing or changing garments, I used every opportunity I could to take note of the reactions of the inmates as they watched our company members perform. Those eyes, which had previously appeared vacant during the speakers' presentations and then had glistened lustfully with Andrea's entrance, gradually began to be attentive with curiosity. Slowly my misgivings began to subside. With each dance piece, the contour of the expressions revealed a revised understanding and perception of what they were seeing. A quiet attentiveness progressively increased as their concentration was captivated. They began responding with respectful applause. As we brought the program to completion, the entire roomful of men rose to their feet in a standing ovation. Their applause seemed generated by a kind of reverent enthusiasm that I shall never forget. It brought tears to my eyes. Two of the inmates, accompanied by a guard, were permitted to talk with us before we left in order to tell us how much they had appreciated the program. These men had been touched and changed. So had I.

Our bodies, joined with mind and spirit, are gifts from God. The visual element of dance and the image it portrays in communication of the spirit validates its effectiveness in touching and transforming people. And sharing this gift of wholeness through the art of dance in a worship liturgy or sacred performance can have tremendous impact not only on the community with whom it is shared, but on the dancer as well. What more can be said?

"Praise Him with timbrel and dance." [22]

• • • •

KATHRYN MIHELICK, former assistant professor and coordinator of the dance division at Kent State University, is founder/director of Leaven Dance Company, a professional dance ensemble in Ohio. She received the National Sacred Dance Guild's Honor Award in 1999 for "Exemplary Contribution to the Field of Sacred Dance," as well as the award for "Outstanding Contribution to the Advancement of the Dance Art Form" in 2002 from OhioDance, and the Akron Area Arts Alliance's 2005 Outstanding Artist in Dance Award. She performed professionally with Orchesis Ensemble, the Heidt Touring Company in California, and Indianapolis Starlight Musicals, and spent five seasons as resident choreographer for Porthouse Theatre at Cleveland Orchestra's Blossom Music Center. Her website address is *www.leavendance.org.*

CHAPTER FIVE

Dancing the Goddess Tara: Praise Her, Embody Her, Discover Your Own Perfection

Prema Dasara

S HE APPEARED TO ME as a dancing Goddess. Tara, Mother Protector, is known for Her excellent sense of humor. I had met Her in different texts and *thangka,* or paintings, introduced by Tibetan Lamas and my Hindu research into the Goddess. And there She was, dancing before me as I walked the hills above my remote Maui home. I'm not sure who started dancing first. It could have been me. Trained in the art of Odissi, a style of Indian Temple dancing, I was familiar with embodying the goddess through dance.

I had been asked by a Tibetan Lama to shape the 21 Praises of Tara text into verse so it could be sung in English. The text resembled the *slokas,* or verses, that comprise the dances that I had learned in India. I was certain that it had been danced before. The 21 Praises of Tara is one of the most common prayers in Tibetan Buddhist practice, akin to the Lord's Prayer in the Christian religion. The Praises are in four line stanzas, describing various qualities and attributes of Goddess Tara. It is said when Tara attained enlightened mind, the entire universe praised Her. This is the source of the 21 Praises of Tara.

As I sang the praises, reaching for the perfect meter, I felt my body forming the *mudras,* the stances and hand gestures that interpreted the text. As I became more familiar with each praise, I could not distinguish if I was imitating the goddess that appeared before me as a rainbow breath of light and joy, or if it was arising out of some deep knowing of my own. It was a transcendent experience and I would arrive home breathless with exertion and wonder.

Lama Sonam Tenzin, a Tibetan Lama who had been assigned to teach at the Maui Dharma Center, had recently arrived on Maui from India. With my few words of Hindi, we were able to communicate and became friends. I had just settled in myself, after having lived in India for six years and married a man whose home was on Maui. My husband's friends were interested in experiencing the dance that was so precious to my heart and so I endeavored to present this sacred experience to them. I invited Lama Tenzin to my offerings. He was quite taken with the experience and invited me to dance in the shrine room of the Maui Dharma Center as an offering during Tibetan festivals. Then he asked me to work with the 21 Praises of Tara.

When I told him of my ecstatic experiences working with the text, I asked if it had ever been danced in the Tibetan Tradition. He was quite certain that it had never been done. Since he seemed to enjoy my dances as an offering during his celebrations, I asked for permission to create a performance piece based on the practice he had given me. He gave his wholehearted permission.

I approached two other professional dancers thinking we would create the dance together. My dear friend, Lauryn Galindo, said she had been dreaming of Tara dancing and thought that it was to be something that would include all of our Maui friends. Knowing that very few of our friends had any dance training I could not imagine how this would work. My idea had been to carefully choreograph each praise according to traditional postures and *mudras*, or symbolic hand gestures.

Lauryn insisted on her vision and said that she would "dream on it." I knew that she had profound guidance dreams so the next morning I eagerly awaited what insight she might offer. She said to me, somewhat discouraged, "I don't have anything to say... all night I dreamt of a golden spiral." As soon as she said those words I could see the dance clearly.

We set to work immediately. Fourteen friends joined us in the dance. I asked them to select a praise that they wanted to represent and I helped them create a solo dance to interpret the praise.

My neighbor, Jeff Munoz, worked with me on the music. Jeff often came down from the hermitage he managed above us and joined my husband and I, singing Hindu devotional songs into the night. One of our favorite pieces was a traditional Indian chant to Tara he had learned from his good friend Bhagavan Das. Using that melody as the basis for the body of the dance, and keeping within the *raga*, or beat, I shaped the rest of the piece.

Lauryn and I worked together on the opening movements. We started with the dancers arranged in a crescent moon mandala facing the audience. I stood in front of them so they could follow my movements and we engaged in a simple version of Refuge and Bodhicitta. These prayers traditionally open any Tibetan Buddhist practice. From there we went directly into the music of the Mandala of the 21 Praises of Tara. It begins with an invocation, "I Pray That You Come, Arya Tara." We had the dancers reaching out to Tara, then turning and walking in a stately, stylized way into a spiral. When the praises started, a dancer would be "born" out of the center of the spiral to dance her praise before the audience. When she finished her praise she would rejoin the mandala at the end of the spiral. We separated each praise by singing Tara's mantra, OM TARE TUTTARE TURE SOHA. The dancers would turn in place with the mantra and advance one position, a new Tara being born during each turning. We unwound the mandala during the prayer of benefit and then "danced the mantra."

I was very inspired by a body of work at that time called "Sufi Dancing." Mantras from the world's religions had been formed into simple folk dances, done in a circle. Kachina Palencia and Dechen Groode had been trained in this genre so they helped me to create a "Sufi Dance" using Tara's Mantra and three traditional Tibetan Buddhist meditation practices.

There were about 100 people in the audience the day we danced Tara for the first time. I had opened the program with several of my Indian dances. When we completed the Mandala of Tara it was the most remarkable thing. Dancers were crying, audience members were crying, and Lama Tenzin's eyes were filled with a beautiful reverence.

I found the experience rather strange. From my point of view, the dance was not very interesting. The dancers were not trained. Their movements were not very expressive. I could not understand why the audience was so moved. Immediately everyone asked us to do it again. Other women wanted to join us. I was certainly willing to do this but I was curious why the big reaction. It took me some years before I began to understand the basis of what we were doing that was affecting the healing, the blessings, the sense of empowerment.

His Holiness the Dalai Lama was the one that clarified it for me. In 1998, Anahata Iradah and I took a group of fifty dancers from around the world to offer the dance to Him and the Tibetan Community of Dharamsala. After the presentation, He granted us an interview.

I had been teaching the dance to groups all over the world for over ten years when we had this momentous meeting. I asked Him, "Whenever the dance is performed, most of the audience members have no idea what we are actually doing. They don't

Prema after dancing for the Dalai Lama

know anything about Tara, Buddhism, Asian thought, or sacred dance, yet they have tremendous inner experiences. Many of them weep. It is not the expertise of the dancers that is moving them. For the most part the dancers are untrained and often insecure in their presentations. What is it that affects people so strongly?"

His Holiness explained that Tara's element was the wind. She represented the energy that moved through the body. Her mantra brought blessings of vitality and well being. "You do not need to know the name of the wind to feel its effect."

It reminded me of a talk that Bokar Rinpoche gave shortly after a group of Maui dancers had presented him and Khenpo Donyo with an offering of the Tara Dance. He told us that the dance creates auspicious conditions. In the Tibetan tradition, this is a very important concept. In order for us to realize our highest spiritual aspirations and the greatest mental health, it is essential that our mind be stable and clear. This enables us to attract beneficial and inspiring circumstances to us. It also makes us receptive to these circumstances so that we can make the most of the opportunities they provide.

He explained. "…associating with Tara's transmission allows us to remove obstacles in our lives, including natural calamities, epidemics, war, and all kinds of danger, harm, and fear… the dance directly communicates not only through words and movement but also through energy, symbol and atmosphere… the dancers who with a genuine heart express the enlightened qualities and activities of Tara can be so inspired that hindrances in their own personal lives can be clarified. This gives rise to longevity as well as from an ultimate point of view the dancer may find herself endowed with the unconditioned wisdom inspiration of Tara."

Rinpoche went on to tell us that those who are witnessing the dance will find clarification from confused preoccupations and will find hindrances removed in the path of pursuing spirituality in their own life. It is that sublime sense of freedom when we experience the truth of our inner nature that is stimulated by the Dance of Tara. Listening to these great Lamas say such wonderful things about this simple dance that I had created forced me to reflect on what in my past had prepared me to give birth to this powerful method.

My mother was fond of saying that I danced out of her womb. I always remember delighting in the feel of being in a human body. I loved to move my body. And I loved music. My parents were passionate about ballroom dancing and from an early age, I was whisked around our living room, standing on my father's feet as he guided me through the waltz, the foxtrot, the rumba, and the cha-cha. They were also passionate about music. I ironed my clothes to some of the greatest operatic voices of our time, and dusted the living room to recordings of great classical composers.

I had some ballet training at a very early age and this was excellent for helping me to strengthen and prepare my body for exceptional dance movements. I lost interest in the form of ballet. I discovered that on my own, in nature, I could move to the rhythms and melody of my own heart. I could dance with the wind, twirl with the mermaids in the ocean, exchange gossip with the trees through the magic of my gestures.

As I grew, there was conflict in my family and I was not very comfortable at home. Fortunately I grew up in Miami, Florida which, in the 50s, was little more than a town. I could easily ride my bike into the most exquisite places in nature and dance and dream. This kept me sane.

I left home at the age of 16 looking for "wisdom." I didn't really know what that meant, I only knew that to find it was the most important thing in my life. This took me traveling throughout the United States and Europe finally settling in India where I worked for the Theosophical Society. Rukmini Devi opened my eyes to another world with her dance school, Kalakshetra. The subtleties of Indian dance had me intrigued.

When I encountered the style of Odissi Dance, I was enchanted and intimidated. The sinuous movements, the lyrical music was haunting, mesmerizing, powerful. The choreography was complex. The feet, the hands, the midriff, the hips, the head, the face, the eyes, the eyebrows all moved independently and yet were highly coordinated.

It took me three months to persuade Guru Ramani Ranjan Jena to accept me as his student. At his insistence, I joined his group class, but it was impossible for me to imitate the nuances of the style. Finally he agreed to teach me privately. Every day he would come to my house. When he stepped through my door, he would bow to the deities I had enshrined about my practice room. I would place his drum before him and then would touch his feet in reverence and gratitude.

The dance was so complicated—so subtle—my mind would focus completely in concentration. There was no room for any thought. The practice was a powerful meditation so far removed from my personal style, abandoned, free. I found my body and consciousness responding in exceptional ways.

I came to live in India because of a series of powerful visionary experiences I had with a teacher called Satya Sai Baba. While living at his ashram in India, we were encouraged to immerse ourselves in as complete a cultural experience as possible. The cultural trappings surrounding Sai Baba were Hindu but trying to understand just what made up a Hindu was a perplexing challenge. After years in India, I came to understand that, etymologically speaking, a Hindu is someone who lives in the Indus Valley. The varieties of worship and belief are enormous.

Being somewhat of an intellectual, I found the need to understand what was happening beyond the personal inner experiences, which were quite unusual and profound. I centered my inquiry around the study of the four kinds of yoga: Bhakti – devotion; Karma – activity in service to others; Jnana – knowledge; and Raja – meditation. At the ashram, we had the opportunity to engage in any of these according to our attraction. For most of us, the atmosphere of devotion was the most powerful. Sai Baba's activity and presence encouraged this.

Every day under the trees in the courtyard, we would meet and sing devotional songs to the various Hindu manifestations of the divine—including Sai Baba. This was an immensely satisfying experience. Waves of bliss would pulse through the crowd. It didn't really matter whether it was Ganesh, the elephant-headed god, or Kali, the wrathful mother, or the previous "incarnation" of Sai Baba as a Muslim fakir that we were chanting to. The openhearted waves of love would flow through the assembly.

I made it my business to try and understand who these objects of our devotion were. There is a vast literature about the gods and goddesses. I found the most child-like legends, similar to the Greek and Roman stories of the very human-like exploits of the gods and the goddesses. I also found commentaries by astute philosophers, both historical and modern, such as Adi Shankaracharya, Vivikenanda, Sivananda, Chidmoyananda, and of course, Sai Baba himself, that translated the legends into exquisite teachings of profound mystic and temporal truths. With all parts of my psyche encouraged by the experiences, it was only natural that I would want to dance them.

Rukmini Devi, the woman who revived the ancient art of Bharatanatyam in Ma-dras, lived next door to the office where I worked in the Theosophical Society. We often greeted each other and one day she invited me to witness one of her students giving a demonstration/introduction to the dance style. It was a revelation for me... to see the deities dancing before me. The gestures, the rhythms, the *ragas* were like a call from my ancient past. I resolved that I would learn the art of Indian Temple Dance.

Tai Situ Rinpoche once told us that there was a science of *mudra*, hand gestures, practiced in Tibet that allowed distant monasteries to communicate with each other. One of the monks trained in the art of *mudra* would go to some high place visible to a lookout posted in an area at a distance. He would hold a *mudra* with intent. The lookout, trained to a high degree in receptivity, would receive the message.

My dance teacher confirmed this in other ways. He said that within all of us were deep responses to certain energetic gestures and symbols. If we assumed the proper pose, it would symbolically and energetically influence the audience. To this end, we were taught almost a hundred hand gestures with their mundane and profound significance. We were taught the *mudras* of body poses and facial expressions. Each worked with mood, color, intensity, emotion. We were taught how to train the eye to follow the hand, the expression to reach from the heart, always with the understanding of the profound effect our aware-ness—our strength of concentration—would have on the audience.

My teacher demonstrated how certain rhythmic patterns would cause the audi-ence to move with the dancer, bringing a feeling of joy and well being. Permeating it all were the deities themselves, active energies that became palpable to me.

Whenever we entered "dance space," we took the blessing of the earth. In this ritual movement, we declared that as dancers we carried the prayers of our community within us. We asked the blessing and forgiveness of the earth, as we thoughtlessly moved upon this great being, taking our nourishment and support from Her. We in-vited all unseen beings to be present to bless the dance and orient it toward the most elevated experience. At this point in the prayer, I always felt a great celestial stirring, confident that benevolent, non-corporeal beings were participating in the joy I experienced as the dance unfolded.

Several years into my training, I told my teacher that I was not interested in performing. My experiences as a performer in the west were not very satisfying. I found the atmosphere of dance schools and performance halls to be stifling. Nature was a temple for me. I could dance with integrity within the embrace of the natural world. The dance space in my home was arranged as a temple. There I could feel the depth of experience that the dance provided. I could not imagine dancing publicly without the trappings of ego, concerning myself about what others thought of me, of the dance. When I danced for myself, there was no question of self consciousness. There was simply enjoyment, the delicious movements of my body either accomplishing a training or stretching in abandon. I luxuriated in the feeling of being alive, in a beautiful and supple body. My mind and heart were open to either the beauty around me or the beauty of my sincere heart opening to its wisdom, its creativity, its love, and it's power.

As soon as there was a witness, the experience of the dance changed. I could manage maintaining my focus if it was a friend. The experience was not tainted if I was free to share without thought of judgment. I really was not interested in anyone having commentary on my dance, determining its value by their standards. I danced because I loved to dance. When I shared these reflections with my teacher, he just smiled. He encouraged me to get a costume just in case I changed my mind.

Returning to Hawaii, my husband's friends heard that I had been studying dance in India and of course they were curious. I thought deeply about how I could present the dance to them yet still maintain the integrity of my inner experience. I decided to offer the dance in a friend's living room which was easy to convert into a temple-like atmosphere. I organized a shrine, made offerings, dressed in a sacred way.

My teacher had blessed each object of my costume. Classical Indian dance, in some traditions, was taught as a form of yoga. When each dancer accomplished a certain awakening she would be given a piece of jewellery to represent this accomplishment. Each piece was oriented toward the *chakras*, areas in the body where the channels of energy met and gave rise to certain mastery. Most important were the *ghungru*, or ankle bells. There are many songs and devotional stories told about the *ghungru* that are an instrument when the dancer beats her rhythmic patterns upon the earth.

I was also careful to translate the pieces I danced so that the audience would not just be looking at interesting movements but would be fully informed of who and what I was dancing. There are several different aspects to the Indian Classical Dance of Odissi. At times the dancer is praising the deity. At other times the dancer is manifesting as the deity. Some pieces are devoted to rhythmic accomplishments. Others

73

are stories, told with great depth of emotion, the dancer acting out all the parts. The last dance of every Odissi performance is Moksha. The literal meaning of the word is "liberation" and the movements demonstrate this ecstatic accomplishment.

When I started offering small performances of Odissi, I kept the audience to people I knew. I was confident of my training and of the exquisiteness of the style. I knew that people would be fascinated. I wasn't sure if I could maintain the sacredness of my work. I didn't need to worry about that. As soon as the music started, I was in that world and my training and inner devotion carried me through to the glorious conclusion of full liberation.

The first few years of teaching the Tara Dance did not really generate that kind of transcendent connection. My focus was on grounding the other dancers, keeping them orientated in the movement and choreography. There was no time for me to relax into my sacred space. But at the end of every dance, there was always a great feeling of accomplishment, a celestial joy. Everyone felt it.

Through the dance, I was drawn into studying the Tibetan way. I went to every class the lamas gave. I served each one that visited Maui. I read everything I could find on the subject. I received many empowerments. And then I went into retreat. Lama Tenzin guided me to engage in a simple practice of Tara. It was during this retreat that I began to understand how profound the dance was.

When Situ Rinpoche witnessed the dance in 1987, he said a number of things to me. He told me I would travel all over the world teaching this dance. He said that a festival would form around the dance, much like in the monasteries of Tibet.

I was reluctant. First of all, I didn't know anything about the Tibetan Buddhist dharma that was the source of the music of the dance. I explained my reluctance about performing. I was concerned about the ego taking over the dance. And I couldn't imagine working with groups of women; the strange conflicts and jealousies that seemed to crop up around me were not at all interesting to me. Rinpoche didn't even acknowledge these objections. One by one, over the years, my objections proved unfounded and his predictions accurate.

Everything became clear in the first silent, isolated retreat I did. It was only a month, but it opened for me an understanding of the depth of Tibetan practice they refer to as "view." It showed me how the methods of practice allow us to align with an inner attunement that eventually results in a profound awakening. I started to understand why the Tara Dance had such a powerful effect on the dancers.

On Maui, each time we danced publicly, we offered the dance to a visiting Lama or other spiritual dignitary. Because of their attunement with spirit and energy, they would be transported, and that would amplify our own experience. Situ Rinpoche's first observation was that the dance appeared to him to have a depth of devotion that he had never seen in dance form before. This much I had been able to communicate in my transmission to my students.

After my first retreat, I began to dissect the different parts of the practice that I had already choreographed, but now I was able to understand the inner significance. It was startling how much of what had been put in place was accurate to the practice. The nature of my teaching of the dance changed. My previous preoccupation was on the movements. I started to focus on the meditations, the inner orientation. One of the big discoveries in retreat was a realization of the basic premise of Tibetan practice. It is common cultural knowledge that everyone has "Buddha nature." We engage in the practices in order to reveal this truth. This was a big departure from the indoctrination I had received growing up Christian. We were born sinners and only through the intervention of an outside agency—God, Jesus, Mary—would we ever be redeemed. This was a profound breakthrough. This discovery was a major part of what needed to be healed, in myself, in the other dancers. This is what the dance, the dharma, the practice of Tara directly addressed, the sense of inadequacy that our culture imposed on us.

We all know that there is something within us that is powerful and precious, wise and compassionate. By dancing Tara, by acknowledging our Tara essence, we are able to touch into this essential knowing. The more we affirm this birthright, the more manageable the world becomes. As I incorporated this information into my transmission of the dance, the energy of the dance changed.

In 1996, we danced for Situ Rinpoche again. It had been ten years since that first dance offering to him. This time he declared it not only a vehicle of devotion and an accumulation of merit, but also an accumulation of wisdom; when he watched the dancers he felt that he was watching Buddhas and *dakinis* dancing.

One of the early challenges in forming the dance was how to organize the mandala. What did it look like? How did I arrange twenty-two women into a golden spiral? I started with the downward pointing triangle, ancient symbol of the generative aspect of the goddess. Surrounding this, a circle of six manifested to my eye as the "Star of David," the symbol of the union of masculine and feminine, union of opposites. This left twelve in the outer circle, the number of sacred activity. Twenty years later, I discovered that in some Hindu traditions this is the mandala of the heart chakra. In the Tibetan Buddhist tradition wisdom rests in the heart. This wisdom is based on a true understanding of our potential as human beings. It is inseparable from compassion.

The dancers are born out of the center of the mandala, out of the heart of the rainbow body of the Goddess, to dance their praise before the community. The challenges of moving through the mandala with awareness and the courage to dance publicly were intense for many women. It was the perfect situation to apply some of the mind training practices for which Tibetan Buddhism is famous. First, we need to get acquainted with our mind. Then we need to be able to discriminate what is helpful and what is harmful. Then we have to engage in activities that will turn us away from the harmful and into the helpful.

The dancers are born out of the heart of the rainbow body of the Goddess

These practices provide stability and clarity. Within these two treasures, inspiration and truth arise. The movements, the rhythm, the chanting, the mantra, the energy, and the support of the leader and the rest of the circle of dancers provide a crucible in which intense emotional and mental restrictions can be examined and discarded. It is extraordinarily liberating. Throughout the dance, the dancer is being encouraged to claim her Tara essence. When she steps out of the mandala to dance her praise, she must be convinced that she is the Great Goddess, bringing Her inspiration and blessing to the world.

She must affirm that within her, the wisdom of the world rests. It is only our confused notion of who we think we are that ties us to ideas of inadequacy. This practice directly confronts this basic confusion. Experiencing through the dance and the practice what it feels like to present yourself as a confident, courageous woman, possessing all the qualities of the Great Goddess Tara, a woman can never again take seriously the undermining impulses of her fractured psyche.

The healing that this experience provides is monumental. I have received countless reports from women who have danced with me over the years. Often they have only experienced one dance workshop. And yet the experience changes them forever. One story is especially poignant. I was teaching a Mandala Dance of Tara workshop in Pennsylvania. On Saturday morning, when we were handing out the praises, there was one woman missing. We found her hiding under the table, terrified with the idea of dancing a praise. We coaxed her out and she completed the public offering.

Anahata and I were taking a group to India and Nepal to dance for the Tibetan Refugees and this same young woman was persuaded to join us by an elderly friend who also wanted to join but felt that she needed some help. This was certainly a long way from hiding under the table. The dance pilgrimage was challenging but she moved through it all with balance.

After returning home, she kept in touch. One day she sent an email telling us that for years she had been dissatisfied with her job, working in a basement warehouse. She decided to get another job. The next thing we knew she was driving a semi-trailer truck around the country. She was not quite five feet tall so the thought of this once timid young woman hanging out in truck stops and barrelling down the highway in one of those big monsters was delightful. Her truck was called "Star," one of the translations of the name, Tara.

Overcoming fear, stepping out and manifesting your goddess essence, acknowledging your inner life, the Tara Dance heals at the deepest level. In our western culture, children are often taught that they are not good enough. They are presented with a concept of what is normal, the ideal for which they must strive. They either try desperately to be "good enough" or they succumb to a sense of feeling that they will never be good enough. They try to hide from their own essential nature. Fear grips them, immobilizes them, and they suffer, feeling they have no right to happiness, to freedom. Something within keeps trying to assert itself, to insist that there is so much more to life. There is an inner knowingness that continues to demand expression. Dancing Tara re-establishes their connection to personal power and wisdom.

As soon as you engage in dancing the goddess, you cannot deny what you have always known. You are the goddess, you are free; fear is a part of the gravity and density of the world that can be overcome by recognizing that there is so much more than just this dimension of consciousness. One of the dancers sent an eloquent letter to me, years ago.

The workshop was absorbing. Though it was focusing and meditative, it seemed less a celebration of a Buddhist deity than an acknowledgment of our own inner self and our infinite potential as women. It was also fun. The Sophia in me was delighted to be playful and creative and full of realizations.

We looked at the mistakes we made in the form as necessary ingredients in our coming to understand the playful accepting of the feminine.

Often we would have to trust the process. A loving, trusting community took shape in the simple rules of the dance. We weren't performing a dance for anyone else, we were being Tara, collectively, for ourselves and for each other.

We wept at our own beauty. **Tara is Auspicious Beauty**. *We were draped in the most graceful feminine attire ever invented, the sari. Prema dressed each one of us as she sang under her breath, "...dressing the Goddess..." We entered the mandala. At every realignment of the energy we heard, "Golden spiral" telling us to send our energy through the spiral, to do our part for the whole. I was living out my dream of redemption of the feminine. The discomfort of being a woman on a planet controlled by men and mate-rial aspirations was forgotten as I danced the Goddess.* **Tara is Victorious Truth**.

"Faith, Surrender, Send Out Light," our chant in the mandala, is barely audible to anyone outside the mandala. We are one voice, one golden spiral of light and energy. The love and happiness in our hearts fuels the fiery energy of each sister's embodiment of Tara's qualities.

"Golden Spiral," we send this invisible yet potent force through our hands into the heart of the dancer we follow. As we progress through the mandala, we infuse each dancing Tara with our power as life-giving women. Each Tara that is born carries the energy of all twenty-one of us blissful mothers, twenty-one loving, light-emanating Taras of glorious feminine divinity, each expressing her quality so that others may see and be liberated. **Tara is Triumphant Joy.**

The divinity expressing through our individuality was nourished into manifestation by the loving presence, the commitment, the constant atten-tion to the golden spiral of our sisters. "Faith, surrender, send out Light." In the spiritual community created by the dance, the bonds of materialist culture are broken. We are no longer its slaves. We do not dance to attract the protection of men. The men who see us do not feel lust or desire but deep realization of our power. **Tara is Worthy of Honor**. *We weep in this realization. The men weep also. We feel wildly happy.* **Tara is the Remover of Sorrow**. *We all know that this power, this loving attention of mind and heart, this community of high purpose, this birthing of Self is the power we all want:* **Tara is Complete Enlightenment.**

This is only a small part of the eloquent letter this woman sent me. And it is one of thousands of communications that I have received telling of the immense change that the experience of this dance has brought to women and men of all ages and walks of life.

As my body ages, the dance changes. No longer leaping and spinning, I use my eyes, my arms, my stance to express the goddess that I am. Music lifts me up and though my hips can no longer undulate, my spirit can, and I soar. Ultimate Healing, Lama Zopa tells us, is the heart open in compassion, based in wisdom. I am healed every moment I turn towards the truth of my essential nature.

As the world spins about us and within us, are we ready to let go of our confusion, our obsessions, our neurotic insecurities and dance? Let us meet each moment, dancing with whatever life offers us, wonderful opportunities for the **Tara of Creative Wisdom**. Each day we encounter the resistance within, trying to push away every hurtful thing. But if we are Tara, then we open the wisdom eye in the center of our forehead, we open the heart of compassion, and we step into life. We insist from ourselves, our friends, our lovers, our students that they, too, demonstrate their Tara nature. We hold each other as we break open and then re-form. Even the act of dying becomes sacred in the light of wisdom.

There are now circles of Tara Dancers all over the world. For some groups, it is an inner practice and they do not perform. For others, they are closely woven into the life of their communities and they offer the dance during all kinds of local celebrations. An organization has formed, Tara Dhatu, the Pure Realm of the Enlightened Feminine, training dance leaders and developing events leading towards a Great Festival of Prayer.

The Great Mother dances, bringing Her message of protection, of compassion, of freedom, of skill, of beauty, and of joy to the world.

Eh Ma Ho – Immeasurably Wonderful.
OM TARE TUTTARE TURE SOHA
Great Mother Who Removes All Fears and Gives All Blessings
So Be It - So It Is

• • • •

PREMA DASARA: Using the vehicles of sacred song and dance, Prema Dasara invites everyone to experience the power of their own human potential through these sacred arts. Prema began formal ballet training at the age of three. She went to India in 1976 and became a student of a master of the Odissi style of Classical Indian Temple Dance. During the six years she spent in India she worked as an editor for the Theosophical Society, immersing herself in the study of comparative religion. In 1983 she settled in Hawaii where she became a student of the Tibetan Buddhist meditation master, Lama Sonam Tenzin. He encouraged her to continue her sacred dance work which culminated in the creation of the Mandala Dance of the 21 Praises of Tara, a group ritual based on the profound mind training practices of Tibetan Buddhism. She has traveled the world since 1986 teaching this dance and the accompanying meditations. She has been invited to present the ritual to many of the most accomplished lamas including His Holiness the Dalai Lama, who proclaimed the dance "wonderful." She is the spiritual and creative director of Tara Dhatu, a non-profit organization that initiates the training of dancers all over the world to share the Mandala Dance of Tara. She is the author of *Dancing Tara: A Manual of Practice.* Her website is: *www.taradhatu.org.*

CHAPTER SIX

Dancing with (Dis) Abilities

Sharon Took-Zozaya

nobody knows her name
yet she comes to the well
hoping to be called to drink
hoping to see her face in the pool [23]

M Y IMMEDIATE AND EXTENDED FAMILY includes people with a variety of mental illnesses and physical disabilities. This has been both a blessing and a curse, for it has given me awareness of and sensitivity to the issues involved, and at the same time, deep scars that are still healing. As a young person, I was never allowed to feel and own my anger or to have my own grief and needs clearly expressed, since the adults around me were consumed by their own pain.

My response to painful and shocking events that inspired fear and other raw emotions was to hide my real feelings or to freeze up. One way I avoided overwhelming feelings was to hold my breath. I also developed a certain resistance to physically moving through my feelings, which sometimes took the form of physical inertia or hiding in my bed. In coming to terms with the fear and resistance that restricted personal and professional aspects of my own life, I began to identify with others who had visible and/or "invisible" disabilities. Through this personal history, I've come to understand that not all disabilities can be seen with the untrained eye, that each individual has unique experiences of life and physical embodiment, and that in some way, we all have special needs or limitations.

Coming from a difficult and unstable family background, where emotions ran high and words could not always be trusted, I began to ask difficult philosophical questions early in life, sometimes looking in risky places for answers. Trying to find out how to live in the world through, with, and in spite of, my fear and resistances eventually inspired me to explore creative expression beyond the confines of the formal dance world for which I was originally trained.

I began ballet training at the age of 4½, but didn't become serious about dance as a career until high school, when an inspiring teacher named Christina Botiller-Feliz introduced me to modern dance. It was a revelation to be able to express thoughts, feelings, and ideas through movement genuinely grounded in my own experiences, and devised to support a particular theme. I went on to study dance and kinesiology at university, earning a B.A. in dance and an M.S. in kinesiology from UCLA, and an MFA in performance and choreography from Arizona State University. My studies emphasized several forms of western theatrical dance, including modern, ballet, and jazz. I then went on to choreograph and dance professionally.

Since my early dance experiences, I've continued to seek ways to integrate movement that wells up from internal sources, with movement learned from outside sources such as classes or rehearsals. I'm fascinated with relationships between content and form, inspiration and technique, as well as the transformative potential of dance. This has led me to explore many different approaches to dance and to develop as a dancer, choreographer, and teacher in unexpected ways.

I've not always found it easy to choose to participate in and practice dance; to overcome the fear, inertia, lack of confidence, and depression that could so easily stop me. Fortunately, inspiring teachers, therapists, mentors, friends, and colleagues have supported me in my healing and growth. In addition to modeling dance techniques and practices, setting tasks, and asking questions, they have challenged, confronted, supported, and held me, both physically and metaphorically, until I developed enough confidence to make it on my own. I'm deeply grateful to all those who have supported this long and challenging process, especially my mentors Gary Bates and Daniel Nagrin.

Sometimes I still have great resistance to dancing, even though I know that it will always take me home to the clearest place I can find within, the essential, spiritual self where the archetypes of love and will intertwine. Even when the journey leads through many layers of pain, physically exploring and challenging the resistance always leads to the beauty and freedom it conceals somewhere under the surface. Over many years, repeated experience with this exploratory journey has given me insight about the nature of our common humanity, and ways to support others to fully embody themselves through dance, whether or not they have disabilities.

During several years of living in community at the Findhorn Foundation in northern Scotland, I researched new approaches to movement on my own and also shared them with others, both as a workshop leader and as a performer. This was one of the most profoundly transformative periods in my life.

Sharon enjoying the present moment

I am dancing with others in the Cluny Ballroom, at the Findhorn Foundation. We are dancing a vigorously cathartic moving meditation using Hindu guru Osho's movement score. Suddenly, my imaginal realm is transformed. I am a Hindu dancer, perhaps a goddess, dressed in a blue and gold sari. I can almost feel the gossamer fabric of the veil wafting through the air at my touch. My center of gravity lowers, my hands articulate detailed gestures and my feet slap the floor with the rhythmic stamp of a classical Indian dancer. I have never personally danced this style before, though I have seen it beautifully performed on occasion by others. Today this dance is effortless and it's as though I'm being danced by an energy larger than myself. The dance continues long after everyone else has gone to lunch. At one point, I'm aware of a male presence dancing with me, Shiva. We twine around each other in a sensual dance of union and finish on the floor in a lover's embrace. I am in an altered state and it's not until I have drawn a richly colored pastel of our embrace that I am ready to return to ordinary reality and the rest of the day. This archetypal experience for me symbolizes the union of masculine and feminine power, spirit and body, human and cosmic. I move on into the rest of the day with an expanded sense of who I am… freer and more able to both hold my ground and give to others. I feel blessed.

As I understand them, dance, images, music, and poetry can be entertainment, yet they are also much more. These art forms call us to wake up to what is alive and moving within us beyond functional, task-oriented activities of movement, images, language, and sound. The arts invite intuitive, holistic exploration, which leads to the discovery of what is most essential. Functioning like myth, they reveal what is "true" without being literal. Participants and audiences alike are invited to imagine themselves into the universes created by the works.

I began dancing with people who have special needs almost by accident. While living in Aberdeen, Scotland in the late 1990s, I worked as a professional choreographer for BE RIOTous, a week-long community dance and live music performance project. The community dance movement in the UK originally began as part of the government funded community arts movement, an initiative to provide access to the arts and give voice to marginalized groups, such as people with disabilities, at-risk youth, and prisoners. The first mixed-ability performance group I worked with included people with cognitive disabilities and developmental delays. The choreographer set a lot of mirroring and repetitive actions, so the cast could follow and remember the choreography. Although interacting with these dancers was fun and fulfilling on an interpersonal basis, I found myself impatient with the amount of repetition required for them to learn choreography. I decided that teaching and choreographing for special needs groups was not for me. However, subsequent events resulted in a change of heart.

A few years later, I accepted a temporary position as Dance Development Officer for North Ayrshire Council, a county government which served economically and culturally underprivileged residents. The job included providing dance for clients of the Social Work Services department. These were people with a variety of special needs, some of whom had complex, multiple needs and had quite profound limitations. In preparation for this, I participated in training workshops and had long conversations with colleagues who taught and choreographed for people with special needs. One of these was Fran Stridgen, a friend and colleague whom I shadowed as she taught dance at a day center for people with complex disabilities and/or mental health conditions. This was the context for a life-changing experience.

I arrive at the center and enter the activity room where about 30 clients and staff are already gathered. Fran asks us to form a circle and then conducts a greeting process and a warm-up. She then passes a velvet pouch around the circle, so each person has a chance to feel and move the noise-maker objects inside it. After this, she leads the students in making simple shakers (maracas) out of rice filled paper cups with tongue depressors for handles. We then gather in a rough circle to play them.

A middle-aged looking woman I'll call K, stands next to me. She is about five feet tall, of slight build and her upper back is markedly rounded so that she is gazing down toward the floor. She appears to be in her own world, and perhaps a bit depressed. A staff member, who seems to tower over K, approaches from behind, places a shaker in her hand, closes her fingers around K's and moves her hand to shake and make sound, as per Fran's instructions.

K remains passive and apparently uninvolved, her gaze still toward the floor. I feel uncomfortable with this. It seems to me that the staff member isn't really connecting with K, or respecting her autonomy. Instead she is enforcing K's participation, getting her to follow the form of Fran's instructions without encouraging her to get in touch with her own will, the ability to make choices and to move her own body.

I remember that my first Kinesiology professor, Sally Fitt, had once told us a story from her student days which made a strong impression on me. During a visit to a mental hospital, Sally sat down on a bench next to a long-term patient who was catatonic. The woman didn't seem to notice Sally, but continued rocking repetitively forward and backward, as she always had, according to staff members. Sally joined in with the rocking in the same direction and rhythm as the patient, who still appeared not to notice her. After several minutes of this, Sally began rocking from side to side instead. At this moment the patient sat bolt upright and appeared to be alert, something the nurses had never seen her do before.

Remembering this story inspires me to attempt to make contact with K by meeting her on her own terms in some way. When the aide eventually leaves to work with someone else, I crouch low in front of K, so that I'm in her line of sight. Then I imagine a column of warm pink light surrounding her, an image sourced in my meditation experiences. To my astonishment, K straightens up immediately! I stay where I am, low and in her range of vision, and we begin a gentle non-verbal communication/dance. I gradually straighten up, as she remains upright, and we continue for awhile.

This powerful experience has remained as a reminder that a great deal can occur beyond the realm of what we can see or know through intellect and the usual five senses. We never really know exactly what is going on inside another person, especially if that person has no language. This awareness has been invaluable as I have continued to deepen my teaching in this field.

There is an ongoing philosophical debate about the relationship between the mind and the brain. I'm personally inspired by the model that the brain is a kind of computer that interfaces between the mind and the body. Wilder Penfield,[24] a world famous neurosurgeon who created early maps of the brain, wrote that he could not find any explanation of the location of the mind based on his experiments, and that the mind and brain are distinct entities. Current research is consistent with this.

There are also many reports indicating that people in comas can have conscious experiences, even when they don't visibly move or interact with others. I'm most familiar with the story of M, a visual artist friend of mine who was in a coma for about a week in the late 1980s. M told me that during this time he experienced himself as if he were floating on the ceiling, completely detached from his body, yet able to hear and understand activities in his room. He said that his minister had sat by his bed for many hours over several days speaking aloud in an attempt to convince M to return to waking consciousness and life. M was seriously ill and knew that returning to his body, and to waking consciousness, would undoubtedly result in continued severe discomfort and pain. However, he decided that it wasn't time to die yet and deliberately chose to return to consciousness to face the pain in his body and to complete his life with a sense of peaceful acceptance until his death a few months later.

This model of the brain as a computer that interfaces between the mind and the body has been very useful in working with people who have a wide variety of abilities and disabilities. It reminds me, that for all I know, they are having a rich inner life, even though they may seem to be unfocused or confused. It causes me to approach them with respect and openness to being surprised.

My first special needs class in North Ayrshire included a small group of students with complex needs who used wheelchairs and were supported by a couple of day center staff. None of these students used spoken language.

P is a new client at the day center and none of the staff know anything specific about her condition. She has a jerky, repetitive rhythmic pattern of arm movement that never seems to stop, though it's sometimes faster and more vigorous than at other times. P raises the back of her hand to her mouth about four times in quick succession. On the last time, she presses the back of her hand into her teeth so hard that it has become red and raw. She never stops this activity. My overall impression is of a kind of repetitive, automatic violence, which might be her way of coping with some kind of internal pressure. The intensity and speed of this action appear to increase both when P is displeased and when she seems to be experiencing pleasure. Neither of her arms ever lifts above shoulder height during this gesture and she appears to be very tense.

I begin to explore ways to connect with P, sometimes joining her movement pattern by mirroring her repetitive movements with a slightly softer dynamic flow. In response, her arm movements continue, but usually slow a little and become perceptibly softer. One day, I bring in some scarves. I try draping one over P's head to see how she will respond. She brushes it away, lifting her arms much higher than ever before and moving in a softer way both on the upward journey and as she lowers them. This becomes a game that continues for five to ten minutes, during which she continues to lift her arms relatively high above her head. I continue this activity, in order to reinforce the quality of relaxation and the increased range of motion she is using.

During this time, P's movements become increasingly more gentle and flowing. We continue without the scarf, but with the same quality of move-ment. We alternate, one of us gently floating our arms upward and the other mirroring the action. This "dance" in itself, seems to me to be a valuable step forward.

However, I'm astonished by what happens next. As my hand passes near P's face, she gently places her cheek into my open palm. We stay that way for a few seconds, and then resume our dance. I am deeply touched that simply mirroring P's movement and joining in with her dance could foster this type of rapport. The staff also comment that this has been a very unusual moment. They have never before seen P move so smoothly and gently or initiate this type of physical contact.

class at Cabrillo College

Through this experience and work with people who had autistic characteristics, I came to realize that a person who has autistic symptoms may seem to live in an impenetrably isolated private world. Yet the quality of their presence and willingness to interact with another may alter radically when someone joins them by mirroring their movement pattern and perhaps entering their world, however slightly. Perhaps this is true of us all. Once someone joins our world in order to communicate, it may be easier to gently follow her to a wider world view and new ways of being.

The moment of unexpected contact with P described above eventually became the core inspiration from which I choreographed a tender duet called *Intimate Distance*. This piece explores the possibilities of contact across seemingly immovable barriers, and the subtle tenderness that can result when communication really does occur. Clients and staff who work with people who have conditions on the autistic spectrum have told me that they clearly recognize elements of their own experiences in this piece. Mainstream audience members in Scotland and in the USA at every performance have told me that they've been moved to tears by how accurately it reflects their own experiences.

In 2003, when I joined the Cabrillo College dance faculty in Aptos, California, the college already had a well-respected adaptive physical education program. However, there was no one teaching adaptive dance. I developed a new curriculum for it and taught my first adaptive dance class there in the summer of 2004. We began performing in our dance department's Winter Dance Concert that December. At Cabrillo, we consider adaptive dance to be dance for, by, and with people who have conditions such as physical disabilities, developmental delays, cognitive disabilities, sensory impairments, diseases, injuries, infirmities due to age, and/or mental health conditions. Integrated dance includes dancers with and without disabilities dancing together on a more equal basis.

Because we believe that everyone can dance, no matter how limited their movement capacity may seem, these classes include students with a wide variety of abilities and experiences of movement. The atmosphere in class is somewhat different from other dance classes I teach, though there are some common elements. Students, staff, and volunteer student assistants collaborate to create a supportive learning community by dancing together and performing for each other. Volunteer student assistants with and without disabilities help all class members get the most out of the activities we do. Much of this occurs through role modeling, rather than actually physically helping people to move.

Student assistants support participants who have very specific, limited abilities and also students who are more "high functioning." In the latter case, experienced dancers provide an important service by challenging these more able students to develop beyond their familiar comfort zones. For example, students with Down's Syndrome are often naturally very able dancers, yet they sometimes need encouragement to express themselves fully and/or to explore new moves that they haven't thought of before.

The job of student assistants is to assist and empower, supporting participants to achieve as much independence as they can within their abilities. Before intervening, student assistants are asked to make sure they're needed and to do the least they can do to accomplish their aims. They are asked to "be real" and to dance full out, whatever that means in any given moment, as everyone in class is expected to dance full out, to

Characters explore a new level of communication in "Intimate Distance"

the extent of their ability. For the most part, joining in as a dancer is considered the best policy and they use non-verbal communication wherever possible to encourage students to participate fully.

Respect for each individual's autonomy is vital. For example, when dancing with a wheelchair user who might benefit from being pushed, we ask if the wheelchair dancer wants to be pushed. When possible, we agree on a system that allows the wheelchair user to be in charge of directing where they are taken. As much as possible, we speak with all students directly, rather than speaking to care assistants about them, even if the students need help answering or implementing activities.

One of the greatest reassuring gifts we can give each other as human beings is acceptance, so we model an allowing and accepting attitude. Mirroring back what we see is one way of expressing this, as mirroring is also important in development and learning. We look for even the tiniest responses to our approach, contact, or instructions for movement, and respond to these subtle cues. A little mirroring and embellishment can go a long way to establishing rapport with dancers of any ability.

> *Five assistants and I gather in a close circle at the end of class, three standing and two in their wheelchairs. Today has been a good day. M allowed herself to be coaxed off her chair and to expand her filigree of arm gestures to incorporate full body leans. J danced a delicate pas de bourée across the room, followed by A in a wheelchair. T, an autistic student, led a group across the floor with uncharacteristic large kicks. One by one, we review the class, evaluating student participation and noting areas for future work for them and for ourselves.*
>
> *Some days there are major revelations, like the day when the apparently shy R unexpectedly volunteered to perform an intricate flowing solo for the class. Most days, there are small successes that add up over time to a general trend toward increased mobility, ease, confidence, balance, and creative expression. We have modest goals, yet know this work enhances the quality of life for these students, and for us as part of this community of practice. Comments from teachers and staff who bring adaptive students to class reinforce this perception.*

Over the past seven years, some of our most advanced student dancers have volunteered as assistants in these classes. It appears that often it is they, as much as the disabled students they came to assist, who have received the gifts of heart-opening inspiration and self-acceptance. Several of them have told me that this experience has been transformational for them, as it has also been for me. Traditional western

"So Light Can Enter," choreographed dance by Sharon Took-Zozaya.

theatrical dance forms are often learned and rehearsed with an ideal of perfection and sometimes competition. By contrast, it's healing for us all to know that we dance as part of a community, where we are all equally invited to contribute our best at that moment, however flawed, yet beautiful. As one Integrated Dance Repertory student wrote:

> *This class has taught me more than just how to move. It's taught me how to trust, and even love, perfect strangers. It's the people in this class that gave me this gift. This gift is timeless, a priceless treasure that I will keep forever. Thank you.*

There are always a variety of people and roles in the dance studio: students, staff and teachers who accompany them, student assistants, and myself—the teacher. In my opinion, we function best when we all join in and meet each other on the dance floor as human beings with creative and interactive potential. Occasionally, however, care staff who accompany disabled students to class can be overly concerned about making sure their clients do what is asked and therefore may intervene more quickly or more often than might be best for empowering the students. Their frame of reference can be more about accomplishing daily tasks and protecting their clients from harm than about experiments and discovery.

The story about K earlier in this chapter contains an example of this. While their intentions are for the best, this can sometimes result in limiting a student's creative potential. Dialogue between myself and the staff who bring students is also part of the classes. I'm in the process of moving us more in the direction of an integrated model, because it is more inclusive and fosters more sense of equality for everyone.

What does this work have to do with spirituality? Everything, as far as I'm concerned, because it has the potential to bring us home to our deepest essential selves and to foster the development of compassion. Dancing together, especially if we are improvising, asks us all to meet and celebrate the many known and sometimes unknown parts of ourselves. As we begin to accept ourselves in all our many colorful movements and moods, we also learn to connect with and accept each other in the same way. My personal experience has been that as I acknowledge and integrate more and more aspects of movement and feeling, I feel increasingly at home and empowered in my physical body, while also more accepting of others. As dance brings us home to our deepest selves, we discover that beyond the obvious separations of everyday personalities, we are inherently connected through the web of life itself. We cannot fall out of that web, no matter how hard we try.

Even though there are days when the last thing I want to do is stand in front of a group of students and take responsibility for directing their learning experiences, overall, sharing dance with others is deeply fulfilling for me. Building community in this way is part of my spiritual practice and I'm grateful for the opportunity to contribute.

• • • •

SHARON TOOK-ZOZAYA, Artistic Director of Stamping Zebra Dance Theatre in California, has taught, choreographed, and performed in a wide variety of professional, university, college, education, and community contexts in the U.S., Scotland, and internationally, working with both able-bodied and disabled dancers. Her teaching and choreography combine training in dance, kinesiology, and counseling, with a life-long exploration of dance as a medium for invoking and celebrating spiritual experience. Currently on the faculty of Cabrillo College in Aptos, California, Ms.Took-Zozaya teaches a variety of dance and somatics-based courses, including adaptive and integrated dance, which she initiated. She has also taught at the University of California, Santa Cruz and previously served as Dance Program Chair at Scripps College, Assistant Professor of dance at Rutgers University, and an education faculty member at the Findhorn Foundation in Scotland.

CHAPTER SEVEN

Why I Dance, to Heal

———

Opeyemi Parham

THERE IS SOMETHING IN ME that has been called to dance my prayers and find my way to wholeness through movement. I am fifty-three, African American, and I dance ecstatically, excessively, and enthusiastically.

I attended a predominately white public high school in a suburb of Washington, D.C., back in the 1970s. There, I felt awkward and disconnected from my body. This was despite being a cheerleader, one of two African Americans on a squad of ten. Our cheerleading style was "white" with lots of stiff-armed, super duper gymnastic moves involving flips and cartwheels. While it was true that we integrated "black" cheerleading moves (copied from squads across the river in Anacostia), I felt uncomfortable rolling my hips and syncopating the movements. My environment labeled these natural movements "wrong" and "sexual." I felt awkward in my body, despite being a drama chorus member with parts involving choreographed dance, and despite being a member of a modern dance group.

I first glimpsed my authentic relationship to dance in college; it was a healing experience, for me. I remember, early in my first semester at Mount Holyoke College, being on a five-college bus on my way to a dance hosted by a Black fraternity at Amherst. I was dressed up, wearing make-up and high heels, and worried about making the right impression. Then I had an epiphany. It occurred to me that I had absolutely no history with the people I would be meeting. I could be whoever and however I wanted to be.

I chose to be seductive and flirtatious, using my body to speak to the young men with whom I was dancing. Here, I found an opportunity to play with edges that I hadn't felt safe exploring within my high school world or within the sphere of my parents. I savored my experiences at those late night Afro-Am dances over the next three years. I learned to love the bump and grind, feeling the closeness of another human, and responding move by move to the invitation and conversation struck up by our bodies. I explored how the rhythm of the music helped me learn nonverbal cues to connect to another human. I remember how the bass voice of a Barry White or an Isaac Hayes was a direct link, to opening my second chakra, if I relaxed into it. In energy physiology, the second chakra is a center in the body that is identified with sexuality and creative potential. In the music of my day (60s and 70s music from Motown), it often had a crescendo built into it. I would stand at the side of the room, and wait for a dark shadow of a male to emerge from the crowd and take my hand.

It was a culture where one was seldom verbally asked to dance; the communication was all in subtleties. Body language of an open posture, eye contact, and smiling back at a fellow dancer were the cues. Once on the dance floor, the nonverbal conversation continued. African American slow dancing allowed for some very, very hot contact. His arms would slide around me, resting on my shoulders, or at my waist or at my hips. The choice of the embrace meant different things, with his arms settling at my hips, being the most intimate of the three choices. My arms, in turn, could go around his neck, rest on his shoulders, or hold him at the small of his back. Then we would sink into the music together. A slow grind meant enough closeness to feel the breath of the partner, chest-to-chest. It was all about what was happening person-to-person between the upper thighs and the lower abdomen. Cultural convention prevented frontal groin-to-groin contact, but a good slow grind was everything but.

I remember the music allowing me to open to the smell of my partner—usually a combination of an aftershave, hair oil for the almighty afro, and his sweat: good smells, mingling with good music. In the nonverbal conversation, we could lean into each other, or hold a distance. I loved leaning in, letting the music cue him to move his hands to hold my hips a little tighter. If my body language said "yes," then he could direct the swaying of our two bodies, using his hands at my hips. If this "yes" offered with the support of the music continued, I could move my hands to the back of his neck and place my head against his shoulder. He could respond by leaning his cheek against the side of my head. Deeper and deeper we would go, one into the energetic/sensual body of the other, and that Motown music would crescendo.

Who needed sex? By the end of our five minutes together, I would feel that I had been transported to a place where pleasure in the moment is good, and safe, and right. Then the music would stop, and it was over. Sometimes, an exchange of a phone number would happen off the floor. The cultural norm was the intimacy ended when the music ended, no questions asked. I had found a culture that allowed for "dirty dancing" without consequences off the dance floor.

I had been raised around many Jewish neighbors and considered myself somewhat "bi-cultural" when it came to Jewish traditions. So I sought out the Hillel community at Mount Holyoke next. This community introduced me to Israeli folk dancing, which offered pros and cons. The pros included the fact that Israeli folk dancing may have actually kept me sane through my first year in medical school. Sick from the trauma of too much to memorize and the smell of formaldehyde in gross anatomy, I created a special, Monday-night discipline. Every week I would put down my books, shower, dress in a flowing skirt, and travel by bus across town for three hours of Israeli folk dancing. Skipping the first hour of lessons, I would arrive in time for the fun stuff. Always more of a kinesthetic learner when it came to my body, I could stand behind the circle and quickly pick up the dance moves. I could then flow into the movement, swirling from one circle dance to another. I got to be good enough that once I was approached by a woman who spoke to me in Hebrew!

The cons of Israeli folk dance for me were that it served as a dating space for George Washington University students. I participated in the circle dances but always felt on the outside when the couple dances would begin. The partner dance time at the Israeli folk dance nights was about courtship and coupling, a tradition I was excluded from as an African American woman. To this day, I cannot hear the tune to "Evening of Roses" without a pang of loneliness and yearning.

Oh, but what I opened to and learned about the space of my heart, body, and music, as I explored Israeli folk dance! Because of the Jewish diaspora, the dancing held elements of Arabic rhythms in the power of the *debkas* or tight line dances done shoulder-to-shoulder, often with ululation as accents to the music. Central European influences could be detected with moves and twirls of such frenetic energy that I had to look deeply into the eyes of my partner to keep from spinning out of control. Intermingled with these were Greek elements with grapevine steps that took my dancing feet forward, then backward, then forward again in a slow and swaying journey around the circle. All of these movements, taken from folk communities that had been dancing these dances for hundreds of years, held mystical, magical power that went directly to my fourth chakra (the energy center most identified with openness in the heart). I would leave feeling uplifted and well nourished. Back to my medical books I would go, so much happier for the dancing experience that had refreshed me.

Dance as stress relief faded out of my life once I married in my mid-twenties, had babies, and settled into the practice of medicine and raising a family. But I remained an enthusiastic dancer when I did get an opportunity. I was the pregnant one who kicked off my shoes and delightedly twirled around the floor at my college room-mate's wedding. Dancing with my three-year-old outside me, and my soon-to-be son on the inside, I was unable to stay sober with live big band swing music playing. The moment the band began Benny Goodman's "Sing Sing Sing," I was intoxicated. I felt that I had been possessed by the spirit of some teenage 1940s swing dancer. Gene Krupta was in the house too, when the drum solo began. Luckily, many of the other guests were intoxicated with a drug of a different kind, alcohol, so my transport into an altered state probably didn't stand out that much.

Generally, my mid-twenties to mid-thirties (the 1980s) were years of working hard, parenting fiercely, and coming to terms with the ways and places I was no longer hearing music in my life. I divorced my husband twelve years into the relationship. I was suddenly a single, full time family doctor with two little ones under seven. While this choice felt like a good one for me, it was a frightening one.

Enter Dr. Mitchell J. Levine. Mitch was a colleague at my progressive Cambridge, Mass., medical office. He kept after me about going to some weekly dance on Friday nights. I thought he was trying to flirt with me and with a newly-divorced heart bruised and battered, I really didn't want to be bothered. This went on for months and months. Finally, Mitch cornered me and invited me to a dance party at his house. "It's my birthday… if you have the kids that night, we can find a place to put them down to sleep in my daughter's room." This sounded clean enough. Little did I know that I would be crossing a threshold that would lead me solidly and irrevocably into the world of ecstatic dance.

I knew I was entering The Twilight Zone as soon as Mitch answered the door to his home in Somerville, Mass. This was *not* the doctor that I worked with, nine to five during the weekdays! Here in the doorway stood a very attractive man in a bright blue sleeveless T-shirt and brightly colored flowing pants. I think the pants actually had flowers on them. His arms were muscular; I had never noticed the physical health of this man before. I got my children settled in for bed upstairs, then joined the party. That is when I noticed the second strange thing: the energy of the dancing at that party had all the characteristics of those fraternity parties back in college without the unspoken rules of who asked who to dance.

The party had that lightness of spirit that I had felt at the Israeli folk dances of my medical school days, but didn't appear to be a Jewish dating service. In fact, I danced with Mitch and knew that this was not the folk dance community. The dance we did was not a slow grind, but held amazing sexual energy in a healthy and honest way. Through Mitch, I had been introduced to a community who danced ecstatically. These people had actually rolled up the rug, to have a better dance floor; something that I had only experienced in African American dance parties. There were at least fifty people, most white, all dancing to music I liked, from "oldies" such as Aretha Franklin and James Brown, to current hits by Annie Lennox and Talking Heads. Whatever the music, whatever the style, this community knew how to be in the moment, with love and openness in their bodies, connection to the music, and connection to each other.

I had a blast at that birthday party, which was my introduction to the Dance New England (DNE) community. Fifteen years old at the time, DNE was a community of people in love with movement and music, but totally disenchanted with smoky bars and other available venues for social dancing. So Barefoot Boogies were created; spaces in gymnasiums or dance studios throughout New England that were alcohol, smoke, and drug free safe containers for freestyle dancing. Participants were welcome to dance alone or to approach another for a partnered dance. Groups could dance in circles. Since many members of this community had skills in Contact Improvisation, dance also occurred on three levels and people would often be rolling around on the floor, or "flying" partners through the air, in stunningly beautiful lifts.

I was hooked. Every Friday, I would pack up both children and head out to Dance Friday, in Watertown, Mass. I would arrive at seven thirty. My three-year-old and seven-year-old children would go hang out with other children, in a play area, while I would have ninety minutes to stretch, synch myself up energetically with the music, dance alone or with others. My "Cinderella Hour" would be marked by the behavior of my three-year-old; I would leave when he had worn himself out, running, running, running around the huge gymnasium floor. As I left, a "second shift" of singles without kids would often be arriving. In that crossover time, I would occasionally find myself dancing with someone in a way that asked a sexual question, to be re-negotiated off of the dance floor. My Friday night dance space became a place for me to let off steam from a week of being a caretaker in a busy family practice office, but not a place to pick up men. I was deeply appreciative of the opportunity to dance away my stresses. That was enough.

Next, I found the DNE summer camp. This community of ecstatic dancers has a sixteen-day summer camp each year off in the rural, lake area of Maine. Not only were there nightly barefoot boogies, there were wonderful dance classes all day long. And great childcare, where my son waved me away when it was time to pick him up at the end of the day. I found myself in community with other people who loved to dance as much as I did. There I was, in the company of four hundred other people, in the tranquil atmosphere of a private lake in rural Maine. I was taking three dance classes each day, ranging from African to Middle Eastern to swing to tango. I thought that I had died and gone to heaven. Never in my life had I experienced so much unbounded energy and creativity, and it was coming through dancing. I took classes all day and still stayed at the evening Barefoot Boogie until midnight. I found that I had fallen in love with this community.

Being the no-nonsense, practical Capricorn that I am, I returned from that experience intent on creating more ecstatic dance space in my life. For three years, I endured several challenging temporary living situations as I pursued this dream of 24/7 dance community, buying land, designing a home, and having it built with my co-conspirator, Mitch. The doctor in the floral pants and I had formed a fast friendship, and embarked upon a platonic but intimate (a shared mortgage is intimate) relationship, focused on creating an intentional family. Ecstatic dance was our core family value. We welcomed the new year of 1994 in the company of about 120 DNE community folks. We had a dance party before we moved the furniture into our home! Our community home was given its name by the carpenter's son. Near the completion of the project, this nine-year-old had asked, after hanging out with his father for a week building the gymnasium-style living room floor for our sacred dance space, "Daddy when are we going back to that purple palace?" In the pale light of December, with snow on the ground, the shade of lilac we had selected for the external paint made quite the impression on that young boy!

I lived in intentional family in The Purple Palace for the next seven years. The living room in the house, equipped with a fireplace and designed for a family to fill with lots of sofas, chairs, and coffee tables, was kept bare. There was the sprung wooden floor and speakers mounted into the walls; nothing else. That amazing dance floor was a space that I used frequently and well. I danced through conflicts with my ex-husband around lifestyle choices for our children. I would come home from a mediation attempt, feeling frustrated and constrained. There was nothing more satisfying than going over to the stereo, putting Gloria Gaynor's "I Will Survive" on high volume, and dancing all by myself through that space. I danced through political intrigues, literally breathing and doing authentic movement as I listened to the Supreme Court's decision after the stolen 2000 elections. I was on that dance floor, listening to chanting by Deva Premal the night of September 11, 2001. My next door neighbor, accustomed to music and dance in odd and unusual venues wafting across the lawn and into her windows, commented the next day that it was wonderfully soothing to hear that music, behind the traumas of that awful Tuesday. Dance and movement at the core of my home helped me stay open to my emotions, all of them, through many overwhelming experiences.

Then I began to connect my spirituality to my dancing. One year after finding the Dance New England community, I found the neo-pagan movement. I began exploring earth-based spirituality after attending a Unitarian-Universalist women's convention in 1989. At that convention, Starhawk, an eco-feminist and prominent voice in neo-paganism, was the keynote speaker. On April 22, she tapped a spoon against her glass in the campus cafeteria at the end of the dinner hour. "This is Earth Day" she announced. "Some of us are planning to celebrate with a spiral dance, on a hill up the road a bit, under the full moon. Any interested women can meet us up there."

All four hundred women attending that conference, including ones who were too infirm to dance the dance, participated. The elder women were driven to the hill in a station wagon, and sat on chairs in the center of the circle. I had never participated in a spiral dance before; a circle dance, practiced for centuries by European people of earth-based religions. The form of the dance allows for eye-to-eye contact with everyone in the circle. I will never forget standing on that hill, in the light of a full moon, holding hands in a circle of women so vast that I could barely see the other side, across the grass. Starhawk began a chant with these words:

"She changes everything she touches and
Everything she touches changes... "

Once the group had picked up those simple words, Starhawk let go of the hand of the woman on her right. Turning to face the woman on her left whose hand she still held, she slowly began to move past each and every woman in the circle, taking the line with her. She sang a descant to the chant:

"Rising, rising, the earth is rising
Turning, turning, the tide is turning... "

The experience felt hypnotically beautiful, and deeply, inexplicably familiar. Soon the circle had become a spiral, as Starhawk wound the group tighter and tighter into the center. At the center, she magically turned again, having acknowledged those elder women sitting on chairs, and we were suddenly moving out of that spiral, as others continued to move in. Like a long sinuous snake, four hundred women chanted, danced, and connected with one another and with the earth, and with the moon, in that mystical dance.

It took me three years to integrate what had happened to me on that hill into the rest of my life. The spiral dance experience set a fire in my heart. I came to understand how my body, mind, emotions, and spirit were connected. Starhawk had said to us, at the beginning of the dance, "Sometimes the Earth will speak to you. Listen to what she has to say." When the chanting stopped and my body came to stillness at the end of forty minutes of dancing on the hill, I heard something; I actually heard a voice in my head that wasn't mine as I bent to the ground and placed my hands on the earth. It was a small voice, but it was clear and "Other." It said, "Stay Open To Me." I was reconnecting to my roots, as a woman, as an African American from people whose spirituality was not originally Christian.

Three years after that Spiral Dance, I connected to the Earthspirit Community, a pagan organization in Massachusetts. I was learning to say the words "pagan" and "witch" without shame. It was then I went to my first pagan gathering hosted by Earthspirit. It was called Rites of Spring and included a fire circle. What is a fire circle? In that context, it was a huge bonfire set and maintained in a clearing deep in the woods. Drummers would assemble on one side of the fire and people were welcome to dance around the fire, between the drummers and the fire itself. Back in 1990, this was a new expression of a very, very old and primal connection. Many of the drummers were playing African hand drums, familiar to me from African dance classes I had taken at DNE summer camp. I was curious about this fire circle and became fascinated by what I experienced in that space. Back in 1990, the fire circle would run from about eleven p.m. until about three a.m. Something happened at these circles that got to be known as "the two a.m. tilt." After hours of dancing and drumming, what would emerge was a heart-to-heart connection that defies words. Back in 1990, it was a fleeting phenomenon; one that almost felt like it had to be "earned" or that other issues and struggles had to be burned away before the yumminess of the heart connection could happen. Sometimes, around two a.m. we would "tilt" into a space of loving connection to one another, for about fifteen to twenty minutes, often circling up and having all dancers hold hands and sing or tone while dancing, with the drummers in synch with our moves.

I became a dancer at the fire circle, learning to feel the magical energy of connection at that circle. If that spiral dance with Starhawk had a familiarity to it that was deep and rich, this experience felt primal. Many of the drummers became interested in the complex polyrhythms from African diaspora cultures, and learned to play these rhythms with skill and enthusiasm. The rhythms were meant to open the way for Spirit, and Spirit often showed up in the dancers. In Haitian or Santeria tradition, this phenomenon of feeling Spirit move directly through the physical body of a dancer is called "being ridden" or "being a horse" for the God/Goddess/archetypal energy that had presented.

We neo-pagans were on an exciting adventure together; learning to reconnect to the earth, learning to honor the earth, learning to use dance as a way of connecting to Spirit, learning to listen to what Spirit said to us, through our dance. Over the years, I became more aware of when energy/Spirit/chi was flowing in our circles and when it was not. In time, our fire circles became longer, deeper, and more powerful experiences. Three hours around the fire, then five, then seven. Sometimes I would go to bed, or to a nesting area of blankets outside of the circle and wait for the heart fires to "catch." Well-rested, I would return to the fire just as that "two a.m. tilt" was happening, to join the circle and ride the waves of bliss. Over the years, I learned to sense when to return to the fire. Magic was afoot. I was opening to ways of knowing that came from my body and my heart, not from my head. Language is an inadequate tool to describe these experiences.

My fire circle evolved, going through a mini-diaspora of this newly found spiritual experience. Several of the facilitators of that early experiment at Earthspirit moved to the west coast. I followed them, attending a yearly, three-day fire dance in the Santa Cruz Mountains. The seeds floated back east, in the form of a fire festival called Spiritfire. By the late 90s, I was able to look forward to attending five days of all-night fire circles, on at least a yearly basis. My dance in these spaces was informed by the freedom that I had found in the DNE community. I was totally at ease with my body and confident of its physical ability to transport me to spaces of bliss. At the fire festivals, I learned to open, through my dance, to Spirit. I learned to open my heart.

And there has been more. My earth-based spiritual practices have included participation in a women's circle for the last thirteen years. Meeting every two weeks, we often have a round of checking-in and then put on evocative music, for dance/trance work. Sometimes a question will be raised during check-in and the dance space allows for answers to flow through, on the wings of Spirit. An answer may come through me for a sister in my group. Sometimes, she will "hear" an answer/advice/guidance for me. I remember one evening shortly after the Barcelona international convention on HIV/AIDS. I came to my women's circle feeling extremely despairing, aware that an epidemic of bubonic plague-like proportions still stirred little awareness in the first world nations. I began to dance and asked, "What is HIV/AIDS about? Should I leave the U.S. and take my skills as a conventional medical doctor to South Africa?" Over the next twenty minutes I got quite an answer as I moved with my sisters through space in that living room. I saw and felt things in my body; beginning before the middle passage of the slave trade. I felt the experience of many girls being circumcised. I heard Spirit say, "You have been delivered into the New World so that you could find your way to whole, healthy sexuality. Do not travel to Africa to help with this crisis until your white brothers are also traveling there."

Dance/trancing into the future, I saw an entire African subcontinent, devoid of Africans and occupied by Europeans, there to loot the natural resources that were left. My vision revealed that these Europeans had developed an entire new cadre of psychological/spiritual afflictions related to their inability to see, connect to, or appease the spirits of the dead around them. I saw myself a healer in that future space; a healer of mind, body, heart, and soul.

I continued to explore. I became a practitioner of Five Rhythms, Gabrielle Roth's dance discipline.[25] Author of *Maps to Ecstasy*, Roth has created a practice that she calls "sweating our prayers." A Five Rhythms practice involves using five distinct ways that the human body can move: flow, staccato, chaos, lyrical, and stillness. I have found that following this moving meditation, I am reliably transported to a space of ecstatic bliss. Dancing for about twenty minutes, I end in stillness, and feel the flow of Spirit in and around me. It is the most wonderful psychic purification/detoxification, and I try to sweat my prayers in a "dance church" space several times a month. DanceSpirit takes place twenty miles from my home in western Massachusetts on Sunday mornings. It is exactly the right place for me to sweat my prayers. Prayers for my children and their health and well-being. Prayers for my friends. Prayers for myself, to help move me through the places in my emotional life where I am feeling stuck. And prayers for a world that often feels overwhelming.

Using the five rhythms as a discipline, I often flow into specific archetypal dramas as I dance. Recently, I drew a card from the altar set up in the Dance Spirit space that said "kick up your heels." As I focused on those words and moved through my five rhythm practice, images from the Hans Christian Anderson fairy tale "The Red Shoes"[26] came into my head. I felt myself moving into an archetypal healing dance, and I danced for all of the young girls of Central Europe who had been harmed by that tale. The fairy tale tells of a child who loves her red shoes more than anything and finds she is unable to remove the cursed shoes, which dance her wildly away into the woods. The wildly-dancing red shoes keep her from eating or resting. Finally, she is "saved" by a woodcutter, who rescues her by cutting the red shoes (and her feet) off. I danced an archetypal dance and literally kicked up my heels, reclaiming the power of my dance, in memory of all of the European Catholic and Protestant girls who were told that passion, lust and love of motion and color were sinful. I danced a healing dance here, honoring those who would not or could not move the way I was ecstatically moving.

Recently, I have been introduced to a new dance community. I attended Forest Dance, a gathering of about one hundred ecstatic dancers and drummers, which took place about thirty minutes away from where I now live, in a sustainable agricultural community that is "off the grid." The average age of the participants was about thirty and at age 52, I was considered an Elder in that circle. The fires began at midnight and continued until sunrise. The "two a.m. tilt" lasted from the opening circle until the closing one. On the third night of the gathering, the dancers and the drummers were able to blend into the most beautiful and profound circle of healing. Music, rhythms, and dance steps from African, Central European, Middle Eastern, and Native American cultures whirled together and complimented each other in harmony rather than a cacophony of sound and sensation. At one point near sunrise, I remember going around and around the circle, doing a grapevine step to accordion music, with rhythmic drumming anchoring the experience.

I recall that back in my medical school days, in that Israeli folk dance world, there was an inspirational woman. She was significantly older than the typical twenty-something student, and she danced with breathtaking grace and fluidity. She was connected to the music and the other dancers, yet she also seemed to be transported by the dance to somewhere else; she seemed to be "more" than the dancer in front of me. I remember that I wanted to be like her, when I grew up. I am all that. And more.

• • • •

OPEYEMI PARHAM is a 54-year-old, retired African American family practice physician, now offering health education, holistic health consultations, and intuitive medicine sessions in western Massachusetts and southeastern Vermont. She uses ceremony to create sacred spaces for people to explore deep feelings; to facilitate this she has become an interfaith minister. She considers herself a healing artist, and an artist, healing. Her website address is *www.ceremonyheals.com*. She produces an hour-long radio show called "Channeling the Muse" with a mind/body/spirit theme and invites the listener to boogie along during the body segment (see *www.archive.org* for audiofiles of podcasts of this program)

CHAPTER EIGHT

Trance Dance as a Portal to One's Self Knowledge

Sandra McMaster

D ANCE HAS BEEN PART OF MY LIFE in a variety of forms over the years. I would like to say I have been dancing everyday and that I live and breathe dance. However, I do not. Dance for me has been what I have turned to in times of stress, as a way to find release from the tensions in my life. When I was younger, that meant going to the nightclubs to dance alone or with others in the midst of the too-loud music, smoke, and alcohol. In later years, I took courses and attended retreats in an attempt to find my center again.

As a counselor at a university, I support others through difficult, stressful, and transformational times. This work is very rewarding and I have had many opportunities to celebrate with students when they have achieved significant and positive change in their lives. It can also be intensely draining. My own training never prepared me for the slippery slope to burnout. Self-care was not an action word while I was at university and although I heard the word a lot, it was a rarity to discuss what it really meant or how to practice it.

It seems that self-care was one of those things that you just learned in the field. I must say, at this point in my career, I appreciate the part about needing experience to understand what self-care might mean to me; however, learning more in training, especially from veteran counselors, would have been helpful along the way.

Over the years, I found myself in aerobics, yoga, meditation, and running classes. I ventured into belly dance, the five rhythms, African dance, and ecstatic dance. In my spiritual life, intuitive and shamanic journeying increasingly played a role in my grounding. Although yoga has formed the backbone of my self-care practice, dance in many forms was a home I often returned to as a way of coming back to myself.

In my experience, burnout sneaks up on you like a frog sitting in a pot in which the heat slowly increases until it is too late and you realize you are being cooked. Although I am happy to say I have not been completely "cooked," I have on occasion noticed my headlong dive into burnout and have been able to make a turn around. In one such scenario, I had just come through four months of being the only counselor on our campus of 3,000 students. In that time it felt like my office had a revolving door as I dealt with all day-to-day student and faculty issues as well as emergencies. Training the new counselor while continuing to carry the same caseload added even more stress during this intense time.

It was in October 2008 that I found myself on the road heading to a women's retreat in Minnesota with the hope that I might find a place to restore myself. Some months before, my friend Jocelyn told me about the First Women's Foundation which held retreats twice a year and suggested I join her for the fall gathering. Held at the Maplelag Resort within the Detroit Lakes, and nestled in the forest, she described the weekend as a wonderful opportunity to rejuvenate in the company of other women. She explained the weekend was designed so that participants could create the type of retreat they needed with the choice of scheduled workshops, a variety of sessions offered by other participants, or by just hanging out. She also noted the bottomless cookie jar, which held great appeal.

On the way to our destination, we came across some unusual billboards that we agreed could be expanded upon and placed along the Trans Canada highway. "BE KIND," "BE GRATEFUL" and, "BE NICE," were inspiring reminders of how simple life can be. How difficult can it be to follow such basic directions? Isn't this something we all learn as children? I have found practicing these to be most easy when directed at others, however more difficult to apply to myself. As I reflected on my need to strengthen my self-care practice and the relationship I had with myself, these simple yet profound statements seemed to set the stage for the retreat.

Arriving at the resort just before supper time we settled into our room. Having come through some challenging weather, we were delighted to arrive in good time. Jocelyn showed me around and explained how to "design" my retreat. I took note of a number of scheduled workshops including an intriguing description of a trance dance session. Before I had time to look over all my options, we were beckoned to the dining room where I was introduced to a number of welcoming women.

Guidance for living can arrive in interesting and inspiring forms

During supper, there were introductions, reconnections, and lively discussions as participants settled into the group and the possibilities of the weekend. There were some newcomers such as myself; however, there were many who, like my friend, were returnees. It felt like a homecoming with much laughter and many "catching-up" conversations. In these situations, it had been my tendency to create a sense of being an outsider and I noticed this creeping up as I watched the many warm greetings the returnees received. I decided quickly that I did not need to fall into this old habit and resolved that rather than recede into myself I would speak to others, ask questions, and sit with different people at each meal. Although I knew I needed solitude, I also knew I did that well and the balance of connection was an important one to explore this weekend.

Later, the high energy was carried into the opening circle where we were greeted by the retreat founder Margie Stillwell, also known as "Two Cooks." The opening circle was a time to create the sacred space in which the retreat would occur. All of us were invited to bring something to place on the altar for the weekend. I noticed the altar had grown since our arrival and seemed to contribute to building the energy and creating a sense of belonging. In Margie's welcome, she noted this was the 10th year that the First Women's Foundation had held this retreat. It was a time of celebration.

The Circle Keeper was introduced and in turn she asked us to introduce ourselves. Eighty women shared who they were and what had drawn them to this retreat. We were then asked to set our intention for the weekend. "Hmmm," I thought, "I just need to rejuvenate." When I looked back into the journal I was keeping at the time, what I had written was much more. "Intention? My intention for this weekend is to find my center again, become centered in self, you know, that thing you teach your clients." Humbling, yet right on. Once again I had to revisit the very thing I often taught my students, how important it is to return to your self, to be "centered in self." How many times would I have to take this lesson?

That first night closed with a drumming circle. Eighty women began to drum in unison. The sound grew louder and louder, the intensity increasing. Women stepped inside the circle to dance as the voice of the drum beckoned them. I remained an onlooker and found myself at times dropping into that feeling of being an outsider. As I drummed, I strengthened my resolve to find my place within the circle.

The following day for me was a balance of coming into community and going into solitude. The resort grounds offered the perfect opportunity for me to go within and pay attention to what I needed; another lesson that I was apparently required to practice again. After spending time on the land, writing, reflecting, and meditating, it was time to step back into the world of other people. I had signed up for the trance dance session offered by Suzannah Martin. Once again, I had to face myself and drop any sense of preconceived notion as to what would happen. I had earlier experiences of trance dancing, ecstatic dance, and shamanic journeying in which my head dominated. I was well aware that this habit set me outside the experience rather than firmly planted in it. I was determined to be present to this experience.

The room we entered was large with chairs moved back to provide the maximum amount of space for us to dance. Suzannah explained the process we were about to undertake and likened it to a shamanic journey. Been there, done that, with little results, I thought. Traditionally, the shamanic journey is done lying down. As one enters a state of deep relaxation or trance, imagination and fast, repetitive drum beats assist the individual in entering other realms to discover such things as helper spirits or animal guides. In my past experience, my mind had run rampant, over-analysing, creating to-do lists and just plain not cooperating. Usually, in sharing, everyone else seemed to effortlessly engage in the journeying and successfully discover her power animal. An outsider once again.

OK, return to non-judgment. Maybe with movement, I might have a chance to experience something different. Suzannah told us she would be playing music that would change in tempo and mood throughout the session. We would also be blindfolded. The music and the blindfold would act in the same way as the drum beat, to assist us in maintaining an inward focus. She asked us to name an intention to take into the dance. Mine remained that of finding my center. She also asked us to summon any guides or helpers we might want to accompany us. Wolf, a familiar totem, came to me immediately as guide and protector. Milo, my friend who had not so long ago died from cancer, surprisingly stepped into my thoughts and became the second guide.

I found a beginning space in the room and placed the blindfold over my eyes. The music began and slowly I allowed my body to move and my mind to stop. Although my body cooperated, my mind did not easily relinquish its control. Along with my mind running its usual negative track, I found myself becoming increasingly frustrated as I kept bumping into other dancers. This seemed odd to me, as the room was huge with plenty of space for all of us to move with ease. I felt hemmed in as if I could not get space and kept checking this out by reaching and stretching my arms around me. I became worried that I was bumping up against others, disturbing their process, and the chatter in my mind took off.

I asked my friend Milo to help and she came to me in the form of a lion. I understood from her that she had not released her worries and was off balance and this was what had brought her ill health. I had the sense that I was dancing to save my soul, to maintain it and my body's good health and well-being. I was dancing to bring harmony into my life, harmony for my relationship with myself, my partner, and my family. I was dancing to find my center. To find my center was to find my true relationship with my true self. I wanted to stop, sit down, and sulk, but the music beckoned me onward, and a small voice encouraged me to "move through this."

As I struggled to keep my mind settled and remain present to my body, a terrifying image came to my inner vision. It was a pack of wild dogs, angry and mean, circling around me, teeth barred, leaping in for the kill. I forced myself to look at those menacing beasts and was struck by the fact that they were skeletons—bones—frozen in the past. Could it be that they represented old beliefs, all trying to stay alive by keeping me fearful? That resonated loud and clear. The more I looked at these creatures the more I saw. They were just bleached old bones, no power in them, just in the old thought. In my dance, I realized that there was no use in keeping them around and I knocked them down.

The bones clattered to the ground and I stood bewildered at the power these old beliefs had on me. Beliefs that I was not good enough, worthy enough, I was unimportant, unnoticeable, and valueless. Where had they come from? It did not matter. However, the awareness of their presence did matter, as with this awareness grew empowerment. I felt my body fill with intense emotion and relief. As the dance came to a close and we gathered in a circle to share, all I could do was allow the tears to come.

The trance dance had impacted me in a way I had not expected. It was a profound experience that has returned to me again and again as I revisit the lessons of self-care and self-love. Past experience had told me this type of practice did not work for me, again, the outcast. Somehow this time I had found my way, allowed the dance to work its magic and open a portal to my true self. Over the months that followed, I looked for ways to connect with myself, show myself respect, and create harmony. Returning to movement as a pathway to self-care was an important step in my own healing.

A very concrete way that I demonstrated to myself that I was serious about self-care was to adjust my daily working schedule to eliminate the revolving door syndrome that had established itself. I capped the number of counseling sessions per day and made time for the other tasks, which included report writing, consultation, and work on other projects. I also began dropping into a local dance studio to participate in ecstatic dance and world dance classes. Within my own discovery, I realized some of the students I saw might also benefit from dance and as appropriate would encourage individuals to explore the role dance might play for them. Although trance dance had acted as a portal for me, my suggestions to students were of a general nature encouraging experimentation in a variety of dance modalities with attention to how they felt.

In the writing of this chapter, I revisited the journal that I kept around the time of the retreat. I was slightly embarrassed to notice that the themes of two years ago continue to be present today. It seems it is a human characteristic to have to return to the important lessons again and again. I am happy to notice that I can identify when I am in the pot sooner and have found I have the ability to control my thoughts more effectively. It seems in the naming of things (such as the bleached out bones) that "power over" can be eliminated and empowerment established.

When I returned home, I chose to create a collage as a way of connecting to my harmonious life. Following the dance, I wrote these words in my journal and offer them to you as a prayer that you might too find your worth:

I accept myself here and now
as I am with all the gifts I have to offer this world,
those I know and those yet to become known to me.
I value myself and know I have a place in this world,
at this time,
just because I am here.
And so,
I always do my best.
I learn and I laugh.
I relax into life and especially into this body,
this temple that carries my spirit.
I tend to it respectfully and care for it in kind ways.
BE KIND BE GRATEFUL BE NICE

Integrating the teachings of the trance dance experience
through the creation of a collage

• • • •

SANDRA MCMASTER is a counsellor at Brandon University in Manitoba, Canada. She is also a student of Hakomi Therapy, a body-centered approach to counselling. Sandra has always found movement to be a path to self-knowledge, which she has accessed through her yoga practice and many dance experiences. She has practiced the Five Rhythms and has participated in the Mandala Dance of the 21 Praises of Tara. Through her counselling and dancing, Sandra has come to know the transformative power of renewing and rebuilding our relationship with our bodies.

CHAPTER NINE

Dancing for Peace

Rhavina Schertenleib

I HAVE LIVED IN ITAMBOATÁ VALLEY, in Simões Filho, Bahia, Brazil for about 16 years and have participated in the Dances for Peace project at the Terra Mirim Foundation (TMF). Terra Mirim is an eco-village founded in 1992, which promotes community-building and sustainability development projects in the region. I first came to the village in 1995 at the invitation of its founder, Alba Maria Nunes Santos, a shaman, to participate in a sacred dance workshop called Sacred Dances and the Four Elements. During this dance workshop, I had the sense that my soul was reconnecting with the spirits of my ancestors and I felt myself deeply connected with nature. The experience was somewhat bewildering and even frightening but profoundly spiritual and very beautiful. It was a transformative time for me.

Participating in these sacred dances gave me the motivation to further develop these dances through shamanic practice, as a student and member of the research group, studying the ethnography of shamanic rituals guided by Alba Maria. I saw the potential of this work as a way to investigate dance as a strategy to enhance the capacity of human senses through rituals and experimentations with the four primary elements of nature: earth, fire, water, and air.

In shamanic ritual, there is an emphasis on mythical time, also known as sacred time or no time, which favors the recovery of unity with nature and with our ancestral lines. In an altered state of consciousness, a "new" identity is created and linked to parallel realities where contact with these "other worlds" reveals a powerful vehicle that simultaneously unites present, past, and future.[27] The shamanic ritual then becomes a sacred space for dance/performance in which one can connect to these parallel realities and access multiple "selves" resulting in the expansion of perception through body and mind. This is a powerful space in which the dancers can immerse themselves in exploring the movement.

Terra Mirim

During my years at Terra Mirim, I have been drawn in through the rich opportunities for creative and spiritual development offered to members and the people it serves. Terra Mirim was created from a dream, an inspiration grown and managed in the heart of Alba Maria. The initial intent was to cultivate a land that needed care and could be transformed into a place of education and healing for people all over the world. In addition, it could provide a place for full human manifestation under the care and reverence to Mother Earth, guided by the beings and elements that are part of nature.

About forty people form the core group of members and employees (residents and non-residents) of Terra Mirim. Many have profound life experience and are committed to common values and dreams. They have dedicated their lives to collectively weaving a dynamic experience and learning to recognize their own place in this world. Resources and tasks related to the community are shared in order to make things happen; personal and collective tensions are faced together. For 18 years, TMF members have managed to deal with all kinds of crises, observing that the truth set in the spirit of Terra Mirim, which we call our purpose, unifies the group and helps it to carry on.

One of the greatest challenges is the quest for self-sustainability of the foundation and the individuals. A great part of the activities are voluntary or come with little financial return, which often results in the need for some members to find ways to financially support the community from outside work. This challenges the faith and patience of the group every day. In order to build self-sufficiency and sustainability, Terra Mirim puts into practice some principles of solidarity economy, such as sharing expenses, collective buying, helping each other, and developing partnerships in the main area projects.

A major principle of Terra Mirim is "Integrative Ecology." It is founded on the belief that the protection of nature and human development are one single, interconnected process. In Integrative Ecology,

The internal nature of the human being and the external nature are considered interdependent in the physical (earth), emotional (water), mental (air), and spiritual (fire) dimensions, in order to assure that the healing of the planet goes through the healing of the human being.[28]

It is, at the same time, an ethical principle and a political vocation, as it gives us a direction to exercise our global citizenship in direct dialogue with the realities that surrounded us.

One core aspect of Terra Mirim's principals is spirituality. Seen as the tool to create community connection, spirituality is understood as the sacred flame that gives daily support to each member and each activity. Although the community is open to all kinds of spiritual traditions and masters, shamanism is the main source of sacred visions and practices. The shamanic perception of nature's sacredness and its multidimensional approach to reality unveils great potential to human beings not only to make us more perceptive of our spiritual nature but also to open up our physical sensitivity. The shamanic rituals and visions that exist at Terra Mirim thus became a unique laboratory for experimentation in all arts expressions, specifically in dance.

Shamanic Practice and Dance

In the shamanic tradition, during the rituals of initiation the body acquires an aesthetic choreography very similar to that of bodies in a dance performance. The rituals of the shamanic tradition can stimulate a physical dimension that creates the state of the imaginary body during their practices. For example, it is not the person who is dancing, but the body; the qualities of the holy fire are expressed in a ritualistic bonfire. This can represent the expanded physical dimension in the individual who is receptive to the experience. The following excerpt from my journal describes a shamanic experience from November 2007:

> The night fell. I was able to light a small fire and later I was awakened by
> the night. I felt the healing space being set and the rain started to shake
> me inside of my sleeping bag and stimulate me to dance. My guidance
> expanded my body sensation, I felt myself bigger, occupying an enormous
> circle where I danced in the night spheres, feeling myself being free from
> fears and attachments.

The shamanic ritual becomes an exercise that allows participants to examine unexplored parts of their being. This important aspect creates the possibility of recovering space for the imaginary body. In this way, redesigning and reconstructing the body image within the dance allows for an experience of expanded perception. There exists the potential of self-investigation through increased self-knowledge that can result in the expansion of the body consciousness.[29] In a journal entry, dated May 2008, I present another personal shamanic dance experience:

I danced for a long time, turning, dancing in the rain, letting myself be taken by the body sensation of surrender. It rained and it was cold but it didn't matter. The freedom of the naked body stepping on the wet ground together with the consciousness of the breath and the fasting amplified my percep-tion, providing a state of body/nature unity. Going beyond the basic needs: warm or cold, hunger and sleep not satisfied, darkness, allows us deepening in these body states that reflect the conscious expansion.

All the shamanistic experience, with the guidance of Alba Maria, showed me the pos-sibility of a great connection between soul and body in the art of dance. I became open to the manifestation of my sensitivity, while also becoming more responsive to nature and other human beings.

The Dances of Universal Peace Project

Within this context, I became part of a group who met weekly to study the Dances of Universal Peace (DUP) and the traditions and instructions that are part of this prac-tice. The bright presence of Alba Maria in these meetings inspired me with confidence to develop a new way of being and contribute to the healing of the world in creative and transformative ways.

The DUP were created by the Sufi master Samuel Lewis, who was inspired by Ruth St. Denis, one of the predecessors of modern dance in the West. Besides Suf-ism, Lewis studied Jewish mysticism and the Kabala. Lewis lived in the period of the two great world wars and felt motivated to build an understanding of peace between the religious traditions using their sacred phrases in the dances. His idea was to build up the comprehension of peace through simple movements accompanied by holy phrases of the world's different spiritual traditions. The DUP stimulate a deeper inhabiting of the body, making it possible to enter states of trance and deep medita-tion. The intention of the dances is to give us back the meaning of human, planetary, and cosmic unity, celebrating this revolution through singing, meditation, and strong, vibrant dances.

The purpose of this dance practice is to expand one's access to the teachings and understanding of mystical order. This practice was restricted in the past, being provided only to the initiated through the gestures, symbolism, movements, and em-bodiment of sacred phrases. Now, through this practice, the aspirant is able to progress through the stages of spiritual development with the conscious use of breathing, con-centration, coordination, and confidence. It seems this practice helps participants to grow on many personal and collective levels.

Dancing for Peace Brazil

In Terra Mirim, the Dances of Universal Peace project began in 2006, eleven years after the original seed was planted in our study group. At that time, I was appointed the dance coordinator at TMF. Anahata Iradah (a DUP Mentor Master and a TMF cooperative friend) and I organized a series of dance workshops for groups of teenagers from neighboring public communities who were interested in getting to know and practice sacred dance.

We organized workshops in public schools and adult associations in the Dandá *quilombola* community, Escola Amélia Rodrigues, and Escola Sepram. (A *quilombia* is a typical Brazilian traditional community formed primarily of African descendents who escaped from slavery.) We also gave workshops to the association of elders and youth groups of the Catholic Church in the community of Palmares, the association of residents and the public school community of Oiteiro, and the children of the ecological school at TMF. All these actions had the effect of empowering the people of the Itamboatá Valley, especially the teenagers and children. Helping to enhance individual potential, these dance projects also gained a political, social, and cultural dimension.

The region of Simões Filho is marked by serious social, economic, and environmental problems, including drug trafficking, smuggling chemicals, early pregnancies, and prostitution. Although these extremely unbalanced conditions go back to colonial times, the process of industrialization only increased the problems. Together with the growth of poverty and violence, the modernization of the region (and of the country) has forced the communities to break with their cultural roots, which were traditionally linked with the land and embraced a synergetic spirituality. To face these extreme and unpleasant conditions, Terra Mirim has been developing many activities addressed to the local population. As with the other activities, we found these dance workshops filled a huge need in the community. They have not only helped the teenagers create new perspectives of their personal lives, but also helped to strengthen their sense of community and political engagement.

Since 2005, the project, "Culture: Right of All," has established Terra Mirim as a cultural center in Bahia, with a considerable educational, social, and cultural impact on the people involved. The workshops have united over 600 people in the sacred dance movement, including children, teenagers, and elders. Dance classes are taught weekly for three hours. There are also monthly meetings for a group of teenagers from the *quilombola* communities on the periphery of Simões Filho. These youngsters greatly enhance our dancing experience, giving classes for the children at Terra Mirim's Ecological School and in the communities.

The value of the dance workshops is demonstrated by the involvement of the youth from the *quilombola* community of Simões Filho who have been developing the Art for Peace Project. They have engaged in the project through the use of methodological principles of DUP interconnected with the sacred elements of shamanic tradition: earth, fire, water, and air. The teenagers were not only curious but ready to change their lives. The consciousness of citizenship in the community, the environment, and the larger culture was nurtured in the young people through the dance workshops. The girls and boys from the *favelas* (slums) cross huge barriers when they come to participate in dance and music classes or to meditate. Through this, they become more aware of their bodies and the states that emerge from them, discovering for themselves how to dance their own movement.

The art of education in this context causes a conscious integration of body/nature prescribed by the integrative ecology philosophy. The shamanic experimentations with the elements make them more aware of the intrinsic bond between the multiple dimensions of their bodies (physical, emotional, mental, and spiritual) and their surrounding environment. This approach not only brings forth an ecological sensitivity in them, but also increases their social interaction and the development of many other skills.

Terra Mirim's social and cultural work with youth includes sixty participants. Of those sixty, there are ten participants, ranging in age from 16 to 23 years, specifically engaged in the DUP. They are more keenly aware of body and movement, creative capacity, and autonomy. They developed a collective sense and solidarity within the interpersonal relationships and the group as a whole became more centered. Some of them have also demonstrated an increase in their leadership capacity.

During the DUP training process with the youth of Terra Mirim, we noticed that five of the young women demonstrated interest and talent in becoming dance leaders. These young women come from dire socio-economic situations and are faced with increasing violence in their communities. They were excited to be able to introduce new, creative possibilities for their families and communities, different from those that are normally available to people in their situation.

Engaging in the process of "dancing one's body" has allowed the young people to access their own cultural matrix and awaken their own creative selves without the need to be professional dancers. Personally, it has been a great source of inspiration to work with these young women as, in addition to developing their musical capacity, motor coordination, rhythm, concentration, and confidence, it stimulates creativity and inner artistic capacity. Their testimonies tell of the changes in their behaviors, which they say is a result of their involvement in dance. Improved confidence and autonomy has increased their capacity in the areas of commitment, participation, compliance to a schedule, and availability and openness to learning new exercises, movements, and approaches. They take on many responsibilities, acting as monitors of new groups, attending to the children in the Ecological School in the TMF and in their communities. They are clearly engaged and interested in becoming agents for social change.

Making a Difference with Dances of Universal Peace

Five key participants, who are now collaborators in the TMF, teach the DUP and other interventions in educational and environmental areas to help support the healthy development of young lives. What follows are some of the observations and comments they have made about their experience in the Dances of Peace project.

Ana Paula is a member of the *quilombola* community of Dandá and participates in an eco-project where people gather to discuss important issues such as environment, citizenship, access to culture, culture for the peace, and the improvement of the socio-economic conditions. Stepping into a leadership role, she has started holding regular dance practices in the public school in her community. Here, Ana Paula expresses her sense of the impact that dance has on her community:

> In each one of the meetings with the adults of the association, or the
> children of the school, I sense that these dances create a positive energy
> in the group, and I take this energy back with me into my own life.

Silvia & Camilla

Every meeting with my community is wonderful, getting them to
celebrate, dance, and sing together. We always include a samba de
roda (samba in a circle) at the end of the Dances of Peace, to make the
children understand the value of their own culture, and to unite us, so
that we can express our culture in a beautiful way. The possibility of this
work amplifies my sense of life.

It is important to stress that these youth come from communities where the Afro-Brazilian dance traditions, like the dances of *orixas* of the *candombé* [30] and other expressions,
are still present. At first, some of these girls, like Eliandra Moreno, another DUP student, had great difficulties sharing with the group the participation of their mothers and
grandmothers in these cultural manifestations. It was clear, for example, that some were
embarrassed while watching their ancestors' dances during visits to *candomble* festivals in
the region. However, after an intense period of collective reflections, dance workshops,
and growing familiarity with Terra Mirim's community, a strong change in their acceptance and understanding of their cultural backgrounds developed. They are now helping
their mothers and grandmothers in their *candomble* rituals. Eliandra, who became a class
assistant and dance teacher in Terra Mirim's Ecological School, observes:

During our dance workshops in the ecological school, once a fortnight, I can
see the changing in the children. The knowledge of the Dances of Universal
Peace, united with the Ecological School learning methodology, brings

119

something new to me and the children. The school enhances the Dances of Universal Peace movement.

Silvia Santos and Camila Santana, also members of the group, lead dances with beauty, humor, and grace. Silvia describes the effect on herself and her students:

> *To dance the Dances of Universal Peace in my community and in the Ecological School encourages my personal and the children's development. Their way of listening to music changes when they practice the movements and the message of peace enters their bodies... I feel more confident when I focus on the work. I see the shine in the eyes of the children, the change in their behavior. This has a solid meaning for me. My soul comes to rest and becomes secure. I have already developed a repertoire of dances and I feel that in this way I can spread the happiness I experience in my everyday life.*

Camila also expressed her engagement with the movement, pointing out the opportunities she has been receiving:

> *After I entered the world of dance, many doors were opened for me. Today I know wonderful people, and have been able to visit nice places, and have fantastic experiences through the invitations I received. I was asked to teach the Dances of Universal Peace to a group of teenagers of the Catholic Church and an association of elders in my community. They like the Dances of Universal Peace and adore the fact that there is a young woman in the community who focuses on messages of peace through the dances.*

The experience of these young women shows us that the shamanic dances, inspired by contact with the holy elements of nature, create a ritual space, bringing each dancer to recognize her place in the cosmos and to rejuvenate him/herself. The dances promote the culture of peace development and help to dissolve conflicts. Their message is widely accessible and provides a greater appreciation of other traditions while creating a deeper understanding of local cultural traditions, which in Brazil are deeply syncretic.

The Invitation to Dance

Brazilian identity is a mosaic compound formed by different cultural heritages: Christian Catholicism brought by Portuguese colonization, African rites, cults, and deities brought by African slaves during colonial times, and all the many indigenous wisdom, practices, and traditions which existed before the foreign invasions of this land. From this ample and intense blending, we were made. From this amalgamation, the history of Brazil and its people continues to be inspired. To understand our history, it is necessary to see it through these colorful expressions, by reviewing our past and present memories. It is to undertake a journey to the core of our soul, a cultural richness manifested in dances, music, rhythms, and all the arts and creativity present in our country.

Dance, in Brazilian culture, is a way of self-expression and communication. The state of Bahia, for example, pulsates in many different rhythms, which include gestures and symbols manifested through the language of dance. Dance seems to be a Brazilian way of expressing creativity and concerns as well as being an avenue for receiving information. Although there are other artistic languages, dance has become an important way of expression and empowerment to the local cultures. It helps us to better understand our roots and our past, as it evokes sensorial beauty and etherial richness.

Over the years, Terra Mirim, as a social organization, has not only acknowledged the importance of this legacy but has also become an open space for its manifestation in the region. The intervention in the Ecological School, that includes dance classes, considers this artistic vocation a remarkable characteristic of the local population. Under the coordination of Mynuska de Lima, and direct links with the other TMF organizational areas, the Ecological School manages to accomplish a great number of intense daily services, which demand from the participants a strong faith in Terra Mirim's purpose. The dance projects and activities are part of this great dream. It is a belief in the awakening of the true potential in each person, even those who suffer from disaggregated social conditions. It is a belief that in helping individuals to fully express themselves, this will also help them to expresses their feelings of love and caring towards others and towards nature, in a beautiful and sacred cosmic dance. I have experienced this myself and have witnessed the transformation of the many children and teenagers in our groups.

If you also believe in these possibilities, you can collaborate by helping the dance or other educational/artistic projects of TMF. Please contact us: *rhavina@terramirim. org.br* or at *www.terramirim.org.br*

• • • •

RHAVINA SCHERTENLEIB studied dance at Brazil's Fundação Cultural do Estado da Bahia's School of Dance and the Federal University of Bahia, focusing on the sacred and native dances of various traditions, specializing in Shamanics. Since 2003, she has facilitated shamanic and *orixás* dance workshops in Switzerland and Germany. She is a member of the Brazilian net of Dances of Universal Peace and is the creator and supervisor of the Art for Peace project in Bahia, Brazil. Her website address is *www.terramirim.org.br.*

CHAPTER TEN

Sun Dancing as Service to Mother Earth and All of Creation

Barbara Waterfall

*B*ooshoo. *Waabshki mshkode bzhiki kwe ndizhinikaaz. Zaawaa nimkii aankwad kwe ndizhinikaaaz. Waabshki jijaawk ndoodem. St. Joseph, Lake Huron ndoogibaa.* I greet you in the customary way of my Anishnabec People: I have been given two names, White Buffalo Woman, and Yellow Thundercloud Woman. I am an educator and a healer. I come from the White Crane Clan and descend from the shores of Lake Huron.

I am a Métis woman of Anishnabe/Ojibwe, French and German ancestry. As a Métis person, I am not a registered Status Indian under the dictates of the Indian Act of Canada (1876). I am a Sun Dancer, and I completed my initial pledge to engage in four successive Sun Dances. The specific form of dance that I have been involved with has been a Warrior Sun Dance. The role of the warrior within Anishnabec society is to protect the People, and to preserve our heritage and cultural traditions. The experiences of Sun Dancing have had profound and unanticipated impacts on my life, for these experiences have empowered me to firmly stand in my own identity, and to assume the sacred roles and responsibilities that the Creator has given me. This has occurred in spite of real, imposing forces that would like me to do otherwise.

I am very cognizant that I live within a dominant colonizing and patriarchal context where the exercising of a Métis woman's traditional spiritual power is contested terrain. Through the rigors of Sun Dancing, I have been tested and stretched beyond what I thought was humanly possible to accomplish. My experiences of Sun Dancing have taught me the importance of surrendering my mind, emotions, body, and my life on an ongoing basis over to the service of the Creator. In doing so, I have learned about the immense spiritual powers that we as human beings can access, both within and outside of our physical selves. I have also become aware that these vast and expansive spiritual powers can make all things possible.

I was excited and honored to have been asked to contribute to this book about women's experiences with Sacred Dance traditions and practices from around the world. I have come to believe that there is great power in the coming together of diverse experiences, particularly when this diversity is positioned both from within a place of integrity and respect, and for purposes of gaining greater harmony and understanding. Indeed, the dream of All Peoples, from All Nations coming together for the sake of global harmony, is the most basic teaching and purpose of the Sun Dance.

It needs to be said that I come to this writing in a humble way, knowing that I do not speak *for* Métis, and/or Anishnabec People. Respecting North American Indigenous protocol regarding the writing about North American Indigenous phenomena, I do not share intimate details about the Sun Dances, out of respect for the power and utility of oral tradition, and for the sanctity of the Sun Dance Ceremony. Given these parameters for Anishnabec writing, I relate information that has been recorded in previously written text, as well as oral understandings I have been given permission to express in written form. At the same time, I speak from my place of my own authority—the place of my heart—about what I understand to be a subjective experience of truth. I have previously referred to subjective heart knowledge as reflective of an epistemology of inner knowing.[31] Leilani Holmes supports this understanding and contends that spirit-based/heart knowledge is a legitimate epistemological foundation for truth telling.[32]

My motivation for writing this chapter is two-fold. In the first instance, I wish to shed light for a broad audience on the past and current plight of Métis/Anishnabec existences. I further desire to promote awareness and respect for the power and utility of Métis/Anishnabec cultures and traditions, and in particular the Sun Dance as a spiritual practice. It is a documented fact that historic and ongoing colonizing forms serve to eradicate, devalue, and to inferiorize Métis/Anishnabec Peoples, and ways of being in the world, inclusive of our philosophies, worldviews, methodologies, and practices.[33] As Maffie[34] observes, the dominant discourses of modern culture often posit the superiority of Western technological knowledges over Indigenous localized understandings. In this context, I write to valorize marginalized Anishnabec cultural practices, using a discursive rather than theoretical approach. I make use of a discursive framework in order to make room for the fact that the social context in which we live, as well as our histories and our lived experiences, are constantly changing, and in order to provide space for Indigenous holistic and interconnected understandings.[35]

Colonialism is not something that existed only in the past. The fact that the reservation system in Canada still exists today speaks to current experiences of colonialism. I therefore employ *anti* colonial understandings to center the current project of Indigenous Peoples resistances and opposition to colonialism.[36] The anti-colonial discursive framework can be defined in three ways. It posits the absence of colonial imposition, the agency for Indigenous Peoples to govern our own lives, and the practice of such agency based upon the life-sustaining ways of our Indigenous ancestors.[37] This framework makes room for the development of Anishnabec positive and pro-active stances and approaches.

Indigenous knowledges have been conceptualized as a body of Wisdoms associated with a People's long-term occupancy of a certain place.[38] Indigenous knowledges are said to be embedded in the spirit and blood of the land through the bones of our Ancestors. They also flow from our relationships and kinship ties with all living beings, inclusive of the elemental spirit forces and life energies of the earth.[39] These knowledges have been accrued through time, passed down through our oral and written histories, such as our pictorial drawings, legends, stories, proverbs, songs, ceremonies, and dances. They also can be acquired through empirical observation and through spiritual sources, such as communion with Ancestor spirits, and through visions and dreams. These knowledges encompass experiential, qualitative, and subjective understandings. Indigenous knowledges by their nature are holistic, inclusive of mind, body, and spirit connection.

The History of Anishnabec and Métis/Anishnabec Peoples: A Legacy of Resilience

Anishnabec Peoples have a rich history. Our birch bark scrolls trace our Anishnabec origins on this continent back through four ice ages, about a million years ago.[40] Anishnabec knowledges and practices remain resilient today, embedded within Anishnabec and Métis languages, oral histories, legends, songs, dances, ceremonies, and within pictorial written accounts.

Anishnabec People have historically believed that the Earth is a female planet, and that our pre-colonial existence was organized by earth-centered ethics, knowledges, systems, and ways of practice. Wub-e-ke-niew[41] observes that Anishnabec were traditionally non-violent People, subsisting on the practices of gardening and on what the permacultural environment provided. Anishnabec People lived in close harmony with nature. Life revolved around an ethic of stewardship for the land. As Wub-e-ke-niew suggests, Anishnabec People took care of their homes, their gardens, their forests, while augmenting their subsistence through fishing and hunting. He also contends that within this context, a prolific oral literature developed. Women played pivotal and central roles in the culture. This understanding is supported by our recorded libraries or pictographic drawings, as well as by our Elders, oral teachings. Wub-e-ke-niew agrees, asserting that Anishnabec men and women had complementary and respectful roles and relationships.

I descend from Anishnabec-Ojibwe People. I am also a Métis woman. My understanding about being Métis is informed by my own localized history. The term "Métis" originates from the early colonial period on this land and originally referred to the offspring of North American Indigenous women and French men.[42] My Métis roots stem from this very early colonial period, where my Ancestors came to be deemed by colonial authorities as other than Anishnabec or Ojibwe. That is, we were constructed as a "hybridized other" and as such, not defined as legitimately a "real" Anishnabec/Ojibwe. With the enforcement of colonialism on this land, all North American Indigenous Peoples in Canada were forced to live under apartheid. A reservation system was put in place where people who were defined to be legitimately Indigenous were relegated and restricted to live on small tracts of land referred to as reservations. Those of us who were not considered to be Indigenous were positioned off reserve, and were allowed very limited access to our non-mixed race Anishnabec relatives.

The impact of this apartheid system for my People was that we were kept strategically apart and isolated from Anishnabec People. Through time, many people took this apartheid system and the legislation of legitimate Indigenous identity for granted. The impact of this history for me personally has been that I have all too often been confronted and challenged, (sometimes violently) about my not having rights to participate in and to practice Anishnabec traditions. In my early life, my ability to live according to my own sense of knowing, integrity, and power was severely disrupted. Yet, as I have critically deconstructed and revisioned my People's history, I have become aware that in spite of colonizing forces, I was raised as a Métis child in a context where I grew up learning about many Anishnabec knowledges. I was raised in a humble agricultural context, subsisting on the bounty of what the land offered. I was taught how to live in accordance with the rhythms and cycles of the natural environment. I was taught how to respect the land, and to preserve the land for the future generations to come. I also learned about the healing properties of many plants.

My early upbringing was a grounded Anishnabec existence, and as an adult I have made it a priority to seek out, participate in, and to support the revitalization of Anishnabec cultural traditions. Through the assistance of my Anishnabec Elders, I have been able to pick up my sacred responsibilities, which includes being an Indigenous educator, as well as assisting others as a healing practitioner. Therefore, in spite of very real barriers and challenges that have been imposed by colonizing legislation, my identity and my ability to exercise the natural gifts that Creator has given me remains steadfast. I contend that this reality speaks to the cultural resiliency of a Métis/Anishnabe woman's spirit.

Anishnabec Cosmology:
We are All Connected and Related

The organization of the Anishnabec Sun Dance reflects an Anishnabec cosmological understanding. Anishnabec People believe an entity constituted as both female and male created all of the life and the world that we live in. Many refer to this being or entity as *Kitche Manitou* or the Great Mystery. Anishnabec People also believe that Creation was not a series of events which happened in the past, but rather reflects a process that is continually taking place. We are also not understood to be passive recipients, but rather active agents of our ongoing Creation.

The implication of understanding our participation in Creation comes with grave responsibility, for we must seriously consider what kind of a world we are actively creating.[43] We must ask ourselves, are we creating harmony and peace, or disharmony and discord? Are we working for the liberty and equality for all, or are we merely concerned with our own individualistic pursuits? Do we take up the call for justice, or do we allow apathy and indifference to motivate our not taking a stand? Are we actively working to ensure that our earth, our air, and our waters are clean and pure, or are we leaving a polluted world for the future generations to come? From an Anishnabec standpoint, these are serious questions which we must reflect upon, since ultimately we are all responsible for the future that is unfolding around us.

For the Anishnabec, life is understood to exist within a circular cosmology. This cosmological understanding is represented within the Sun Dance Ceremony as the Sun Dance Lodge constructed within a circle. The circle reflects an Anishnabec truism that "we are all connected and related." This understanding is consistent with a most basic Anishnabec tenet that we as human beings are inter-connected with all of life within a rich web of kinship relationships. Antone, Miller, and Myers[44] articulate that there are complimentary clan-based relationships between humans and other areas of creation. As well, they assert that our human role in Creation is limited, as our existence is dependent on other beings and life-giving forces. A concrete example of this understanding is reflected in our relationship with the Sun. Anishnabec refer to the Sun as our Grandfather and are also fully cognizant of our reliance on the Sun, for all of life would perish without the Sun's sustenance.

Traditional Anishnabec ethics, systems, ceremonial practices, including the Sun Dance, and every day social relations were organized to ensure and maintain a spirit of respectful co-existence with all of Creation. From a traditional perspective, human beings are expected and required to live a life of balance.[45] That is, through conscious effort in all aspects of their lives, humans are responsible for maintaining equilibrium within themselves and the world around them. Anishnabec ceremonies, including the Sun Dance, are of grave importance in this world view, for they are carried to ensure the maintenance of this intricate ecological balance with All of Creation. Working primarily with the energy of the Sun's rays in harmony with other elemental forces, the Sun Dance ensures that the heat of the Sun remains present and drought is prevented. Given that we currently live in a world with global warming trends, the ongoing practice of the Sun Dance bears particular relevance.

The Import of Indigenous/Anishnabec Ceremonies as Maintaining Balance with All of Creation

My Elders have shared with me that Indigenous ceremonies around the globe have a particular role and a purpose. As one of my past teachers, Oh Shinnah Fast Wolf[46] has written, ceremonies work with and influence the electromagnetic poles of the Earth, in the south, north, east, and west. Oh Shinnah also teaches that the axis of the Earth at this time in Earth's development is changing, and as consequence it is paramount that Indigenous Peoples continue working with the ceremonies to facilitate a positive outcome for these changes.[47] She prophesies that if the major poles are disturbed during the axis change, the electromagnetic field of the Earth is also grossly impacted. If this comes true, without drastic spiritual intervention, a possible outcome could be the destruction of life on Earth.

I am not sharing this potential reality to elicit fear. Rather, I am merely sharing what my Elders have passed down to me, for it seems very clear that we have all reached a most critical juncture on this Mother Planet. Indeed, Anishnabec Elders have asserted that we have moved into a new and changing time on Earth. Many Indigenous Peoples have described the context that we are living in as the time period of Great Purification.[48] Anishnabec People speak of this time as the lighting of the eighth fire, where we as Human Peoples have great potential to learn to respectfully co-existent in harmony with the natural world around us.[49] Our Elders also report that we have reached a critical juncture in our development on this Planet where great changes and shifts are taking place.

When we look to the natural world around us, we see this understanding mirrored in current events. Anishnabec legends foretold of this time, where natural forces, such as hurricanes, tornadoes, tidal waves, flash floods, earthquakes, forest fires, and volcanoes would bring the Earth and her Peoples back to a needed balance. Every day we read or listen to the news, we are reminded of this reality. Not only Anishnabec, but all Peoples, are affected by these changes. The Katrina hurricane on the Gulf Coast and the great fires in various parts of the globe are examples of these effects that are being felt around the world. Anishnabec Elders tell us that while these events are tragic, they are the means by which the Earth is able to heal herself and come back into balance. As a Human Species, we are being called to live in harmony with the four great forces of air, water, earth, and fire. Anishnabec Elders also say that there are ultimately two paths to choose in life. One is the way of modern technology, which has been guided solely by an economic profit. A recent example of the ramifications and consequences of this economic driven pathway has been the Gulf Coast oil disaster. The other pathway is an Indigenous spiritually-based way, of co-existing peacefully, and in harmony with the world around us.[50]

Anishnabec Elders, as conduits of Indigenous life-sustaining wisdoms, are asking all of Humanity to seriously come into balance with the Earth. They also warn that if people continue following a path which is motivated only by economic gain, humanity will experience more natural disasters of greater frequency and of vast cataclysmic proportions. Indigenous Elders around the globe assert that Indigenous Peoples are keepers of integral life-sustaining wisdoms.[51] Indigenous Elders speak urgently to the need for Indigenous Peoples around the world to return to our traditional teachings and ceremonial practices. That is, when we engage in our ceremonies, such as the Sun Dance, we foster healing and restorative energies, thereby facilitating a healing change in this critical stage of Earth's development.

The History and Significance of the Anishnabec Sun Dance Ceremony

Sun Dance ceremonies take place in many sacred sites of North American in the summer time when the sun is at its hottest. An account of the spiritual practice of the Sun Dance is made reference to in our Anishnabec Creation Stories, and was originally referred to as the Thirst Dance.[52] The Thirst Dance was considered to be the holiest and central of all ceremonies. The Sun Dance or Thirst Dance occurs within a circle, reflecting our circular cosmological understanding about the universe, and the circular and cyclical characteristics of life. At the center within the circle is a Poplar Tree, represented as the Tree of Life, as well as a focal point for reflecting upon the Creator.

The Sun Dance was and continues to be a rigorous ceremony, and one that should not be taken up lightly. Some of my Elders have said that, "One does not choose to be a Sun Dancer;" rather, "The Sun Dancer is chosen by the Creator." Some of the recorded purposes of this dance were to promote peaceful relationships and harmony, gift-giving, and the celebration of important events.[53] It has also been acknowledged that participation in the Thirst Dance opens people up to experiences of love and righteousness. As has been previously indicated, the Sun Dance establishes and ensures the maintenance of a delicate ecological balance with the natural world and its life-giving forces.

It is an understatement to say that it is a physical impossibility to complete the pledge to Sun Dance without supernatural aid. Sun Dancers are called into the Sun Dance circle around the Tree at the onset of the Sun Dance by the Sun Dance Chief, or the conductor of the ceremony. Sun Dancers remain within this circle in the hot sun without the nourishment of food and water for two to four days. In the Sun Dances that I am involved with, the Sun Dancers are taken out of the Sun Dance Lodge as the sun is setting each day, and are given an opportunity to rest, or sleep during the evening. In the morning, the Sun Dancers are called back into the Sun Dance circle to resume their Sun Dance.

To successfully Sun Dance, the dancer must let go of his or her ego and limited physical self, in favor of receiving immeasurable strength from spiritual forces and powers. The Sun Dancer then becomes a conduit of spiritual powers and is given the stamina to complete the Sun Dance. As a vessel of spiritual energies, the Sun Dancer can be privy to spirit-based communication from Ancestors and other Spirit-forms through the receiving of visions, auditory experiences, and dreams. The nature of these messages can be for personal use and instruction. However, many people receive messages for the betterment of their families, communities, and Nations, as well as for the betterment of All of Creation.

The Thirst Dance or Sun Dance was outlawed by Canadian legislation in 1880.[54] However, Anishnabec oral history attests that while the practice was made officially illegal, some Anishnabec people continued to hold this and other ceremonies "in the bush" away from the watchful eyes of colonial authorities. This understanding has also been recorded in written accounts[55] thereby attesting to the cultural resiliency of Anishnabec People. However, because the Sun Dance was outlawed, the ability to maintain this practice was severely limited.

Present Day Practices and Outcomes
of the Anishnabec Sun Dance

It has been recorded that after World War II, a revitalization of an anti-colonial spirit took root in many North American Indigenous communities. That is, North American Indigenous veterans during war time experienced the same liberties as their non-Indigenous comrades. Returning to their homes after the war, these veterans found it impossible to live within conditions of apartheid, and other forms of colonial oppression.[56] In response to anti-colonial resistances, some changes were invoked, such as the lifting of the ban on North American Indigenous ceremonies. Currently there is a revival and a resurgence of North American Indigenous ceremonies, inclusive of the Anishnabec Sun Dance ceremony.[57]

I have witnessed three positive outcomes of the Sun Dance as it is practiced by Anishnabec people today. In the first instance, the ceremony has created a context for the healing and empowerment of many Anishnabec People. That is, Anishnabec People have been given a place, and a space for feeling unresolved historic grief and traumas associated with experiencing colonialism. In so doing, many Anishnabec are able to release negative feelings and to come to terms in a positive way with the impacts of our colonial oppression. Duran, Duran, Yellow Horse-Brave Heart, and Yellow Horse-Davis,[58] referring to the Lakota experience of reviving the Sun Dance, cite a similar outcome for their People. Through the rigors of Sun Dancing, I have observed many Anishnabec people earning the right to pick up sacred responsibilities, such as picking up the mantle of spiritual leadership and becoming carriers of Anishnabec ceremonies.

Secondly, during the Anishnabec Sun Dances that I have attended, people from diverse backgrounds and cultures have been invited to participate. I have observed people attending Sun Dances from many parts of the globe, and in so doing, a spirit of greater respect, harmony, and peace between Anishnabec and non-Anishnabec Peoples and knowledges has been achieved. Thirdly, living in a current context where we are experiencing such phenomena as global warming and other climatic changes, the Sun Dance draws upon the energies of the Sun to assist in the restoration of the balance to our Mother Earth. Indeed, I have readily observed conditions of intense and unprecedented summer's heat eased by the Sun Dance, bringing along the spirit of cooling rains. That is, even though the weather report had not predicated rain, my Elders have informed me that through the focused prayers of some of the Sun Dancers, the outcome of rain was achieved.

Sharing my Motivations for Sun Dancing and the Process of Preparing to Dance: Picking up the Mantle of a Warrior of Light Serving Mother Earth and All of Creation

I first learned about the practice of the Anishnabec Sun Dance seventeen years ago. At that time I had a desire to learn more about the Sun Dance, but also knew that it was a ceremony that one had to be invited to attend. I was very pleased when I was asked to become involved with a Sun Dance nine years ago, as a helper for a woman who had pledged to Sun Dance. I served this Sun Dance as a helper for two years, where I primarily was involved with cooking and the cleanup from cooking for the Sun Dance Chief and his helpers, as well as for the drummer and singers, and for other persons who had come to support the Sun Dance from outside of the Sun Dance circle. It was a life changing experience for me to witness the commitment made by the Sun Dancers. I was aware that the dancers were praying for the good of their People, for all of Humanity, and for the continuance of all that is good and true on this Earth. It was at that time that I was emotionally moved to become a Sun Dancer, and shortly thereafter, came into contact with people who sponsored me into my first Sun Dance as a dancer.

My reasons for deciding to pledge to be a Sun Dancer stemmed from my deep awareness of all the blessings that were in my life. I was aware that Creator had given me many gifts and talents, and I had a community of family and friends who respected me and gave me opportunities to utilize these gifts and talents. Aware that so many Anishnabec and Métis People live on this land in conditions of extreme oppression and poverty, this was not my circumstance. While in the early part of my life I lived well below what is referred to as the "poverty line," firmly believing that acquiring a university education was the "ticket out of poverty," I had become very well-educated by Western standards. As a result, I now had not only a middle-class income, but I also had a career to look forward to. I lived in the comfort of a beautiful home, and all of my physical needs were easily met.

I had as a young woman dedicated my life to the service of Anishnabec and Métis Peoples as a community activist and a healer. However, I felt deeply convicted that there was more that I could do in service to Creator, Mother Earth, and All of Creation. I asked myself, "What is it that I can do to give back to the Creator for all that I had been given? How can I show the Creator how much I care?" I was aware that as a Sun Dancer I could offer my life as prayer. I could, through Sun Dancing, offer my body, giving up comforts such as a cozy bed, and plenty of food and water over intense and focused time periods, and thereby, fast and dance in the hot sun in service to prayer. I could become a prayer warrior, praying for the resurgence of the traditional Anishnabec way of life, and for the end of all forms of colonial oppression on this land. I could pray for the healing of Mother Earth, and all our Relations. I could pray that humanity would learn to live from a spirit of respectful co-existence with all within the circle of life. I had also witnessed many Sun Dancers making even deeper commitments through the Sun Dance piercing ritual,[59] and I knew that if asked by the Creator, I could offer this service as well.

Perhaps, more particularly through the Sun Dance, I could pledge myself to Greater Service, being willing to take a stand as a warrior at whatever cost to myself personally. That is, I could utilize the privileged positions that I occupied in life to speak out against oppressions and injustices, even if that meant loss of economic security or physical comforts that my life afforded. I could serve as a role model utilizing all of my gifts and talents in service to not only my own People, but to All My Relations. I could teach people about and emulate what it means to live according to the principle of respectful co-existence with All of Creation. I aspire to live an impeccable life, upholding my sacred stewardship responsibility to Mother Earth for the preservation of life on this Planet.

I have previously stated that the Sun Dance is considered to be the holiest of all of the ceremonies, and that one must approach this ceremony with deep humility and respect. It needs to be understood that it takes an entire year to prepare for the rigors of the Sun Dance. Each Sun Dance ceremony has its own protocol for preparation, which stems from the oral history from where the ceremony originates. Some of the ways that I was instructed to prepare for Sun Dancing were the following: each day, I was expected to get up before dawn to pray and meditate, offering my day in service to the Creator. It was also advised that I eat nutritious food, and that I was to fast from food and water for at least one day each month. I also was expected to attend numerous sweat lodge or purification lodges[60] throughout the year, and in so doing to let go of any emotional blockage or physical limitations that would impact on the ability to Sun Dance. In the spring I was also expected to go out on the land, under the direction of an Elder, and fast without food and water for four days. Having stayed true to this regimen, once summer arrived, I had earned my right to enter the sacred Sun Dance Lodge as a Sun Dancer.

Sharing Heart Knowledges Concerning my Experiences as a Sun Dancer

I will only share in a very general way about the Sun Dances that I have been involved in. It is important to realize that there are many Sun Dance ways or practices. In the Sun Dance way that I have danced in, the Sun Dance begins in either July or August, at the time when the Moon—contextualized as our Grandmother—is at her fullest. In this way, the masculine and feminine principles of life are in harmony, or are balanced. On the evening before the dance, we as dancers are given a feast to eat many nutritious foods. Following this feast, we begin our fast, and enter the Sun Dance grounds where we remain for a four-day and four-night period. When the sun rises on the following day, we as dancers are awakened, and required to enter a sweat lodge, to ensure that we are pure at heart to enter the Sun Dance lodge. After the sweat lodge, we prepare for our day in quiet prayer and meditation, and then are called into the Sun Dance lodge by the Sun Dance Chief.

The purpose of Sun Dancing is to pray for the People. I was advised to focus my prayers on the first day for the healing and blessings of All the Earth's Peoples. We remain in the lodge and dance to the beat of the drum, dancing until the Sun Dance Chief calls us out of the lodge for a break. In some ways I have found the first day to be the hardest to achieve, as I am still very connected to the physical realm, and as such am aware of little aches and pains, as well as the hunger pangs and thirst that my body is feeling. However, I have learned that the secret to successfully Sun Dancing is to surrender your own physical needs, and in so doing to focus on your prayers for the good will of others. Consequently, my attention is no longer on my limited self, but rather directed at that for which I have pledged. At the day's end, it is a welcome relief to be called out of the Sun Dance lodge, and to be allowed to retire for the day.

On the second day of the Sun Dance, and every day thereafter, the morning begins in the usual way, being awakened to go into the sweat lodge. My focus on the second day of dancing has been to pray for my own People. As a Métis person, I have prayed on the second day specific prayers for the needs of Anishnabec People, Métis People, and for all North American Indigenous Peoples of this land. As a mixed-race person, I have also prayed on the second day for my White relatives and for European Peoples in general. I have specifically prayed that North American Indigenous Peoples heal from all the pain and traumas that are the result of our colonization. I have also prayed that Anishnabec and Métis Peoples are able to take their rightful place on this land, and to uphold our responsibilities. I have prayed that the divisions amongst people that have been created by apartheid and other colonial imposition are healed, and that we learn to treat each other as kin. I have also prayed that European/Western Peoples see the error of colonizing ways and learn to live in harmony with All Our Relations.

The second day has historically been a very emotional day for me. It is also the day that I am able to let go of my physical body, and allow my spirit to lead the dance. This is an exciting day, for this is when the magic begins to happen. I become open to immense spiritual powers that come from my Ancestors, spirit helpers, and guides. The practice at the end of the second day, at least in the Sun Dances that I have been involved in, has been for dancers to be given a feast of fresh fruit and vegetables. This gives our bodies needed sustenance, and also serves the purpose of cleaning out toxins from the body.

On the third day of the Sun Dance, I have dedicated my prayers to my own clan, to both my extended and immediate families. This is a day when I focus on the individual healing needs of people who I deeply love and cherish. This can be a time when I experience expansive spiritual insights and understandings, as I am well in tune with the spirits of the dance. Indeed, throughout the duration of the dance, during times of rest I have experienced numerous instructive dreams, auditory information, and visions. Sun Dancing is a much focused time and the more I focus on attending to the Tree and my prayers for the People, the greater the spiritual rewards.

The fourth and final day of the dance is one of great celebration. I often feel on the fourth day, that I have reached such a spiritual high and have gathered such spiritual power that I could dance for many, many more days. The limits and weariness of the human body seem far away, and the realm of spirit(s) is the central focus. It is time of great joy. Day four also comes with a deep sense of accomplishment as I recognize that I have almost fulfilled my Sun Dance obligation for the year. I have experienced great delight, happiness, as well as ease in the dance. On the fourth day, having focused each day on the needs of others, it is said that the dancer has earned the right to pray for him or herself. I have learned that on the fourth day, with prayers for the self, comes clarity and purpose. With these prayers for self has come a renewed commitment to live according to spiritual principles and values, and to live in service for the Creator, for Mother Earth and All of Creation. It was on the fourth day of my fourth Sun Dance that I pledged to continue dancing for as long as Creator enables me to do so.

When the dance comes to an end, I become profoundly aware that as rigorous as the Sun Dance is, the dance itself is merely a representation of the deep level of dedication and commitment that is needed to live a spiritual life on this Earth at this time in Earth's development. That is, I have become cognizant that as I came full circle with my pledge to dance, the life of a Sun Dancer is an endless journey of service and commitment to the Earth, and All Our Relations. I have learned that within the context of the dance, we as Sun Dancers, whether blood related or not, are all part of a Sun Dance family. I have also learned, deeply, in an experiential way through Sun Dancing that we are indeed "all related" on Mother Earth, within an interconnected web of kinship ties. With that understanding is imbued deep responsibility, for as kin we are all obligated to care for Mother Earth and All of Life, for the future generations to come.

At the conclusion of the Sun Dance, there is another feast. There is also what is referred to as a "give-a-way," where people who have completed their fourth year of Sun Dancing offer gifts that they have made throughout their four year commitment to dance.

The end of the Sun Dance is a time for celebration, yet, as I have intimated, there is also an awareness that the real job of the Sun Dance is but before us. Having danced in the spiritual realm, now the hard warrior work begins. Informed by an anti-colonial spirit, my Sun Dance pledge invokes making manifest the dream of anti-colonial realities and legacies from within the perspective of respectful co-existence with all of life. In so doing, I work to manifest in the physical realm Creator's dream of our living in peace and harmony with Mother Earth and All of Creation.

I have presented the perspective that Anishnabec/Métis Peoples are resilient with rich cultural histories. I have shared with you the historical and current significance of the Anishnabec Sun Dance from both the stance of recorded history, and from my subjective inner knowing. My primary reason for engaging in this discourse has been to promote greater understanding and respect for my People, and for Anishnabec cultural traditions. It is my deepest aspiration that I have fulfilled this purpose. Indeed, I hope this discourse promotes a broader base of support from persons who become allied in my People's and other Indigenous Peoples struggles, as the spirit of Anne Bishop's work, *Becoming an Ally*, suggests.[61]

I have presented the perspective that the Sun Dance practice is a very sacred ceremony, and one that must be approached with reverence and respect. I have also relayed my own experiences of preparing for and engaging in Sun Dancing, and in so doing, intended to portray the deep rigor that accompanies this distinctly Anishnabec spiritual practice. I have argued that there is great utility in the preservation of Anishnabec ceremonial practices, such as the Sun Dance, as these practices promote healing for Anishnabec and Métis People, as well as contribute to ecological balance during these times of Earth's critical planetary changes. I have also participated in Sun Dances where non-Anishnabec Peoples have been invited to attend. I have witnessed that the respectful sharing of Anishnabec spiritually and heart-based experiences promotes positive Human relations, such as greater awareness, peace, and friendship. I contend that these types of cross-cultural experiences create future possibilities of respectful co-existence.

I am cognizant that the ideal of respectful co-existence is a lofty goal, since we as Anishnabec/Métis Peoples continue to live in a colonized context. Indeed, as the realities of this world include pollution, warring, greed, and corporate led dictatorship, there is much to do to create a world of harmony and peace.[62] Ultimately, the forces of oppression must surrender to the will of divine and just authorities. Empowered by my experiences of Sun Dancing, I hold within my being a profound sense of duty and obligation. In so doing, I pick up the mantle of my own power and authority to speak and stand up for the truth as I see it. I also pledge to anti-colonial resistances, actively working to correct imbalances within the world that I live in. I intend to be a power of example, or a beacon of light in service to my People, Mother Earth, and All of Creation. I conclude this discourse on the sacred path of Sun Dance in a customary Anishnabec way by affirming our cosmological understanding. *Kina dewa we maag*, or All My Relations.

• • • •

BARBARA WATERFALL is a Metis-Anishnabe-Kwe, and Grandmother. She is also an Anishnabe healer. She has been trained as both a social worker and a Traditional Anishnabe healer. She has maintained a healing and counselling practice for the last twenty years, where she infuses spirituality into her practice. Barbara is an accomplished writer, having published articles and book chapters on such topics as teaching as activism, the inclusion of spirituality in curriculum and pedagogy, reclaiming Indigenous identities and Native Women's knowledges, and decolonizing Indigenous higher education. She is also an accomplished singer and songwriter, and conducts numerous workshops on topics such as Music as Medicine, and 'Finding Your Personal Medicine and Empowerment,' Barbara has taken up a new faculty position in the Indigenous BSW and MSW Specializations in Social Work at the University of Victoria.

CHAPTER ELEVEN

Women's Ritual Dances:
An Ancient Source of Healing
in Our Times

Laura Shannon

KYRIA LOULOUDA *calls to her sister to help her wind the yards of woven girdle around and around my waist. Kyria Stella's aged fingers, still strong, tuck the sash ends in tightly, smoothing down the fabric she and Loulouda wove themselves. The snug embrace of the sash supports my back and encourages me to stand proudly upright. As they help me with the intricate tucks and pleats of the festival dress, and the careful tying of the flowered headscarf, I see their tired, careworn faces come alight with joy and expectation. When they are satisfied, they turn me towards the mirror, smiling. We gaze at ourselves, a row of three women, dressed alike. Like the butterflies embroidered in bright silks on the dark cloth of the bodice, we too are transformed. The food is prepared, the housework is done, the animals taken care of for the night; the other women await us in the square where, by tradition, they will open the dance as they have done countless times throughout their lives. We are in the village of Pentalofos in Greek Thrace in the early twenty-first century, living a timeless scene which has been repeated through the generations for hundreds, perhaps thousands of years.*

Since 1985, I have been researching Balkan folk dances and teaching them in women's circles all over the world. Common symbols in dance patterns, textile motifs, and archaeological artifacts from southeastern Europe have remained the same from ancient times to the present, which leads me to suggest that the dances may be descended from ritual practices dating back to Neolithic times. In my view, these patterns serve as a symbolic language, expressing reverence for the cycle of life. Emphasizing connectedness and continuity, homecoming, and support, women's ritual dances can rekindle ancient values of sustainability, empathy, and equality, and provide an antidote to the alienation of self which is epidemic in the Western world. In my twenty years of teaching, I have found that women all over the world respond to these dances as valuable tools for healing and self-discovery, as quotations from some of my students will show.

> To me, dancing is connection. Connecting my body and soul, connecting
> my womanhood with other women, connecting my Scandinavian culture to
> other cultures, connecting my urban era with agricultural eras.
>
> **(SUSANNA HELLSING, SWEDEN)**

Surviving texts and archaeological evidence show that ritual dance was a primary means of women's worship in ancient Europe.[63] Images of women dancing with joined hands have been depicted in rock art, pottery shards, vases, and frescoes, as much as ten thousand years before the present. Flutes made of animal bones, 35,000 to 40,000 years old, have been discovered; musicians are often shown accompanying the dance.[64] The many portrayals of women dancing and drumming indicate that these activities were considered important in the earliest civilisations. Furthermore, images of women's ritual dance in antiquity are often directly reflected in customs which can still be witnessed in Eastern Europe today.[65]

The archaeological record confirms the significance of the dance in a wide area of Eastern Europe and the Near East. At the heart of this region is the area known as Old Europe, birthplace of agriculture, whose indigenous inhabitants lived in peaceful agrarian settlements for thousands of years.[66] Excavations there have yielded countless goddess figures in bone, wood, stone, and pottery, dating back to the origins of agriculture some 8,000 years ago and even back to the Paleolithic period, over 25,000 years ago. Because the area where the goddess figures are most widespread corresponds to the area where circle dance traditions are still most concentrated and most intact, I suggest that women's dances surviving today can be seen as living remnants of the Old European Goddess culture, which may have persisted for over twenty thousand years.[67]

According to archaeologist Marija Gimbutas, the Goddess of the earliest Old European civilisations was a deity of birth, death, and regeneration.[68] Feminist theolo-

139

gian Carol P. Christ identifies an essential function of the Goddess symbol for women as the affirmation of the female body and the life cycle embodied within it.[69] This connection to the cycle of life is also a key aspect of women's ritual dances.

Women's Ritual Dances

I would like to clarify my term "women's ritual dances." The circle dances at the heart of my research come from areas of Eastern Europe and the Near East where dance is still part of people's lives.[70] There are several reasons why circle dances and related folk traditions continued to thrive in Eastern Europe long after they had mostly vanished from the West, including cultural isolation and the slow pace of industrialisation during the 500-year Ottoman period. The fact that the Orthodox Church did not have an Inquisition was also crucial, as rural healers and "wise women" were not persecuted or burned as witches, and dancing was not forbidden. Free from this systematic persecution, which in Western Europe lasted for several centuries, women in Eastern Europe—although they suffered other forms of patriarchal oppression—were able to keep many of their dance and ritual practices intact.

Balkan circle dances have been part of ritual celebrations since ancient times, on feast days such as midsummer, in preparation for a wedding, at planting or harvest, or in times of drought as a prayer for rain.[71] Some patterns are danced exclusively by women, while others may be danced by women in women's style at some times, and in mixed or men's groups at other times. Even when women's ritual dances share the same steps as those danced on non-specific occasions or in mixed circles, they are differentiated on ritual occasions by a particular intention and context.

Women's ritual dances are also distinguished by aspects of women's work and culture which are interwoven with the women's dance experience. These aspects serve the purpose of affirming women's connection to, and participation in, the sacred cycle of life. On occasions where ritual dances would be danced, such as an engagement, wedding, or baptism, for instance, women would wear the festive dress of their village, as did their ancestors before them.[72] These costumes differed from everyday clothing in their vastly more elaborate decoration, laden with a specific vocabulary of aesthetic motifs, and corresponding symbolic meaning. Spun, woven, and embroidered by women using their own wool, flax, cotton, or silk, the clothing demonstrated their own abilities while strictly replicating patterns passed down for generations without change. In this way, the textiles served both to express individual identity and skill, and to affirm the code of the culture.[73]

Food served on occasions when ritual dancing takes place is likewise prepared by women with the fruits of their own land and labour, the literal distillation of their connection to cyclical agricultural work—again, largely done by women—which supports the whole community. Ritual breads and sweets may incorporate symbols identical to those embroidered on the clothing and encoded in the dance steps. The younger women present absorb these practical and ritual skills from those who have, in turn, learned them from their own elders.

Women's tasks of growing and preparing food, making and decorating clothing, bearing and raising children, and passing down traditions from mother to daughter are thus intrinsic to the women's ritual dance experience. Because men do not do these kinds of work, their dancing may serve other ritual purposes but does not inherently refer to this matrix of ritual and practical tasks as women's dances do. Therefore, I use the phrase "women's ritual dance" to refer to women's dance steps interwoven with other aspects of women's culture, as an embodied affirmation of the life cycle which both sustains, and is sustained by, the dancing women.

These women's traditions communicate the egalitarian, cooperative, and peaceful values of societies deeply connected to the land and appreciative of art. These qualities—of connection, equality, inclusiveness, balance, sustainability, empathy, and mutuality—are the principles of Partnership, as proposed by Riane Eisler, or Belonging, as Carol Lee Flinders calls it, and are also the values of the matrifocal Old European Goddess culture as articulated by Marija Gimbutas.[74] It is my belief that women's ritual dances can be of great service to dancers today, by renewing our faith in these values at a critical time.

These dances have a huge amount of wisdom for our present age. They may be about a seasonal life that we no longer live on the surface, but they plug in to our deeper rhythms and to our experience of birth and death in a way that can never be out of date.

(CLAIRE HAYES, SCOTLAND)

Journey to Healing

I first came across traditional circle dances in the early 1980s, in international folk dance groups in the USA where I grew up and at the Findhorn Community in northern Scotland. Folk dances with symbolic content had been brought to Findhorn in 1976 by German dance master Bernhard Wosien and his daughter Maria-Gabriele Wosien, and from there spread around the world. Under the name of Sacred Dance, the folk forms were adapted as a means to encourage group awareness and facilitate a conscious connection with the divine.[75]

As I searched out and studied diverse forms of folk dance and sacred dance, I was led to focus on traditional women's dances literally by accident. When I was twenty, a serious knee injury threatened to end my career as a dancer. The only circle dances I

141

was able to engage in were the slowest, simplest ones, which turned out to be women's dances. I did not know much about them at that time and was surprised to find them so compelling. With no complicated variations to distract me from myself, I learned to let the repetition of the steps, like the repetition of a mantra, bring me in touch with my truest self and deepest feelings. Just as in meditation, this simple, yet powerful process created a trancelike atmosphere which invited me to be fully present.[76]

Women's ritual dances gently yet firmly invited me back into my body. In their ancient patterns, I felt I could perceive the living, compassionate presence of the grandmothers of the human family who had initiated the dances and passed them on. In the same way that meditation practice is supported by a *sangha*, or community, I experienced how a circle of women all dancing identically allows each woman to feel deeply held. The kinesthetic unity of the circle transcends difference without denying it; competition and conflict are transmuted into co-creation. The dances strongly connected me with an understanding of life—in all its variety, with all its ups and downs—as sacred. The sensation of energy which flowed through me while dancing in this meditative way, along with intense intuitive flashes, and unexpectedly practical insights, eventually wove me back into the web of life.

Although specialists had told me I would never dance again, the deceptively gentle "medicine" of the women's ritual dances helped my knee to heal without surgery and brought me out of the depression that had come in the wake of the injury. Dancing has remained at the heart of my life. Deeply fascinated with the dances and what I perceived to be their healing potential, I used my training as a dance movement therapist to focus as much as possible on the therapeutic use of circle dance and devoted every spare moment to what has become a lifelong dedication to this quest. As I spent more and more time both researching and teaching these dances in Europe and all over the world, I found that they fulfilled my deep longing for meaningful connection. They brought me back into rightful balance with myself, with other women, and with an ancient lineage of dancing women going back through time. Looking back, I feel profoundly grateful for the initial healing crisis which led me to discover the hidden power of women's ritual dances.

Over time, I saw that they fulfilled similar longings in other women too, even for women whose own background is far removed from the areas of Eastern Europe and the Near East where the dances have their origins. These experiences led me to focus on working consciously with the dances in women's groups as tools to access a source of wisdom greater than ourselves. Just as women's ritual dances are differentiated from other dances by the context of a ritual occasion, in my circles it is the context we create for our dancing, and the consciousness we bring to it, which facilitates a dance experience we may name as sacred. The dances are not a performance; everyone present participates. We dance for ourselves and not for an audience. In the absence of an external onlookers' gaze, our attention is directed away from concerns about how we look and what others might think, and toward a more focused awareness of our own inner being. Paradoxically, this inward focus may also help us connect with something larger than ourselves, a sense of oneness with all of life.

> *Slow, simple, three measure dances have been an important part of my healing journey from cancer. When I was deeply fatigued, I would focus on letting the earth's energy rise through my steps. When I was feeling afraid, I turned to dances that remind me of my resilience and dignity even in the context of loss. Dancing directly reconnected me to the joy and trustworthiness of the life force in a way that nothing else could.*
>
> **(EMILY JARRET HUGHES, MINNESOTA, USA)**

An Unwritten Language

Many scholars consider the symbols of Neolithic art to have served as the language and writing of primeval humankind.[77] Bulgarian mother and daughter ethnographers Anna Ilieva and Anna Shturbanova describe archaeological and mythological symbols in ritual dance as the means by which living dances continue to transmit messages embedded in them since antiquity.[78] Hazrat Inayat Khan writes of symbols as living manuscripts which serve to keep ancient wisdom intact, transmitting ideas in unwritten form long beyond the lifetime of the teacher.[79] Jean Shinoda Bolen speaks of poetic imagery as compressed information drawn from the symbolic level of the psyche,[80] while Marion Woodman calls the symbolic language of the unconscious the "original mother tongue."[81] In my view, women's dance steps, embroidery patterns, and song texts can be seen as ancient forms of women's "poetry," containing compressed or encoded information handed down through many generations.

Many dance sequences incorporate clearly discernible symbols in their movements. The zigzag, for example, is a pattern frequently drawn on the ground by dance steps which move both towards and away from the center as well as around the circle.[82] Gimbutas and others interpret the zigzag symbol as the serpent, lightning, flowing water, the rhythms of sun and moon, and the seasons of the year, as well as the cycle of life containing all the mysteries of birth, death, and regeneration. Very often, the zigzag appears together with Goddess figures on carved or painted pottery finds.[83]

Other key symbols found in the dances include the circle, cross, crescent, serpent, spiral, meander, triangle, and Tree of Life. The same motifs are depicted on the ancient goddess figures and other artifacts found throughout the area of Old Europe and the Near East, where, as we have seen, the Goddess was worshipped for thousands of years in the earliest indigenous European civilisations.[84] They still appear, virtually unchanged from Neolithic to contemporary times, in folk arts including weaving, embroidery, pottery, jewellery, woodcarving, ritual bread, and Easter eggs, wherever the dances are found. Ethnologists observing this continuity of folk motifs from Neolithic times to the present day tend to concur that these motifs are native to Europe and the Near East, not imported by trade.[85] Although the ephemeral phenomena of dance steps cannot be carbon-dated, this suggests that the dances may have their roots in the original, autochthonous Goddess culture of Old Europe, and may be at least as old as the other folk arts in question.[86]

The fact that similar dances, melodies, and rhythms are found among all ethnic groups and religions in this vast geographical area also suggests a common heritage predating religious divisions. In the same way, the dances can carry meaning for women today, whatever their personal beliefs, as the unwritten nature of the symbols makes them uniquely resistant to dogmatic interpretations. The dances foster an atmosphere of acceptance, where everyone's experience is equally valid, and each has her place in the whole. These qualities of inclusiveness and respect for diversity are key aspects of the ancient Goddess paradigm.[87]

> It is not only dancing with others, but dancing the steps of the ancestors;
> it helps me remember that those before us have come through many cycles:
> ups, downs, surges, reverses, waxing, and waning. Whatever happens, we
> are not on this journey alone.
>
> **(KAREN FLEISCHER, CALIFORNIA, USA)**

The "Text" of Textiles

As we have seen, the radiant lines, zigzags, and meanders emphasized in the incised "costumes" of Neolithic goddesses also feature in contemporary and antique folk textiles from Eastern Europe.[88] Other Neolithic motifs frequently represented include plants, seeds, birds, cosmological symbols, female figures, or goddesses, and often a strongly emphasised central tree. The butterfly or double axe is one of the most widespread motifs associated with prehistoric goddess figures, going back at least eight thousand years; Gimbutas identifies it as a symbol of transformation and the epiphany of the Goddess.[89] Even today, it has pride of place on the women's costume of Pentalofos.

It is clear that the symbols had meaning to those who kept them alive through the generations; the significance of the motifs is stressed by the care with which they were preserved through time and the frequency with which they still appear. I suggest that these textiles and their encoded meanings can be considered as a form of text, to be "read" by those who have eyes to see. In the village of Soufli in Greek Thrace, for example, bridal aprons featuring time-honoured goddess and fertility symbols are known as *grammènes* or 'written' aprons.[90] In Vologda villages in Russia, the winter festival of "embroidery reading" gathered all the young women near a church where the oldest women in the village would examine their beautifully embroidered blouses, dresses, and aprons, and explain the significance of the ancient patterns.[91] In this way, both motif and meaning were passed down through the generations. According to Linda Welters, the creation and use of ritual clothing embellished with such symbols to promote fertility was an act of empowerment for women.[92] In cultures where women were often illiterate, the intelligence and sophistication of women's wisdom was no less for having been codified and passed down in nonverbal ways.

Embroidered butterfly goddesses on woman's chemise,
Pentalofos, Thrace, Greece

The process of transmission is beautifully illustrated by the pattern of the Birth Goddess, found in countless examples of Balkan embroidery and weaving.[93] This motif, dating back to Neolithic wall reliefs at Çatal Hüyük,[94] shows a vertical chain of mother-daughter goddesses, one smaller than the other and portrayed sheltered in her womb or emerging between her legs. In similar fashion, the Tree of Life often bears one or more smaller trees descending vertically from the central figure,[95] perhaps depicting the line of matrilineal descent, the transmission of information, or the blessing of the ancestors. Mary Kelly writes that the Birth Goddess motif survived well into the twentieth century due to the strength of women's belief in its power to protect fertility.[96]

Fertility was a primary concern in Eastern European cultures, where the necessity of living from the land gave rise to an elemental respect for the natural world, and the invocation and protection of fertility was a central aim of folk ritual. Carol P. Christ identifies fertility as the universal principle of life, death, and rebirth encompassing all of known existence.[97] Far from being limited to reproduction alone, fertility was the sum total of women's overall power—expressed in gathering and storing food, bearing and raising children, safeguarding the plants and animals, fulfilling ritual obligations, and providing nourishment, shelter, and clothing. Women's work was therefore the key to the ongoing survival of the human community.[98] This resonates with Gimbutas' assertion that the Goddess worshipped in ancient times was not merely a Mother Goddess related to childbearing, but the very embodiment of Creation, Source of All.[99]

The Dancing Priestess of the Living Goddess

As I experienced for myself when Kyria Loulouda and Kyria Stella dressed me in the costume of their village, the securely wrapped layers of traditional folk dress strongly shape the posture and movements of the women wearing them. Variations in costume from village to village naturally correspond to variations in dance style, determined, for example, by skirts being long or short, narrow or full. The dance and the costume worn while dancing are thus inseparable. As we have seen, the same symbols and patterns may be expressed in both forms, so that the one helps us better understand the other. Just as the style of the dance depends on the costume, the costume reciprocally depends on the dance, as details such as fringes, sash ends, jewellery, and headdresses are shown to their best effect only in movement.

The relation between costume and dance is emphasised in the common embroidered motif known in Bulgaria as *horo*, or dance. The pattern, showing a row of identical female figures holding hands, neatly mirrors the row of identically-dressed women in the dance line. Goddess figures in both embroidery and archaeology tend to lack distinguishing facial features, indicating that they were not intended as portraits of individual women. In similar fashion, the ritual dance circle where all women are dressed alike also subsumes individual characteristics. I suggest this is intended to help women overcome the limitations of personality and to serve on ritual occasions as archetypal representatives of the feminine. In my view, ritual dances can facilitate an experience of both transcendence and immanence: the dancers become aware of the divine feminine embodied within them, as a force vastly larger than themselves but of which they are inextricably a part.

Textile researcher Sheila Paine identifies as "goddess-derived" embroidered female figures which appear in repeated symmetrical patterns such as the *horo* motif

Dancing grandmother with upraised arms, Razgrad, Bulgaria

described above, or which themselves display a symmetrical, centrally focused ritual stance.[100] Repeated symmetrical patterns, rhythmic gestures, and ritual stance are basic characteristics of traditional circle dances. Through taking on these attributes, I believe the dancers are enabled to transcend their individuality and enter a state which is "goddess-derived." As Iris Stewart points out, since ancient times this has been the role of the priestess, who employed ritual dress, jewellery, and headgear in order to move beyond personal identity and embody a larger power.[101]

147

Goddess of the Sun

The encircling presence of the headdress, always a feature of traditional folk costume, encourages women to stand taller and fully upright as they dance. Many goddess embroideries depict energy radiating from the head like a halo or aura, and many styles of headdress feature shiny, radiant objects such as beads, sequins, and coins together with rain-like falling fringes.

According to Bulgarian belief, this fusion of sun and rain represented the divine marriage between heaven and earth, and brought the blessing of fertility.[102] By replicating the "sun-headed" quality of the embroidered divinities, these elaborate headdresses symbolically transform the wearer into an embodiment of the Goddess herself, channelling the benevolent forces of sun and rain to benefit the home and community.[103]

The radiant sun energy so clearly depicted in archaeological artifacts and ritual costumes can also be experienced in the dance, as I found during my recovery from illness and injury. Very often, participants in my workshops comment on a tangible sensation of warmth or energy in the circle. This sensation of inner heat is easiest to perceive in women's dance movements that are smaller and more restrained; it is quite distinct from the warmth of aerobic exertion that results from the more energetic, athletically demanding movements of mixed or men's dances. Many participants liken it to the experience of *kundalini* or *chi* in yoga, t'ai chi, reiki, and other body-based meditative or healing disciplines. Interestingly, many folk dance styles lift and lower the heel in a way which stimulates the center of the ball of the foot, the acupressure point known in Chinese medicine as Kidney 1, or the Bubbling Spring. Considered to be the source of fertile, creative, and sexual energy and our point of connection with the earth and with the ancestors, this point can be activated with shiatsu therapy or acupuncture to bring a sense of heat into the entire body. In my view, this energy or *chi* is the same as the radiant force illustrated and protected by the dances and costumes.

Therefore, I suggest that women's ritual dances, in their strict discipline, transmission, use of symbols, and activation of inner energy, can be understood as an ancient form of physical and spiritual training. However, unlike systems of yoga and meditation passed down by a male elite, here women are the teachers, taking turns to lead the dance and returning afterward to their place in the body of the circle or dancing in a closed circle entirely without a leader. The egalitarian sharing of the leadership role ensures that leadership in dance does not result in codified roles of power and rank in the society itself. This egalitarian or partnership quality is a central aspect of women's ritual dances, and a key value of Goddess culture.[104]

Dancing women's ritual dances with Laura has given me a new relationship
with my body and with the traditions that hold the dances. I am aware
of my core or power center and of the way that the dances replenish and
strengthen it. As a result, I walk taller and more surely. I am full of gratitude
to the women who have taught these dances through the generations and
bequeathed us with such richness.

(CATHERINE SUTTON, CALIFORNIA, USA)

Sacred Sound

The radiant energy lines streaming away from the head in embroidered goddess figures, and made visible in the festive headdress, may also be understood as sound waves.
Women's dancing was originally accompanied by women's singing. Giving voice to
love, longing, loss, grief, joy, and celebration, the dance songs affirm the wholeness that
comes from embracing and integrating the full range of human experience.[105]

Folk songs often relate a woman's beauty to images of trees, flowers, birds, fertile
fields, or other attributes of nature, the very motifs likely to appear on the clothing she
wears. These metaphors draw parallels between the woman and culturally-encoded
symbols of the Goddess whom, in her festive costume, she is dressed to resemble. Balkan, Greek, Turkish, and Armenian songs may address the Divine Mother directly
either in her Christian personification as Mary / Maria,[106] or by symbolic reference to
Aphrodite, Goddess of Love, or the death and resurrection mysteries of Persephone
and Demeter. Other songs feature birds or animals long-associated with the Goddess,
trees with specific characteristics in the language of folk myth and poetry, or aspects
of the landscape such as holy shrines, sacred hills, springs, wells, or rivers. These songs
often accompany the oldest and simplest traditional women's ritual dances.[107]

The Goddess and the Tree of Life

The dances make me feel whole and harmonious, particularly the Tree of Life
dances, where opposites come together and create synthesis.

(EVA ULLNER, SWEDEN)

Just as the image of the tree is present in many dance songs, so the Tree of Life is one
of the most important and widespread symbols in both ancient and contemporary
textiles and artifacts.[108] Trees were revered as sources of food, medicine, shade, fire-
wood, fodder, and building material, and also as landmarks, boundary markers, and
sacred places set aside for ritual.[109] Since Neolithic times, the Tree of Life has been

identified with the concept of the Goddess, the source of life; woven or embroidered tree and flower motifs which resemble or incorporate goddess figures are still extremely widespread, as we have seen.

Embroidered Goddess / Tree of Life on woman's costume,
Sinasos, Cappadocia

The Tree of Life symbolises the cosmic balance of the worlds above and below, seen and unseen. Uniting earth and sky, horizontal and vertical, it is also the crossroads of the crone goddess Hecate. Marion Woodman describes this crossroads as a symbolic place where consciousness and unconsciousness meet, and where ego must be surrendered to a higher power.[110] In the same way, we as dancers must surrender our individuality in order to embody a power greater than ourselves, the wisdom of the Goddess.

I believe the three-measure dance pattern (by far the most popular dance form throughout Eastern Europe and the Near East) to be an encoded representation of the visual motif of the Tree of Life.[111] I came to this conclusion in 1991 through my own observation of three-measure dance patterns, and by relating the increased frequency of three-measure dances on ritual occasions to the increased frequency of the Tree of Life symbol on ritual textiles.[112]

Gold seal ring from Isopata tomb near Knossos, Crete, ca. 1500 BCE, showing dancing priestesses with upraised arms, descending Goddess and Tree of Life

The basic pattern of Tree of Life dances, as I choose to call them, incorporates an automatic rest: the step back to the left gives a pause in the forward momentum of the dance, which we can experience as a time for reflection and renewal of the impulse toward growth. It is like a peaceful winter after the activity of spring, summer, and autumn; a night's sleep after a full working day; or a feast day in the busy harvest season where everyone must put down their work and join the dance. These moments of rest are essential to our health, and also enable us to store up joy, through connecting to one another through the dances and to the divine energies of earth, sky, and fertility, the benevolent cosmic forces of life.

I see the three-measure dances as a hidden mantra of the Goddess, secretly spoken in the soft touch of our feet on the ground, following footsteps laid down for us by women of long ago. When I dance Tree of Life dances with my groups, I feel that we, too, are repeating this mantra, consciously affirming the timeless message of the Goddess: life in rhythm, life in balance, we remember; life with joy, life with connection, we remember. As we dance, we know ourselves to be daughters of the Goddess, silently "writing" her name in the dance steps, which vanish without a trace after the circle disperses, leaving no outward sign.[113]

The Dancing Mirror

Synchronized movement gives each woman a similar kinesthetic experience. Kyria Loulouda, like her mother and grandmother before her, can look around the dance circle and see her neighbours, friends, and relatives dressed as she is dressed, moving as she is moving, sensing what she is sensing. When all the women are dressed alike, their costume ensures a unified dance style and creates a cohesive visual image which magnifies the harmony of their collective movement. The circle of identically-dressed women mirrors the rows of radiant dancing goddesses embroidered on their costumes, invoking the universal energy of the divine feminine which transcends individual identity.

Recent research into women's neural functions shows that mirroring gestures, body postures, and facial expressions is a way for women to discern what others are feeling, through physical sensations that convey meaning to particular parts of the brain. Neuroscientists have discovered that the skills of empathy, observation, and mirroring come more easily to the female brain than to the male. This is the physiological basis for female intuition.[114]

Neural networks called mirror neurons enable us to watch and imitate another's action, and thereby learn. The mirror mechanism creates a bridge between individual brains for communication and connection on multiple levels, and facilitates a direct experiential understanding of another person's act, intention, or emotion. This neural process ensures that meaning within the message is the same for the sender as for the recipient, while no previous agreement between individuals is needed for them to understand each other. This accord is established through shared movement and mutual observation and reflected in the neural organization of both people.[115] This may offer a key to understanding how the nonverbal transmission of meaningful content in the dance event can still take place among women today.

Dancing Grandmothers, Rodopi, Bulgaria

Dancing together thus creates a shared state of emotional congruence and mutual understanding. This benefits the collective by establishing a system of reciprocal empathy and support which is continually refreshed and strengthened among women who dance together regularly. It was a social imperative for women in Balkan cultures to dance together, ensuring that the repetition of unified movement and dance style would automatically reinforce a sense of community and social harmony.

We learn dances in a circle, from women who learned them in a circle, from others who learned them in a circle, and so on back through time, which means that the kinesthetic patterns experienced in the dances have been imprinted through moving feet, gazing eyes, and joined hands in an unbroken line for hundreds, perhaps thousands of years. I believe the shared physical and neuromuscular experience of circle dancing is a mechanism which enables the transmission of nonverbal information throughout many generations in the dance.

The Healing Container

When I dance a traditional women's dance, the feelings range from power and pride to warmth and tenderness. Sometimes I get insights or receive messages. I connect with a sense of compassion for the women of other times and the women in my life. I feel a strong sense of community and common destiny.

(MARIA MARTA SUAREZ, ARGENTINA)

153

The dances affect our brains and bodies just as powerfully as they did the women of the past, but they serve us in a different way. Whereas Balkan village dances served to underscore cultural values of community, solidarity and interdependence, modern Western culture has emphasised opposite priorities, giving most of us an overdeveloped sense of individual "freedom" and entitlement. This leads many women in the modern world to suffer a crippling sense of loneliness and alienation.

Marion Woodman observes that modern women can be overly conscious, intellectual, and controlling in the masculine way that our culture has taught women to copy, and urges us to learn again to surrender to the healing unconscious as a source of connection with something timeless which is greater than ourselves.[116] The ritual of the dance circle can safely allow us to do exactly that, as the dances help us to bond with each other while celebrating our own and others' uniqueness.

The safe container of the dance experience is created through the supportive space of the circle and the unchanging structure of dance steps and style. Simple repetitive movements invoke the universality of human experience in space and time. The dance circle invokes the circle of the cosmos, universal symbol of unity and totality, and serves as a kind of mandala, which allows each dancer to center herself while bringing the different energies of the individual dancers into a balanced whole.[117] The movements remain objectively the same for all women, while each woman's subjective perception of the dance, and the significance it can have for her, is unique.[118]

Women's workshop with Laura Shannon, Schlehdorf, Germany,
with musician Kostantis Kourmadias

This experience—that the different viewpoints of the individual and the collective are not mutually exclusive, but mutually affirming and strengthening—can come as a revelation for many women. Many of us have never felt before that we could engage fully with our whole selves unless we were absolutely alone, protected from the gaze of others; many of us still feel we cannot be in tune with others unless we suppress large parts of our inner truth as we learned to do in childhood. This way of dancing can transform and heal both of those imbalances and bring them into equilibrium.

The more we bring loving awareness to our unique feelings, memories, and hopes, the more completely each woman can be present in the circle. A fully present circle, in turn, holds each woman even more strongly, creating a positive feedback loop. The level of joy rises and becomes palpable. We recognise it. We know we are welcome exactly as we are. We are invited to bring all the parts of ourselves, to gain and give acceptance, to be safely seen by others in our wholeness. This opens us to a deep experience of love that can dissolve past blockages and release a flood of feeling at one with all life. This is the message of the dances, the territory to which they show us the way back. In this way they give us the opportunity, as Woodman describes, to bring the light of consciousness into the matter of the divine feminine, and to bring body and soul into balance in a deeply healing way.

Rest in the Rhythm

Allowing myself to "listen" to the movements, meanings emerge that guide me in my daily life: with so many forward steps, remember often to stop, step back, or to the side. No need to rush ahead without rest or contemplation.

(EVELYN TORTON BECK, WASHINGTON, D.C., USA)

When Kyria Loulouda and the other women of Pentalofos celebrate a feast day by dancing and singing, eating and drinking, and dressing up in their finest clothes, they are obeying a cultural requirement to regularly rest in the rhythm of their lives.[119] As the three-measure dances show, the necessity for periodic rest is mirrored in the dance patterns themselves, which teach us to rest, to take a break from work, and to connect with other women to sources of joy. Not only is this our birthright, but as Barbara Ehrenreich's research suggests, the spirit of Dionysian celebration expressed in dance may actually be the key to successful human society.[120] Joy is another aspect of the sacred life energy of the Goddess. Quite simply, dancing makes us happy, and that is why we do it.

Tragically, the regular experiences of joy and rest that were obligatory in past societies have become virtually unattainable in our own. Women today, suffering an epidemic of isolation, burnout, and exhaustion, already understand in our bodies that the pace of modern life is not sustainable. It consumes too much of our own energy and does not allow time to recharge nor access to the sources of replenishment. Captive to a linear, patriarchal economic and social system driven towards the illusion of infinitely increasing "progress," at great cost to the finite resources of our planet and our society, we find that the precious resource of our own life energy has also been dangerously over-exploited.

Women's ritual dances affirm a sustainable, cyclical rhythm of life, interwoven with all aspects of women's work and culture. They reflect ancient patterns connected with the Goddess and support a sense of community, equally valid for women dancing today. They provide a safe container for our experiences, guide us through life's passages, and facilitate deep insight and understanding.

Dancing on the earth: Laura Shannon in Findhorn

In the past, women danced to ensure their own survival and that of their families and communities; in our time, what is at stake is the survival of the earth and all living beings. The skills which the dances can help us develop are needed now, not only in the service of our own transformation, but also for a collective return to safety and peace. Women's ritual dances can help us joyfully reconnect to the life-affirming worldview at the heart of indigenous Old European culture, and which we in the modern world must now reclaim, if the planet and those living on it are to survive into future generations.

I see the dance as a vast and complex tapestry, of colour and beauty, of joy, passion, and grief. I am a strand connected to every other, even though some have gone before me and others are yet to arrive. I am stronger because of the support that is offered around me. In turn I offer support too. I know that I am not and have never been alone. Each strand has shared my joys and sorrows or will in the future. To be a woman and dance the rituals is to be blessed.

(DEBBY FLAVELL, AUSTRALIA)

• • • •

LAURA SHANNON is a dance movement therapist and dance teacher known worldwide for her work exploring traditional circle dances as a source of healing and transformation. Inspired by her mother, a pianist who filled the house daily with music and rhythm, Laura graduated in intercultural studies and dance movement therapy, and in the U.S. and Europe intensively studied modern, African, Oriental, Balkan, expressive, and sacred dance, as well as ecstatic dance with Zuleikha and Authentic Movement with Janet Adler. For more than twenty years, Laura has researched and taught Greek, Armenian, Balkan, Romani, and Kurdish dances, particularly women's ritual dances, seeking to rekindle the worldview of community and sustainability which the traditional dances embody. Laura gives workshops and trainings in twenty countries and her writings on dance have been translated into many languages. She is on the sacred dance faculty at the Findhorn Foundation in Scotland, and resides both in Findhorn and in Greece. Laura's website address is *www.laurashannon.net*

CHAPTER TWELVE

Kathak, Dance of Healing

—

Deepti Gupta

K ATHAK IS THE CLASSICAL dance form of Northern India. It is a complex, evolved, and rich dance tradition with centuries of history behind it. A sublime blend of music, poetry, percussion, and drama, Kathak developed in the temples and royal courts. During its evolution, it has imbibed the passion and vigor of rural India as well as the subtle nuances and high aesthetic of Mughal courtly culture. Today, it is practiced as a contemporary stage form with a rich and varied repertoire. It has a codified technique based on rhythm patterns and its repertoire shares a context with many other Indian art forms, all inspired by Indian mythology and ancient Sanskrit texts.

I went to India in 1984 to take six months of intensive training in Kathak. I was already a practicing dancer with training in modern dance and Bharatanatyam, south Indian classical dance, as well as some basic knowledge of Kathak. Six months should be sufficient for me to grasp the technique, I thought. I didn't know then that Indian dance, particularly Kathak, would become a wondrous journey and a powerful force of healing in my life that continues to this day. When I began my work in dance, it was a form of artistic expression for me. I had no notion of dance as a healing art or as something with therapeutic qualities.

And yet, the concept of dance as an art of healing or with healing capabilities has never been more powerful for me than now... a dancer healing from breast cancer. Dance has played a central role in my encounter with cancer and also my entire healing process. This experience has etched out clearly and brought to the surface a process that has been subtly occurring within me all along. This health crisis helped me to experience how each aspect of dance has helped me to grow healthier, stronger, more aware, and more fully alive. This chapter focuses specifically on my experience with Kathak. Some of this analysis could also apply to other classical Indian dance forms.

Training:
A Journey into Kathak

My training began in 1984 with some private lessons in the home of Mrs. Reva Vidyarthi, one of my first teachers in Delhi. Little did I know, when I stepped into her living room for my initial lesson, that my relationship with dance was about to be transformed. The first clue came when she asked me to stand with her in front of a tiny altar on her dresser. We were both in bare feet and she handed me a few fresh flowers to hold. She then led me in a Sanskrit prayer to *Saraswati*, patron goddess of artists, the goddess of knowledge and learning. I repeated the strange and difficult words and phrases after her with little understanding of what I was saying. It occurred to me then that the dance we were about to perform was in some way a sacred ritual. During the opening prayer, she said that the words *ta thei tat* were the seed, *beej*, syllables of Kathak and that I should consider them my *mantra*. *Ta thei tat* are rhythmic syllables and are the base for rhythm compositions in Kathak. The syllables are repeated countless times by dancers as they learn the rhythms of the dance.

No studios of dance I had frequented in Canada had prepared me for this. I had no expectation that dance would have a sacred or spiritual dimension. I now know that Sanskrit verse in praise of *Saraswati* intimately and have danced to its poetry countless times in a variety of choreographies from solo to group. Twenty-five years of practice later, I am still benefiting from that little prayer. This attitude of prayer did not end with the small worship ceremony that began my journey in Kathak, either. It permeated every aspect of my study, practice, and performance of the form.

Sanskrit is an ancient language and is the language of Indian scripture. I have never studied Sanskrit and yet through dance, I was able to learn several other Sanskrit verses which invoke the powers and blessings of various divinities of the Hindu pantheon. Such invocations are a regular part of the Kathak repertoire and are danced at the start of a recital to create a mood of peace and reverence, for both dancer and audience. Already my notions of dance were being challenged. By dancing these invocations, I was learning about the divinity of art and how it connects us to the divine in ourselves.

What's in a Salutation?

The first thing a student of Kathak learns, before a single step or movement of dance, is the salutation, which is done before every class, every practice session, each time one begins to dance. The salutation *namaskar* or *bhoomi pranam*, seeking the blessings of the earth, is a choreographed movement phrase with slight variations from school to school, but with common elements. Graceful movements of the arms offer a prayer to the divine powers above, to the world at equal level with the dancer including audience, teacher, musicians, and fellow students, and finally to the earth. The dancer actually kneels to touch the earth. Finally, the dancer rises to stand with eyes closed for a moment of internal prayer while holding the hands at chest level and then stamps her right foot to signal the beginning of the dance. My guru used to say that when we enter the classroom to dance, we should leave behind all other thoughts and problems. Every morning he prayed when he entered the classroom before beginning any work. Thus, we students always came into a room filled with the fragrance of incense and an atmosphere of reverence for the divine power of art.

The simple movements of the salutation performed by all become a momentary meditation for the dancer, cleansing the mind of distraction and bringing it to focus on the dance. Over the years, the gesture becomes habitual, but at the same time its impact deepens. Performed day in and day out to both start and finish every dance session, be it practice, class, or rehearsal, the gesture takes on meaning and becomes effective in helping the dancer to bring her entire attention to the dance. It also imbues the entire practice with a sense of respect, both for the self and those around us. Without realization or intent, I had learned and developed a habit of meditation that helped me to empty my mind of clutter and bring together the energies of mind, body, and spirit every time I started dancing.

The Elements of the Dance

Deeply immersed as I was in the study and performance of Kathak at the professional level, I never realized that it had power. It has the power to *empower*, to make aware, to make intelligent, to heal, to rejuvenate. More than just a dance, Kathak is a *vidhya*, a form of wisdom or a system of knowledge. It is an ancient form of learning which works on many levels. The study of Kathak provides a challenging array of practices that develop and strengthen us on the physical, the intellectual, the emotional, and also the spiritual level.

The basic technique of Kathak has three main components: movement, rhythmic footwork, and dramatic expression or mime. In combination, these elements of dance

require a concerted involvement of body, mind, and spirit to perform properly. The training process is highly developed and it doesn't take things in simple, easy steps. Rather,
it is a full-on menu that engages the student on all levels at once: physical, intellectual,
and spiritual. Each aspect of the dance is complex, intricate, and challenging to learn. By
engaging the body-mind-spirit of the practitioner, the dance offers a holistic practice for
self-development. In this sense, it is yogic in its approach. In this chapter, I will touch on
major aspects of the technique and how the training and subsequent practice of Kathak
can promote powerful healing and serve to develop us as human beings.

Tatkar: The Power of Rhythm

The foundation of rhythm training in Kathak is footwork called *tatkar*. The dancer wears
hundreds of tiny brass bells on her ankles and learns to play them as a percussion instrument by stamping out rhythms with her feet. Imagine yourself counting long chains of
complex rhythms from memory, to the metered tic-tic of a metronome, with the precision
of a master drummer. Then imagine beating out these same compositions with your bare
feet on the floor. The mastery of *laya*, tempo, or the flow of time, is a primary skill of
Kathak. Dancers must master difficult rhythmic patterns that are executed with precision
to live rhythm accompaniment on the *tabla* or Indian drums.

This type of interaction with rhythm requires tremendous discipline of the mind
and the body. In Kathak, this discipline is achieved first through footwork, which is
a unique, powerful, and pervasive feature of the form. Training in footwork is a long
process that takes determination. Dancers spend hours each day memorizing and per-
fecting their footwork patterns. This daily early morning practice is called *riyaz*.

During my first year of training, I was inspired by the dedication of my hostel
mates who rose every morning at 5:30 to practice footwork. I learned that dedication
is required to work at a practice that takes years to perfect. In time, I noticed that
repeated and prolonged concentration on rhythm and tempo sharpens the intellect
and focuses the mind. Once the mind is fully tuned to the precise flow of rhythm, then
practicing footwork becomes a meditation on time and sound.

Often I practiced footwork to the beats of the *tabla* playing a fixed time cycle,
or to a metronome. At any moment during the practice, the dancer is focusing
on the tempo given by the external accompaniment, the pattern she is counting
against, the tempo, and the inherent stresses and nuances of the feet dancing the
patterns. The patterns are performed at high speeds and include difficult time divisions such as 5/8 time, 6/8 time, and 7/8 time. The compositions are arranged in
long chains with many permutations and combinations of a basic rhythm pattern.
Eventually dancers also learn to improvise within a rhythmic grid and it is only

when the dancer has a thorough grasp of rhythm and footwork that she is taught movements.

This disciplined focus on rhythm is a true challenge for the distracted mind and can be very difficult to sustain. In my own experience, I found that as I practiced ever more complex and longer patterns, I would go into a trance as my mind became transfixed with the rhythm and the flow of time. Each time I practiced, my concentration improved and within moments the sound of the *tabla* and the sound of my bells would merge into perfect unison. It was like a powerful mental exercise that would leave my mind clear, fresh, and quite sharp.

In addition, stamping out footwork patterns in bare feet is an incredibly grounding process connecting one to the earth while strengthening and flexing every tiny muscle in the feet. As we know from reflexology, the soles of the feet are known to have nerve endings that are connected to the entire body. The Kathak footwork gave my feet a great workout and seemed to make them both intelligent and expressive. I will never forget the comment of a senior Canadian dance educator who saw me perform in Montreal once. She said she had never seen such expressive feet!

The Artistry of Alignment

The wonderful thing about dance is that it directly involves the body. The first and most important aspect of dancing is alignment. Every dancer works to balance, stretch, and adjust the body until it is rid of weaknesses, poor physical habits, and becomes properly aligned. Indian classical dance has powerful basic stances that align the body and also give it energy. Many of these postures are ancient and derived from yogic and martial arts practices or emulate stances of divine figures. Basic stances are described in ancient texts on the dramatic arts such as the *Natya Shastra,* which codify minute details of positioning for the body including hands, feet, shoulder, neck, etc.

In Indian dance, alignment takes the form of *ang shuddhi*, or purity of limb. The simple meaning of the word *shudh* is clean or pure. As the Indian dancer works to achieve physical perfection, she is actually creating a physicality that is pure, free from negativity, weakness, and errors. This has the effect of engaging both the mind and body in a positive process, while strengthening the body, and improving the flow of energy.

Furthermore, Indian classical dance is unique in that it doesn't stop at the gross body parts when detailing postures and alignment. So meticulous is the understanding and taxonomy that the body is divided into *ang*, major limbs, *upang* and *pratyang*, minor and supporting limbs. The dance technique involves codified movements for each of these body parts that extend to obvious minor limbs such as the hands, but also to less obvious body parts such as the eyes, the eyebrows, the wrists, the cheeks, and many others. The overall effect is a symphony of movements of greater and lesser body parts in every dance phrase.

As I studied Kathak, my notion of the body grew to a finer awareness of many body parts and how they worked together. I was challenged to extend my concentration to multiple tasks as I coordinated the isolated movements of eyes, hands, and neck, with larger movements of the torso and legs, while stamping my feet and maintaining a correct facial expression. But gradually I found that the different parts of my body came alive and a clear energy flowed through them.

Indian classical dance has powerful basic stances
which align the body and also give it energy.

Correct alignment and preparation of the body for dance requires the active involvement of every part of the body and is also imbued with an expression or attitude. This attitude is of *ang shuddhi* or purity, and also develops purity and clarity of the mind. Once my feet, hands, shoulders, and all the other body parts were working together, I felt that the strength of the rhythms and expressions could move through me, while my mind remained clear and quiet.

Mudras : Intelligent Hands

The best known of the codified movement patterns is a series of hand gestures called *mudras. Mudras* are ancient hand gestures and described in great detail in a variety of Sanskrit texts. In 1999, while training a class of five-year-olds in Delhi, I decided to try teaching them the *mudras* as described in the tenth-century dramatic text *Abhinaya Darpan*. The 28 single-hand and 25 double-hand gestures are complicated to execute and have difficult Sanskrit names. My very young class stunned me with their ability to physically execute the *mudras* as well as recite their names within a few short days. They seemed suddenly charged by focusing on their hands and fingers in this detailed way and the regular practice of *mudras* improved their concentration. The parents returned with stories of how their children were behaving better in school and how they were enamored with this newfound ability to make beautiful shapes with their hands. We never think of the hands as being intelligent, but of course they are. Ancient hand gestures work the hands and fingers along with all the joints and use them for multiple and complex expression. One can only imagine the benefit of these *mudras* for the nervous system.

Of course, there are texts that also record *mudras* that are specific to yogic practice and designed to promote healing in the body. Dance *mudras* are primarily designed for their decorative value and expressive potential. They depict images from nature and form a mimetic or evocative language for storytelling. Often they are used for their physical beauty to adorn grosser movements of the body.

However, to learn the *mudras*, the mind and body are required to work together in a process of refinement. It is not that one is simply exercising the hands for strength and flexibility. Rather, one is fully engaging the mind in verbalizing Sanskrit names and creating multiple images with barely a movement of a finger. The hands thus become potent methods of communication. Once again there is *ang shuddhi* as the dancer masters each distinct *mudra* and aspires to a perfect physical representation. There is an added layer of mental and emotional involvement as she imbues each gesture with the appropriate emotion and expression to complete the image being suggested by the *mudra*. For instance, a gently-falling rain is depicted by the hands gently vibrating, as they descend from above in the *mudra* for rain. At the same time, the eyes blink as if keeping out the raindrops and the feet beat out a gentle pitter-patter with the ankle bells.

While I was recovering from my chemotherapy treatments, I was given the opportunity to teach *mudras* and chanting at a yoga institute in Toronto. I found the daily practice of *mudras* rejuvenating as circulation to my swollen fingers and arms improved. Trying to execute each configuration of fingers in the correct order and repeating the Sanskrit name of each gesture was a challenge for my chemo-riddled brain, and yet, after a few days, it was as if a fog was lifting. Soon, my mind retrieved the memory of hours of practice and the *mudras* came to life as images of a bird, animals, or a woman's veil. My thoughts went back to my five-year-old students and I realized that sure enough, my mental focus increased as I concentrated on the physical and expressive details at my fingertips.

Expressing love divine and love mundane

Building the Energy: *Tukras*

The movements of Kathak dance technique are fluid, fast, strong, and precise. The technical repertoire consists of rapid spiraling movement phrases and turns (pirouettes) composed as a series of rhythm and movement poems called *tukra*. A *tukra* is essentially a piece that is broken off from a whole. The *tukra* sound poem is made of short rhythm syllables and composed according to strict mathematical rules. Every dancer first learns to recite a *tukra* verbally in correct meter. Once it has been memorized and internalized as a sound poem, the dancer learns the movement choreography and brings the rhythm to physical and visual life.

There are many varieties of rhythmic poems within the broad category of *tukras*. These are distinguished by the types of syllables used and the rules for structuring the composition. They may be inspired by music, nature, or anything else that strikes a composer's fancy. In this way, Kathak compositions are a kind of abstract sound poetry, which dancers must commit to memory. Most dancers pride themselves on knowing a vast repertoire of these short compositions and are able to perform them extempore to basic rhythm accompaniment.

The recitation of all compositions in Kathak is a core aspect of the practice as well as the oral transmission of this tradition. During recitation, the meter is maintained with a system of clapping and counting on the hands that is complicated yet highly logical. Reciting even the simplest compositions in this manner takes focus, coordination and a steady mind. Once again, this type of training posed a challenge for my brain. Learning to recite compositions with every rhythmic intricacy intact was like learning a new language complete with a new accent. While I struggled to memorize my repertoire orally, I realized that the process sharpened the intellect, improved memory, and required me to multi-task on simultaneously maintaining divergent patterns with the hands, the mind, and the voice.

Technical repertoire in Kathak is performed according to a strict matrix of rhythm and melody created by two accompanying instruments. A percussion instrument, usually a *tabla*, provides a repeated time cycle of a fixed number of beats. The melody is provided by a stringed instrument, a bowed fiddle-type instrument such as a *sarangi* that plays a melodic refrain, which mimics the rhythmic cycle. The intricate *tukra* compositions are executed with speed and precision within this rhythmic framework and often form an exciting counterpoint to the basic rhythm. The dancer must remain alert to begin and end every composition on the first beat of a rhythmic cycle.

In classroom practice as well as performance, this structural requirement creates suspense and excitement for the dancer and audience. The dancer is challenged to execute the *tukra* accurately in order to arrive at the first beat simultaneously with the percussionist. The audience waits with bated breath as the dancer moves through complex rhythms almost in competition with the percussionist and then both reach the end of the composition in a climax of virtuosic bravura.

The physicality of the dance revolves around spirals and circles. Although the dancer is firmly grounded through footwork, the body, arms, and hands create multiple curving spirals in the air. The movements are executed as a smooth continuum and interspersed with fast circles in which the dancer turns on the axis of her left leg, the left heel planted firmly on the floor. It is reminiscent of Sufi whirling. Many traditional compositions seem to marshal the dancer's energy in upward sweeping spirals and then coalesce in a series of turns that send the energy upwards.

A *Thumri:* The Sweetest of Love Songs

One cannot say anything meaningful about Kathak if there is no discussion of the expressive or dramatic aspect of the dance. In its early incarnations, both rural and courtly, Kathak has been a storytelling art, regaling audiences with tales from India's religious epics and vast body of mythic literature. This rustic art was particularly enriched by the *bhakti* movement; a religious movement that swept through north India during the medieval period. The philosophy of *bhakti* centered on devotion and love as the central religious expression of the devotee. Love songs in both secular as well as religious manifestations became a mainstay of the Kathak repertoire.

The *thumri* holds a special place in this repertoire of love songs; a musical form originating in the soulful and passionate folk songs of rural north India but fashioned with the refined sensibilities of classical music and courtly aesthetics. The subject of a *thumri* is the heroine's love for her beloved. The poetry of the *thumri* expresses the myriad nuances of love in every instance, in every season, in union and separation, and in every changing heartbeat of the lover longing for the beloved.

Once the dancer has mastered movement, rhythm, and gesture, the technique is put to use to express love divine and love mundane. This is the apex of the dancer's art and craft, and requires more than mere precision, discipline, and physical prowess. It demands an emotional involvement and an exploration of the human spirit in its two aspects: togetherness, oneness, and union and separation and division from one's beloved. It is this philosophical exploration that is at the heart of Kathak as a practice and makes it a *sadhana,* or spiritual practice.

Indian dance works with the concept of unity, or oneness, with music and rhythm as cosmic impulses and cosmic phenomena; also oneness with the divine in form and in emotion. The practice of the traditional art of Kathak is to become one with *sur* and *laya* which can be broadly translated as music and rhythm. *Sur* is both pitch and musicality, whereas *laya* is a measured passing of time, the pulse. The body-mind complex is an instrument to be trained in order to become one with these two cosmic phenomena and also to express their mystery through sound and movement. In this way, Kathak is a meditation which I experienced as I mastered each element of the dance. Gradually my mind became one with the rhythms and the music till I, the dancer, disappeared and there was only the dance.

In *thumri* and other storytelling repertoire, the dancer is taking this sense of unity to a level of allegory and seeking oneness with the expression of love, often evoking images of the divine. A *thumri* is filled with images of beauty from nature as metaphors for deep human emotion. The depiction of a simple emotion such as teasing one's lover takes on a myriad of nuances in the dancer's subtle interpretations. In one of my favorite compositions, the heroine has been waiting for a lover traveling to distant lands. She compares her tear-filled eyes with the rain-filled clouds and begs the clouds to take the message of her tears to her beloved. As her tears drop into the river, she begs the river to be a messenger of her love. Next, it is the flower she wears in her hair, which she tosses into the flowing river, sending it on an errand of love. And so on. In this way I could unravel layer upon layer of ways in which the heart finds echoes of its love in everything it touches. In the best tradition of Greek theatre, performing or watching a performance of *thumri* generates a deep emotional catharsis.

Dancing Durga

All of these experiences of the dance as a physical, an intellectual and a spiritual practice, came together for me in June 2008 when I learned a five-minute dance describing and praising the Goddess Durga. Durga is a powerful Hindu warrior goddess famous for defeating demons and establishing the order of good over evil in the universe. She is depicted riding on a lion with ten arms, each holding a different weapon. Yet in the legend of Durga slaying the mighty buffalo demon, the goddess herself is smiling, calm, and awe-inspiring.

The dance celebrating Durga was the first piece I attempted to learn after a year-long break during which I was on a whole gamut of cancer treatments, beginning with surgery, through radiation and chemotherapy. I chose this as my first piece to resume dancing hoping it would inspire me to win the battle against my own demons.

As the dancer describes the many attributes, characteristics, and strengths of Durga, she is required to personify the goddess through postures and actions. More than ever before, I was aware of the strength it took to stamp my feet with the power of a goddess or to focus my eyes on a far distant point as a devotee in awe. As I lifted my left foot and raised my arms to wield her iconic weapon, the trident, in the quintessential pose of the goddess, I needed to summon the actual feeling of power and victory that belonged to Durga.

The hymn describes her as a destroyer of evil who gives strength to her followers. In one line, she is praised as she holds up the severed heads of two demon brothers Shumbh and Nishumbh. The dancer mimes the slicing movement of a sword and holds up a severed head by the hair. Mastering and skillfully executing these movements with conviction was powerful therapy for me as I imagined myself slaying the evil around me and within me. Strength and power flowed back into my body as I practiced. As I raised my hands to my lips in the *mudra* depicting her conch shell, I was aware of the power of its cosmic vibrations to cleanse the environment of negativity. I visualized the dark diseased cells being incinerated in the brilliance of her vibrational field. As I danced and depicted her cosmic form with multiple arms, with the inner third eye, and with her ruthless destruction of evil, I became aware both of her awesome power as well as her blessings. At the same time, in every line of the song, the devotee is aware of her humility before Durga's cosmic awesome form and is asking to be bathed in her radiance. It was a powerful return to dancing that healed the sense of helplessness, which can come from surrendering to a long and damaging process of medical treatment.

Summary

During the many years of my practicing, performing, and teaching Kathak, I have found tremendous fulfillment as an artist. I have enjoyed the movements, been challenged by the intricate rhythms, and deeply moved by myths and poetry. But never before was I so acutely aware of the intrinsic healing power of this dance form whose beauty I took for granted. As I have returned to practicing and teaching, I found the dance lived in me as a powerful life force. The *riyaz* or footwork provided intellectual rigor. The *mudras* provided healing to my hands and brought awareness back to my extremities. The attempt to memorize and recite compositions helped me to regain my memory along with my breath. Learning to dance love songs and devotional songs helped me to focus on positive emotions and created a frame of mind filled with compassion and gratitude.

There is no doubt that any form of artistic self-expression gives the artist a sense of confidence. Performing dance also gives one a sense of joy and exhilaration. The Kathak repertoire full of love songs, invocations, and mythological stories, imbued me with a sense of beauty, love, and devotion. All of this was permeated with the philosophical underpinnings of a process that leads one to strive at all times for unity and perfection and which continuously cleanses the body, mind, and soul of negativity.

Truly there is much to learn in this tradition that encompasses literature, music, percussion, and movement. A great deal of deep analysis can be done to learn more about how the various aspects of Kathak engender healing. There are also many aspects of the teaching traditions and the actual performance of Kathak that are worth exploring for their contribution to healing. But there is little doubt that the skills and attitudes I acquired in my study of Kathak were powerful tools in my recovery to health, for which I am truly grateful.

• • • •

DEEPTI GUPTA is an accomplished exponent of the elegant Kathak style of dance from north India. She is artistic director of Arzoo Dance Theatre in Toronto, Canada, an organization dedicated to creating new works in dance that transcend geographical and cultural boundaries. She has performed extensively in Canada, India, U.S. and U.K. She has received numerous awards including a Dora Mavor Moore Award and the MyBindi.com award for outstanding classical dancer. She has conducted extensive research on the teaching of classical Indian dance in Diaspora communities and has created many contemporary works for children and professionals, which have been performed in major dance festivals and venues in Canada, U.S., and India. Her website address is *www.deeptigupta.com*.

CHAPTER THIRTEEN

Healing and Community Building Through the Art of Hula

Māhealani Uchiyama

"A'a i ka hula, waiho ka hilahila i ka hale." [121]
"WHEN ONE WANTS TO DANCE THE HULA, BASHFULNESS SHOULD BE LEFT AT HOME."

I AM A KUMU HULA, a teacher of Hawaiian dance. Some of my students are from the islands. They never learned how to dance the hula while living in Hawai'i they say, because it was just another part of the place that they took for granted, much like the weather. Some of my students fell in love with the hula after vacationing in Hawai'i. Others have never been over the water.

People have been drawn to the hula for many reasons. Some started lessons because they wanted to learn how to move their hips so prettily, just like the dancers at the *lū'au* shows in Honolulu. Others wanted an excuse to wear a grass skirt like in the movies. Younger students are brought to class by their elders who themselves would have taken hula when they were younger, if they had had the opportunity. A large number of my students are in their mid-life. Having raised a family and worked diligently for years, they are now doing something for themselves.

I have students who tell me that they never thought they would be able to dance, because they didn't have the desired body type typical of Western dance forms, or they were told that they have two left feet. I have just as many students who thought that they couldn't sing, who now find themselves learning to play the 'ukulele or gourd drum and being encouraged to sing or chant along with the dances they learn.

My students are Mexican, Filipino, Hawaiian, Chinese, Japanese, Indian, African American, Caucasian, Native American, and every mixture of these one can imagine. My students are gay and straight, elders, children, adolescents, and young adults. They are attorneys, teachers, engineers, physicians, gourmet chefs, and florists. I have students who are Hindu, Jewish, Muslim, Christian, Buddhist, and celebrants of earth-based religions.

I myself am an American of African and Native-American descent.

What we all seem to have in common is our love of and respect for hula and the culture from which it evolved. We have formed a rich and diverse community around the appreciation of an art form few of us can claim as part of our own cultural heritage. We all have committed to a discipline requiring regular hours of practice each week, plus many collaborative efforts centered on practical necessities such as helping one another with costume making, and keeping each other fed. What is it about hula—a dance form from a group of islands in the middle of the Pacific Ocean—that has called us all together as *kaiaulu*, as community?

The hula is a conduit between the material world and the world of the ancestors. Through immersion in the metaphors of a time long past, hula teaches us how to absorb the sublime energies of the forest, the wind, and the waves. In expressing these powerful energies with our hands, feet, hips, eyes, and voice, we learn to perceive the world of our forbearers. The practice of hula exposes us to a variety of related art forms that support the dance, deepening our respect for such a multifaceted tradition. Learning about the tradition's recent history of exploitation, and the tremendous efforts made to reinstate it to its proper place in modern society, has given me hope that other similarly maligned cultural traditions elsewhere in the world will also survive. In addition, hula encourages us to recognize our place on this earth, not as owners of the land, but as an integral part of creation.

The Hula Tradition

Kuhi nō ka lima, hele nō ka maka.[122]
"WHERE THE HANDS MOVE, THERE LET THE EYES FOLLOW."

The hula is Hawai'i's richest form of artistic expression. It evolved from spiritual practice and is a complex system of preserving historical records and legends, of honoring chiefs, and of celebrating the beauty of the land. Hula has a dual nature, manifesting as both prayer and as entertainment. Birth, love, warfare, death, epic migrations, and ancient legends are all commemorated in its sung poetry. Unlike dancers of other theatrical traditions who become the characters in a story, the hula dancer describes the story with a rich vocabulary of manual gestures. She becomes the visual manifestation of poetry and prayer. In this way, the hula serves as a medium between the spiritual and the natural worlds.

Ho'ola i nā manu i ke aheahe. [123]
"THE BIRDS POISE QUIETLY IN THE GENTLE BREEZE."

The hula was conceptualized by nā Kanaka Maoli, the indigenous people of Hawai'i. Through meditation on their natural environment, they learned to move in imitation of the movement and the rhythm of the surf and captured the swaying leaves of the forest with upheld arms. In the old days, the dance was taught in a *hālau* (hula temple), dedicated to Laka, the patron Goddess of the hula, and presided over by a *kumu hula* (source of dance) who was a member of the priestly class, and supported by royalty who maintained the institution for the honor and prestige of the court. The hālau was an area separate from other households where the hula lifestyle, protocol, and skills were taught to a select few.

The Goddess Laka is manifest in the verdant growth of the land. Certain plants are sacred to her, and utilizing these plants to encircle the ankles, wrists, neck, and head of a hula dancer, confers her blessing and the performer becomes a living, moving *kuahu* (altar, physical abode of a deity). A second *kuahu* to Laka is erected in the *hālau* and placed at the eastern-most wall. The third and greatest altar is the forest itself. The movements of the dance have always reflected nature's energy.

Hula involves a fusion of the arts; dancers chant and play music and chanters move in rhythm as they provide accompaniment. Hula practitioners learn how to construct intricate and beautiful musical instruments and regalia from elements found in their environment. Hula is a way of living and the dancer is an instrument of the divine, conveying the beauty of the world.

Hula evolved not as a solo art form, but one in which a large company of dancers moves as one body, working together just as paddlers in a canoe. In its essence, hula is not competitive, commercial, or egotistical. It is a discipline of the body, mind, and spirit. The energy of the dance is centered at the lower torso, at the area behind the *piko* (belly button) called the *nā'au*, where all thoughts are felt and all life begins.

Until the modern era, there was no concept of lessons on-demand. Hula disciples were chosen, some at birth, to be trained as *'olapa*, or consecrated dancers. These initiates lived together as a hula family, with the *kumu hula* as their guide into this sacred world. Here, they began their training in how to move and to give voice to a rich oral tradition. Because the body of the dancer is the repository of the sacred, they were also trained to regard themselves and each other with utmost respect.

After Hawai'i was brought to the attention of the Western world in the late 1700s, the island kingdom became deluged by waves of newcomers, most of whom completely misunderstood many aspects of the indigenous culture, including the hula. The ruling class found themselves pressured to withdraw their support of their *hālau*, and without the support of the chiefs, the community of dancers faced the hard choice of starvation or compromising the integrity of their sacred dance. While many *ali'i* (chiefs) no longer supported a retinue of dancers, there were whalers, sailors, traders, and other outsiders who were very willing to pay to watch bare-breasted native women swing their hips. The sacred dance of Hawai'i eventually became relegated to the areas of illicit activities rooting themselves throughout Honolulu's waterfront area. Many of the newcomers intermarried into the ruling class. As Christianity spread throughout the islands, it eventually became illegal to teach or perform the hula.

When King David La'amea Kamanakapu'u Mahinulani Naloiaehuokalani Lumialani Kalākaua came to the throne in 1874, the Hawaiian nation was in crisis. The population of Hawai'i had been decimated by foreign diseases, and was further stressed by concurrent attempts by powerful expatriates to repress all indigenous cultural practices. In response, King Kalākaua initiated many reforms, including the restoration of the dance to its former place in the royal court. By this time, however, the performing arts of that era reflected the many Western influences that had become ubiquitous in the islands; such as the use of the 'ukulele, guitar, and other European instruments in popular Hawaiian music. In addition, dancers were clad from neck to floor in loose fitting *mu'umu'u*, and they performed a more delicate, less earthy style of hula.

By the 1900s, the hula was again considered an acceptable part of Hawaiian life, due largely to American and European tourists who responded enthusiastically to this new westernized form of hula. Hawai'i also drew the attention of Hollywood in the post World War II era, and there were many non-native entertainers who made the dance less abstract and more easily understandable for those who did not speak the Hawaiian language. The outside world often preferred this more sensational form of the dance, and tourist demand led to an extended period of time when Hawaiian entertainers themselves performed dances to songs sung in English and about themes that were not reflective of Hawaiian cultural values.

In the wake of the self-determination movements of the 1960s and 1970s, Hawaiians have since achieved popular acceptance of all the traditional arts of Hawai'i, including the hula. It is now common to find traditional *hālau* all over the islands, and they are swamped with *haumana* eager to submit to the rigors of serious dance training. There are also committed and thriving *hālau* communities in Mexico, Japan, Canada, the United States mainland, and throughout the world. Through the hula and the *hālau* structure, traditional Hawaiian values of *lōkahi, kuleana,* and *kaiaulu* are being disseminated to the world community.

Lōkahi: The Relationship of All Things

The concept of *lōkahi* is central to Hawaiian spirituality. It refers to the full integration of the physical, emotional, and spiritual, of youth, adults, and elders, and of Creator, the natural world, and mankind. All part of the greater whole, the absence of one would result in disharmony. So integral is the concept of *lōkahi* that prayers are often repeated three times. "What good is a one-legged stool?" one of my *kumu* once told me. "If you have a stool with two legs, you can prop it up against a wall. But only a stool with three legs will be able to support you."

In the *hālau* paradigm, *lōkahi* is conceptualized as a triangle. The top point of the triangle is *Akua* (creator), the left *vertice* is Nature, and the right *vertice, 'Ohana* (family). The triangle is divided into four sections; the top most is the abode of spiritual consciousness, as represented by the *kumu*. The second level is that of mental accomplishment, and is represented by the *ho'opa'a*, or trained chanters and drummers. The third is physicality and is represented by the *'ōlapa*, or trained dancers. The base layer is the foundation, the abode of the *haumana,* or students. Together, these four levels represent proper balance. One cannot exist without the other. One should not override the other.

Before practice begins, prayers are chanted to invoke a sense of *lōkahi* to become manifest in the *hālau*. These prayers, repeated three times, enable the dancer to leave the stress of the outside world at the door and to open the heart and mind to the learning of hula:

> *"E hō mai ka 'ike mai luna mai e*
> *I nā mea huna no'eau o nā mele e*
> *E hō mai, e hō mai, e hō mai e"* [124]
> "GRANT ME THE KNOWLEDGE FROM ABOVE
> OF THE SACRED WISDOM WITHIN THE SONGS
> GRANT ME THIS, GRANT ME THIS, GRANT ME THIS!"

When chanted consciously and with intent, difficulties with co-workers, a long commute, and other frustrations of day-to-day living fade into the background.

Kuleana

A *hālau* is a community of people brought together by a love of dance and music and held together by recognizing the value of indigenous culture, the community at large, and each other. Members of a *hālau* are encouraged to recognize the unique gifts we each bring, to freely share those gifts and just as importantly, to be willing to accept the gifts of others. We are each important and our involvement is not only needed, but also highly valued. Recognizing our personal responsibility to community confers a sense of belonging to that community. *Haumana* (students) are encouraged to enter their community through the prism of a culture that recognizes the interdependence of humans and nature. They listen deeply to the many voices of the wind, tread gently on nature trails, and remove trash left by others. When it is time to gather materials for adornments, they only take what is needed, after asking permission of the nature Spirits and always offering a prayer of thanksgiving. This Hawaiian concept of personal responsibility is known as *kuleana*.

> *"E hana me ka ʻoiaʻiʻo*
> *E hana me ka haʻahaʻa*
> *E ʻolelo pono kākou"* [125]
>
> "LET US WORK WITH SINCERITY
> LET US WORK WITH HUMILITY
> LET US SPEAK AT ALL TIMES WITH GOODNESS."

It is the *kuleana* of the *haumana* (students) to come prepared to learn, on time, and with a positive attitude. Our *kupuna* (elders) have the responsibility of passing on their knowledge to the next generation, as well as providing hospitality to guests of the *hālau*. It is their *kuleana* to ensure that the proper protocols are adhered to so that guests are well cared for at all times. It is the *kuleana* of the *kuamoʻo* (literally backbone, the *hālau* organizers) to support the vision of the *kumu* and the elders and organize *hālau* activities. The *laulima* are those who assist with that work, and are always ready to lend a hand.

The *poʻopua* are the managers of the *hālau*. It is their *kuleana* to stay on top of the many details. They are the "right-hand" of the *kumu*. The *ʻalakaʻi* are the teaching assistants. They model the style and execution of the dance for the other students. It is the *kuleana* of the *ʻohana* (family) to support their family member during the time of their training. The *kumu* is the source of knowledge of the *hālau*. It is his or her *kuleana* to ensure that the integrity of the tradition is upheld at all times.

The Transformational Power of Hula

'Ukuli'i ka pua, onaona i ka mau'u. [126]
"TINY IS THE FLOWER, YET IT SCENTS THE GRASSES AROUND IT."

Our beginning *haumana* first arrive at the *hālau* eager to learn how to dance. Senior students and *'alaka'i* are on hand to assist them in constructing their practice outfits, and organizing their class materials. They are encouraged to get to know one another, work together, and to regard each other as hula brothers and sisters. As they learn each new dance, they are given information about its historical context, locale, and natural setting. They may learn a bit about what type of rain and wind are to be found at that place, as well as a local legend. They are encouraged to chant and sing the poetry. They are given the opportunity to learn how to construct a gourd drum, and may take the seeds they scrape out from the gourd to plant in their own gardens. Some may even be inspired to learn how to play the 'ukulele. *Haumana* are encouraged to meet with each other and practice outside of the *hālau* to reinforce the teachings.

Traditional Hulu dancers,
KaUaTuahine Polynesian Dance Company

When we prepare for a performance, we find that there are some who have an interest in learning how to dye and lash the yards of fabric used to make the regalia of the dance. Others may enjoy growing a garden of herbs used in Hawaiian medicinal practices, or gourds used to make instruments, or perhaps some of the sacred plants of our tradition. There is always a need for *lomilomi* or *hakihaki*, forms of traditional Hawaiian massage, to nurture sore muscles and prepare the body for the rigors of the dance. Some find that they enjoy learning about island cuisine and share their experiments with their grateful *hālau* sisters and brothers. Once an interest or skill is identified in a *haumana*, it is nurtured and they are encouraged to share their gift with the *hālau* community.

Once each year, we have an examination period. Students are tested not only on their dance technique, but also on their background knowledge. They are taught ceremonial prayer chants appropriate for going into nature and asking Spirit permission to gather foliage for the making of their leis. The senior students teach the newer *haumana* how to construct their first ti-leaf lei.

We invite our extended *'ohana* to celebrate the birth of our new *haumana*. We all contribute to a tasty feast, and the younger *haumana* are encouraged to serve their elders first. Our *kupuna* (elders) are cherished and held in high esteem as examples to us all. We are a growing community of *po'e* hula, hula practitioners, and we are grateful that *nā kupuna* come to witness and acknowledge the accomplishments of the dancers as they take their place as keepers of the hula tradition.

"Kūkulu ka 'ike i ka 'opua." [127]

"REVELATIONS ARE FOUND IN THE CLOUDS."

Our *kupuna* tell us about the times of their youth when it was more common to have a deeper understanding of our environment than it is today. At one point in time, Hawaiian people studied the phases of the moon. Each night of the month has a different name and is associated with traditions about what and when to plant, fish, or gather. One *hō'ike* year, our novice *haumana* learned a hula describing the different phases of the moon. One student memorized the entire Hawaiian moon calendar and could, upon gazing at the moon rising over the East Bay hills, name that night, and then recite the kinds of plants that could be harvested and whether or not it was a good period to go fishing. She was applauded during our *hō'ike* as she was recognized in front of the *hālau* with the name *Māhinahina*, "the bright light of the moon." Together with her classmates who were also given Hawaiian names, they were welcomed into the *hālau* as dancers who had developed their own personal relationship with one of the many aspects of Hawaiian culture that are a part of the hula.

My name, *Māhealani*, is the Hawaiian name for the "second night of the full moon." It is the sixteenth night of the month and the fullest appearance of the moon. Plants are also large on this day and fishing is good. People born on *Māhealani* are known to strive hard in their endeavors.

After a difficult few months of preparing for and directing the *hālau* through a competition, my husband and I visited the islands for some much needed rest. The setting was the Moana Terrace at the Waikīkī Beach Marriott, in the presence of many friends old and new, the ocean breeze, and the night sky. And the musicians, one of whom turned out to be an old college friend of mine who has since become one

Dancing that fills the soul

of the leading slack key artists of our time! I was invited to dance and heard his voice guiding our attention back to the night sky by mentioning the beautiful full moon, a *Māhealani* moon, in the second night of its fullness. And to hear the voice of yet another *Māhealani* who was singing with all his heart a song chosen as a tribute, to his beloved *Kahana'olu*, a former *haumana* of my *hālau*.

The three moons. All part of the greater whole. It was a time of magic, full of *mana* (divine essence) in that uniquely Hawaiian way which fills up my soul.

As *po'e hula*, we are bound by our spirituality in our quest for *'ike* (wisdom), *pono* (righteousness), and ultimately, *lōkahi* (harmony). If successful, the *hālau* is a place where one not only learns dance and music, but also respect for the culture and the natural world, understanding of the greater community, self-confidence, self awareness, and leadership. The hula is a journey to oneself and to a place within one's community. It extends a welcome to the dancer and recognizes what gift he or she brings to the collective. It is in the dance, the giving of the self to Spirit and community that the dancer is brought to her own fullness.

Glossary of Hawaiian words

'Alaka'i – Leader, to lead

'Ali'i - Chief

Hālau – Long house, a place of learning

Haumana – Student

Hō'ike – To test, to show

Ho'opa'a – Chanter and drummer; lit. "steadfast"

Hula – Dance, to dance, a hula dancer, a song used for the hula

'Ike – To see, know or feel; knowledge, wisdom

Kaiaulu – Community

Kanaka Maoli – Full-blooded Hawaiian person

Kuahu – Altar

Kuamo'o – Backbone, spine

Kuleana – Responsibility, right, authority

Kumu – Foundation, base, trunk of a tree; teacher; source

Kumu Hula – Teacher of Hula

Laka – Name of the Hula Deity

Laulima – To work together (lit. "many hands")

Lōkahi – Balance, unity

Lō'au – Young taro tops used in cooking; Hawaiian feast named for the taro tops

Mana – Supernatural or divine power

Mele – Song
Mu'umu'u – Long loose-fitting dress
Nā'au – Intestines, mind, heart
'Ohana – Family
'Olapa – Dancer
Po'e Hula – Community of hula practitioners
Piko – Navel
Pono – Correct, righteous
'Ukulele – Instrument of Portuguese origin popularized in Hawai'i (lit. "jumping flea")

• • • •

MĀHEALANI UCHIYAMA is a dancer, musician, composer, and teacher. An advocate for cultural understanding, she is the founder of the Center for International Dance, (M.U.C.I.D.) and is Kumu Hula (hula teacher) of Halau KaUaTuahine. She approaches dance as a manifestation of the human spirit, encouraging her students to explore and celebrate their cultural differences and common humanity. She holds a BA in dance ethnology and an MA in Pacific Islands studies, both from the University of Hawai'i at Manoa. Māhealani was trained in traditional hula and ori in Hawai'i and Tahiti. Her Kumu was Joseph Kamoha'i Kaha'ulelio. She has produced numerous recordings of traditional Hawaiian and Tahitian music. Her CD, "A Walk by the Sea," is a compilation of the sounds of her cultural and spiritual heritage and was awarded the Hawai'i Music Award for Best World Music Album of 2007. Her latest CD of Mbira music, "Ndoro dze Madzinza," is currently on the Entry List of the 53rd Annual Grammy Awards. Māhealani is a member of the staff of World Arts West, the producers of the *San Francisco Ethnic Dance Festival*. Her web address is *www.mahea.com*.

CHAPTER FOURTEEN

Dancing Lotuses

—

Shahrazad Catharina Huisman

From Bud to Bloom:
My Journey into Dance

AS A THREE-YEAR-OLD little girl in Holland, I learned my first dance steps from my father, standing with my feet on his feet while he held my hands. I felt my socks sliding on his slippery, shiny shoes, keeping my balance and the rhythm at the same time, trying to understand the regular pattern of movements, feeling protected, uplifted, loved. A tall, dark, wooden, Chinese statue of the Goddess Quan Yin, inherited from my grandmother, ignited my love for oriental cultures. It was my secret wish to be a temple dancer, but I felt light-years away from its fulfilment.

My mother and father's influence on my path to dance was significant. They both played the piano and I grew up with their music seeping into my body and heart. I danced freely at home much inspired by my father's collection of records and my parents' piano playing. In our house, there were occasional art exhibitions and jazz concerts when priests and eccentric artists would visit. This field was fertile ground for me, my three brothers, and my younger sister to develop artistically in so many ways.

Ballet would be my first exposure to dance lessons, which I found boring. From the age of fourteen, I went to discotheques and discovered little by little that my dancing talent was more than average. When I was sixteen, I had freed myself of the shyness of puberty and from the frustration of having to wait for and not being asked to dance by a boy, as was the custom at that time. When I loved the music, I would just step onto the dance floor and do my thing. This "thing" was a mix of soul dance and what I had read about Indian temple dance in a book that my father got from his Indian teacher for comparative religious sciences, Dr. Ronald Sequeira from Bombay.

This book, *La Danse Sacrée*, enabled me to get closer to my secret goal of being a temple dancer. It gave intricate descriptions of the postures and steps, hand gestures and mime, inner devotional attitudes and disciplinary rules of the dancers. Beautiful, full-colour pictures showed me every detail of the costumes, jewellery, and make-up.

Mythical dance

I practically learned the book by heart, glued stars next to my painted eyes and brow, dressed up like someone out of a fairytale and danced, danced, danced in the local discotheques. Moroccan people thought that my dance resembled dances from their country, while others said that I danced "like heaven and hell at the same time." When I danced, people always moved away from the dance floor after a song or two to sit down and watch me. I would not look at them but I felt their glances resting on me. I often danced for hours and hours. Without realising it, I would be inducing a trance state through dance, which gradually transformed me. People's minds became more transparent to me. Dance opened me to states of being beyond everyday reality.

In 1974, I made a two-month trip overland through Turkey, Iran, Afghanistan, Pakistan, and stayed another two months in India. The story of this trip could fill a whole chapter, of course. Let me just say that visiting these countries for that length of time had a lasting impact on me, it left me with the sense that the distance between people from that part of the world and myself is very small in my mind. I feel like I'm part of them and they of me. These early experiences formed the basis of my future dance career, where improvisational abilities in dance and intuitive adaptation to foreign cultures and music were of first importance.

On my 22nd birthday, I returned to Holland to start studying fine arts.

The first years in the academy I lived like a recluse, meditated a lot, and studied Buddhism in my spare time. I met the 16th Gyalwa Karmapa of Sikkim and was secretary of several Buddhist organisations.

My first dance teacher was Dr. Ronald Sequeira from Bombay, the man who had given my father the book on Indian dance. He taught me so much more than just dance. Unfortunately, after two years of studying classical Indian dance, I was the only one left of 40 students. As Dr. Sequeira could not maintain a class in my level; it was necessary to find another dance class. That was where Middle Eastern dance came into my life. My new teacher, Samyra, seemed to me like a dancing princess. I found that the dance lacked the spirituality of the Indian dance, but it was fun! And it was a lot easier, compared to the pain and difficulty of the classical Bharat Natyam. After one year, I did my first performance. The people roared with appreciation!

My career began when I accepted the offer to dance weekly in a little Tunisian restaurant. I was learning by doing and took part in occasional workshops in Germany to improve myself. This country "discovered" and claimed me, so I moved to Cologne. I danced in Turkish weddings and galas, in parties for the embassies of some 15 countries, in exclusive Persian carpet stores, in circumcision celebrations, in Arabic and Iranian New Year's parties and concerts, for openings of exhibitions, private parties of all kinds of people, during the intermissions of fashion shows, in small restaurants, in sports stadiums, and in all kinds of theatres, including the Royal Albert Hall in London. Eventually I danced for almost every possible occasion, even funerals.

From time to time people, came up to me and told me about their personal feelings. One woman had hurt her neck in an accident. She entered wearing a special collar to keep it in place. During my dance, she took it off and never put it back, feeling that she did not need it any more. She cried as she told me that she had just seen the most beautiful performance in her life. I was very surprised and thankful. I began to pray that the healing might occur more often during the performances I did, as was said to have been the case with the famous Isadora Duncan, where people had their beds and wheelchairs positioned in front of the stage to be healed by her dance. Indeed, many have told me about strong emotions that cleansed and changed them, sometimes years after it happened. I began to notice the relationship between the amount of time I spent in meditation before a show and the intensity of the people's reactions afterwards. From there on, I saw it as my duty to meditate.

In 1989, I opened up a dance studio with my colleague, Hayat, and started travelling to other cities and countries to teach and perform. Through the work in our Studio Mashallah, in Cologne, I was able to form a troupe with my best students and perform with them. I organised big shows which included live musicians and guest dancers. At first, these were pure Oriental shows, however, they later evolved into much more. I created an African-Oriental show, a Chakra show called "The Story of the Lotus," while "Dreams of Peace" and "The World of Tara" were about the Buddhist Goddess of compassion. Each of these shows had a concept and a story. Mythological themes and historical lines of development were woven into colourful dances with a message. I learned tremendously during the process of choreographing and putting on these shows. However, what I found most striking was the process of transformation, of becoming more complete, the healing that often took place in each of my students and troupe members during the lessons and on stage. What follows are some of their experiences.

Opening Lotuses:
Transformation and Healing through Dance

The first years of teaching were mainly dedicated to Middle Eastern dance. The women who came to our studio, Mashallah, were very eager to learn the Egyptian dance form known as Raqs Sharqi or Oriental dance. It meant that they had to make their bodies flexible, learn a whole new repertoire of movements and, above all, to become elegant and flexible in their minds and souls. They needed to understand the Arabic music and learn how to interpret this with their body and facial expression. Each part of the body can be seen as a treasure box of power, beauty, joy, light, blessing, and medicine. Conversely, it can also be a prison in which old frustrations, pains, humiliations and fears can be hiding.

When I teach a movement, I can see which part of the body is stiff. It can be the chest, the hips, the neck, the shoulders, or the hands that are blocked. There may also be a lack of rhythm or the inability to smile. It is my job to help the student find out why her body is as it is and how to improve its condition. There are physical exercises such as stretching and coordination training that help. Sometimes a blockage is stubborn. We need to be in flow to be a good dancer. A blocked chest shows fear and a lack of self-confidence, for example. Blocked hips may be the effect of child abuse trauma, while stiff hands betray a rigid mind. Stiff shoulders and necks are often seen with caring, worrying, hard-workers. There are many subtle elements, invisible at first sight, that need to be brought into consciousness. This allows the body to become the perfect instrument for a perfect dance, or at least in good enough shape for the first performance on stage. Mind and soul must be in shape as well.

Christa, a woman who looked much older than the mid-forties she was, began attending dance classes. She was unsmiling, very stiff, and did not talk with the other students. I was unaware that she parked her sports car a few streets away so that she would not be seen in it. Also, I did not know that she drove a hundred kilometres each week to attend the lessons and another hundred to return home to her small castle and her rich husband whom she was afraid to lose.

When I approached Christa to correct her position, I tried to explain the importance of a warm smile, first to the dancer, as she will feel better when she smiles, and then to the audience who would be unable to enjoy the performance if the dancer does not smile. I showed her many hand exercises and sometimes I rubbed her hands and fingers to improve their flexibility, as she could not open her hands completely. I talked about inner and outer flexibility. Whatever I said to her, and I always chose different words and spoke softly, she would seldom speak back to me. Still she kept on coming and little by little learned how to dance. After about five years, there were twelve women in this class. They had learned a wonderful Egyptian folklore dance with a chandelier on their heads, the "Shamadan." Christa had never considered dancing on stage, but the choreography was designed such that groups of two and four dancers interacted in patterns, and if she would not perform the eleven others would have a problem. We convinced her to perform.

I bought a turquoise costume that we fitted to her for the performance. The evening she came to my house for the fitting, she finally began to speak and I was completely flabbergasted. She told me that no one had been able to reach her, to enter into her heart except me. She had no friends and did not trust anybody, except me. She said that, especially in the beginning, each time she returned home after the classes she would cry and think about what I had said to her. She cried as she shared

The "Shamadan"

with me her determination to change and how difficult she found it. Dancing was the medicine she had needed. Her body had softened up, her hands began to open, and she started to smile.

She danced well in the show and from that moment on, she began to look younger every time I saw her. It was truly amazing. She learned one dance after another, had beautiful costumes made, and began to perform for her husband and his friends. The relationship with her husband was repaired. She developed friendships and began living a healthier lifestyle. Christa grew in many ways having reclaimed the strength, self-worth, and source of creativity within. When she participated in a weeklong seminar in Austria, I bragged about her, saying that she looked like a flashy eighteen-year-old in her new Russian Art Nouveau peacock costume. She laughed and said that I would probably expect her to come to classes with a weaning bottle next! She is now a generous, warm-hearted lady with many interests who enjoys her life tremendously.

I initially learned the dance of the whirling dervishes in 1980. My first teacher for this was Mira Bai, a French-Indian Kathak dancer, who had learned from a Turkish Dervish Sheikh. This was unusual, because women did not whirl in Turkey at that time. He had taught her because she was already dancing Kathak, a north Indian style of classical Indian temple dance that uses lots of spinning as well. Kathak was influenced a great deal by the Muslim Mogul rulers. They had forced the Kathak dancers to substitute the Hindu story-telling parts of the dance by abstract rhythmical footwork and spins. For Mira Bai, the spiritual component of the Sufi whirling was evident. I stayed in her house in Amsterdam, learning for three days and nights.

In 1982, when I first visited Egypt, I studied an Egyptian form of Sufi dance and whirling during the month of Ramadan. This particular Sufi dance form is the perfect preparation for whirling if one does it for at least 10 minutes. It consists of one turn left around and one turn right around repeatedly, using a precise step and arm movement, as well as a particular way of fixing and closing the eyes alternatively. In 1985, I began to teach it as well, first to a fixed group of 16 dancers in the city of Dusseldorf, very carefully, checking their states of mind each time we whirled and interviewing them about their experiences. I have now initiated hundreds of women into the whirling technique. In 2005, I travelled to Istanbul to learn from the famous Mevlevy dervishes who guard the tradition of Jelaluddin Rumi. They have only started to teach women since 2004. The whirling Dervish is a form of prayer, devotion, and meditation, rooted in old, Middle-Asian shamanic practices that induce trance for spiritual healing. Women dance in immaculate white, as this represents the light of the eternal soul.

The dance of the whirling dervishes provided further opportunities for my students to experience personal transformation. I had spent some time training in the art of the Sufi dance and whirling and began to teach this in 1985. Every year, I teach two or three intensive week-long seminars on different dance topics in northern Germany in a place called Hof Oberlethe. During one of those weeks, I had combined daily whirling with the study of the Indian chakra system that explains the anatomy of the different forms of energy in our body. Chakra means wheel or energetic center. Each day, the participants wore a different colour, corresponding to the chakra we were working with that day, starting with red, then orange, yellow, and so on until we came to white on the last day. Each day, we also whirled at the same time on the same spot and observed the changes in our minds and bodies. The whirling would go on for 20 to 30 minutes at a time. The group was divided in half and, during the preparatory exercise, one group would whirl while the other watched over them as guardian angels, one-on-one. Then the roles were reversed. As the days went by, we noticed the phenomena of spontaneous telepathy. The group grew together more and more.

One of the dancers, Rosel, was not able to whirl, although she is a very good dancer. The others grew more and more concerned. I have discovered that the inability to turn, even after the preparatory exercise, is based on a lack of fundamental trust in the universe, often due to early childhood experiences and trauma. The group began to pray for her. Rosel means little rose. One woman had the vision of Rosel as a "Desert Rose," a crystal rosette formation that tends to occur when the crystals are in arid, sandy conditions, expressing that perhaps Rosel had petrified part of her soul. Another woman said that there are plants in the desert that can look dead, even be completely covered with sand for years and years, but then can flower suddenly and abundantly after rain.

We all prayed for rain to make this Desert Rose bloom, and it came. On the sixth day, Rosel tried to whirl again and this time it worked. She allowed herself finally to cry. She drenched her handkerchief and told us that she had not cried since she was four years old, 40 years ago, when her mother would have no pity on her. At certain festivities, her mother wanted Rosel to be more beautiful and used a pair of hot curling pliers to make the little girl's silky blond hair curly after the latest fashion. Rosel cried so much because the skin of her head was burned time after time. She begged her mother to stop, but she just went on and Rosel swore to herself never to cry again.

On the seventh day, Rosel spun in both directions in any speed and for half an hour. She collected her precious tears in a handkerchief and said that she wanted to bury them in her garden. Another woman immediately offered to send Rosel a package of flower seeds that bloom all year long. We were all deeply affected by this strong experience; however, the most striking moment had yet to occur. Rosel was performing in one of my shows, "Dreams of Peace," and her mother came to the theatre to see her daughter dance for the first time. During the performance her mother cried, something Rosel said she had never seen. We were amazed and grateful.

The chakra teaching resulted in a chakra show, "The Story of the Lotus." It was based on three components: 1) the Indian chakra system, 2) the spiritual development of women, and 3) the spiritual development of mankind as reflected by the history of oriental dance. The full production came on stage in 1995 and included an Arabic orchestra of nine musicians, a dance ensemble of twenty-one dancers, and some actors. There were about twenty-four dances performed. In seven tableaus corresponding to the chakras, I illustrated Pharaonic mythological dances, Indian temple dances, Mongolian power dances, Oriental Gypsy dance, Persian court dances, Arabic court dances and New Age dances. It was the first time I had ever undertaken such a huge production with the idea of educating and entertaining the audience at the same time.

Prior to the performance, I explained the chakra system to the audience in a 15-minute lecture and provided a handout for them to read later. At that time, few people knew anything about this system. The show was staged in a number of large cities, with audiences of 400 to 1000 or more at each performance. For my dancers, who were non-professionals but very devoted, it was quite a challenge to slip into the many different roles that they were dancing. Of course, they also had to understand their own energy anatomy. Some went through many personal crises before they realised the enormous growth they were experiencing; others just went with the flow. The dance classes were no longer just dance classes. We were all in the school of life.

The biggest learning potential and challenge to the students was when I asked them to do a particular solo for the 5th chakra (communication), where each one told a little story through her dance and pantomime. One performance, the Seven Dances of the Seven Princesses, was based on the tale of the 12th century Persian poet Nizamy. Each princess came from another country, had her own pavilion decorated with her color and planet, which the king would visit on her day of the week. The dancers had to leave the security of the group and embody another skin, culture, vocabulary of steps and gestures, and do the acting with the required facial expression. They all mastered it beautifully.

The ability to become someone else occurred even more in the "The World of Tara" depicting Tara, a Himalayan Buddhist Goddess of compassion. In the multi-media show, I combined different dance styles to create a theatrical production with Buddhist religious material that would be understood and appreciated by a western audience. In 21 dances, we showed Tara's origin from the tears of the Bodhisattva, the different forms in which she is venerated, to what she represents in this modern time. Each dancer in my troupe interpreted one particular Tara form, based on the traditional 21 Tara Praises within the Buddhist practice.

To dance a princess is one thing, to dance a Goddess is another, so while learning the choreographies, the dancers were immersed in a process of introspection and meditation. I visited each dancer at home and instructed her personally and I came to know more about her particular situation in life. I chose the roles in such a way that they would optimally fit the dancers' characters. There were the slender, elegant Golden Taras; strong, tall Red and Black Taras; quiet introspective and concentrated White Taras; and vital Orange Taras. Heidi, a mother of seven children, and Steffie acted as Tara's guardians Ashokakanta Marichi and Ekajata. Karin and Marita were special characters: the Bodhisattvas Avalokiteshvara and Manjushree, which symbolise Compassion and Wisdom, and also two black Taras of the most dangerous kind. It was fascinating to see what happened to all of these German women once they had on their crowns, wigs, costumes, and make up. They jumped over their own shadows and brought out their enormous potential.

We had the powerful help of the Tara Mantra, OM TARE TUTTARE TURE SOHA, that worked for us in removing countless obstacles on our way. Numerous little miracles happened and there were many helping hands. On the evening of the premiere in Cologne Hürth in 1999, it was as if the whole earth was participating in our event. The show had been splendid and we were all backstage still in our silver Space Tara suits from the finale, embracing each other and crying with emotion and relief of the tension that had been building up during the long preparations, when outside an incredible rain storm burst loose. It flooded the streets around the theatre so that people could not even drive their cars because they could not see where they were going. People told me that they

The Goddess Tara and all her qualities

were waiting in their cars behind the gushing windshields until it was over, and they were meditating! Some people came to see the show three times to understand it better. Many more people told us about their moving experiences after this show.

A much more down-to-earth form of oriental dance is American Tribal Style Bellydance which originated in California in the seventies and progressively found its way through all the continents, especially in the last 10 years. The main idea was to show dances that looked like they came from ancient tribes. The costumes were an assembly of all kinds of garments and pieces of jewellery that were actually old or looked like it, and that had come from Middle-Eastern countries such as Morocco, Egypt, Turkey, Afghanistan, and Yemen. Just as in the Tara show, there was the factor of changing identity through costuming. Where the golden Tara crowns had hidden blond or red hair, now black turbans with silver trinkets also successfully transformed the dancers' identity. This style attracted women who had no or very little dance experience and united them in newly formed "tribes." They found strength in gathering together around a style of dance where, instead of choreographies, the code of dance was a system of group improvisation with certain rules.

While in the cities the style developed further into what is called Tribal Fusion, a much more difficult, high-tech form of dance (which is no longer improvised), the "tribes" in the rural areas stayed together and developed their own creative ideas. I have come to know many of these tribal dancers and observed how much they have grown. From rather isolated and sometimes frustrating existences as housewives, their life situations gained a new quality from this community dance experience. Childhood dreams of becoming dancers, which had been buried due to strict rules, lack of money, or just being too far away from where it was happening, returned to the surface of their consciousness. Some women had problems accepting their own physiology and thought that one must be slender and beautiful to dance. But once they saw wonderful tribes like "Ganesh" dancing, whose members all weighed at least 80 kilos (176 lbs.), they decided to try it themselves. Dressed in gorgeous outfits with many yards of fabric and belts that required strong hips to hold the weight of all the silver clasps and coins and woollen tassels, they would sweat, have rosy cheeks, and lots of fun.

Healing energies of dance

Many of these factors came together in Heidi, the Tara guardian that I mentioned earlier. She lives in a tiny village with only a few farms around her in a picture-perfect old German framework house with a huge garden. When I first met her, she was pregnant with her sixth child. She had baked pastry for all of the students in the workshops that I gave and that she attended. She washed the dishes and stayed in the background. Hidden inside her was a wise, creative, endlessly precious dancer. But this she came to discover only after many years of dancing in the background through many of my seminars on dance and spirituality in Hof Oberlethe. Now she teaches, dances, and has formed a troupe that performs in the villages of her Protestant area, where dancing was out of the question for a long time and spiritual female dancing equated with witchcraft and blasphemy. She has danced as a Mongolian shaman and calls herself "Solongau" (Rainbow), representative of her colourful being. She dances whirling dances with several veils or with candles and is also Wolf Woman. She dances the "Four Seasons" with her friends and is the Gypsy Mother. There is no end to the creative ideas she has, including ideas for church celebrations.

In contrast was Ute, a slender, beautiful, red-haired banking professional, who used to be a successful ballroom dancer in her free time, winning many prizes before she came to Middle Eastern dance. Spirituality was not her thing; she would come to the workshops in full make up and pretty outfits and discuss the price of the best gemstones. After having perfected herself technically in the art of Oriental dance through many seminars in Hof Oberlethe and elsewhere, she finally began to discover the deeper foundation underneath the tip of the iceberg. This began to happen because she had not been able to show any emotion on her face. Although this emotionless mask was very good in her banking career, interpreting the Arabic music demanded emotional expressiveness and a warm heart. False eyelashes can only enhance good expression, not create it.

Dancing itself is trance-inducing if one does it with enough vigour for a long enough time. That is the clue for the transformation that can change even the most rigid conditioning. So Ute discovered that there is more under the sun and the stars than the sexiest costume. I saw her change come about in a course dealing with the interpretation of Arabic songs and the discovery of the deep poetry therein that touches the human soul, regardless of the nationality of the person hearing it. Through her participation in the whirling exercises, however, her materialistic cocoon began to open. She became curious about the spiritual seminars and attended the intensive weeks on "Chakras and Goddesses" and the "Dancing Fairies." Her dance studio now boasts two large brass Tara statues and many other Indian pieces. At the autumn equinox in 2009, she brought a fantastic Goddess Show to the stage in which goddesses from all different cultures were shown in spectacular settings doing very beautiful dances. While the banking world was crumbling in the huge financial crises, Ute danced the Sumerian Goddess Inanna rising from the underworld.

The ability of dance to heal has shown itself time and again with my students. Karla, who has suffered from severe headaches since the age of 14, shares her experience of the healing power of dance:

I can't count the number of therapies that I have done anymore. Starting from Autogenic Training to very painful neural therapy, I have tried every-thing. Nothing helped in the long run. The origin is a misplacement of the spine, a birth defect. Coping with everyday life is sometimes very difficult with these enduring headaches, in addition to which there are acute attacks of migraine that can last up to three weeks. Of course, these acute pains af-fect my psyche, I often feel weak and helpless. At the age of 19, I discovered Oriental dance for myself. Since then, it has become my profession and my life energy. Oriental dance has enabled me to have completely different body awareness.

Pains make me stiff, immobile, fearful, and unfree. When I dance how-ever, it is not the deficiency that's in the focus but my strength, my lightness and agility of the body, that I had forgotten completely until that moment. When I dance, I don't feel the pain or just barely. I feel complete and whole, free, in union with myself. I feel clean in my spirit and my body. I feel my body as positive and powerful. I could also say "I feel healed."

The energy that flows through my body when I dance I can only describe as healing energy. Sometimes it is such as if I am not dancing — but I am being danced. Especially when I improvise and when I do Dervish whirling, I can feel this cosmic energy very strongly, sometimes also in stage situations in which I feel like growing beyond my limits. It gives me strength for the moments in which I don't feel well — and it is not only about the moments when I dance. Dancing has given me many precious moments on stage, in shows, in training, with other people that are an absolute treasure for my life. When I feel bad, I sometimes look at videos of past shows. Often I have to cry at such occasions, because of the deep feelings that break loose in me. It gives me the power and motivation to continue in spite of the pains!

Where would I be without the dance? I can't imagine, can't imagine my life without dance. It has become my life energy and heals my soul and therefore also my body. It's a process that through its multilayeredness is never finished.

Birgit, Karla, and Marita were my students for ten years. They also experienced the transformative power of dance. Birgit used to be sick and depressed by the injustice of her work as a civil servant in the unemployment department. She quit her job and became a fantastic Oriental dancer and dance teacher with unique creations inspired by the European Medieval, Celtic, Mayan, Indian, and other cultures. Marita was very, very shy, hiding somewhere in the back of the class, a habit that she transcended. All three of them are now very successful under different stage names. They do hilarious and ingenious alternative Oriental dance shows and refresh the German dance scene with their unconventional and brilliant dances. As with these three, many of my former and current students have formed their own troupes. I see the same processes of transformation take place in their students and troupe members. Dancing has created community from which has sprung friendship, collaboration, and generosity of heart.

As you can see, dance takes us to many places inside and out. I discovered that as dancers, we have the ability to (re) connect with everyone and everything, because when we dance we are in flow with the stream of life. We see ourselves as a mini cosmos, whirling and dancing in this amazing universe on this beautiful planet and thank God for this Prayer, Offering, Gift, and Medicine that Dance means to us.

• • • •

SHAHRAZAD CATHARINA HUISMAN was born and raised in Holland as the daughter of a philosophical goldsmith and a ballet-dancing, piano-playing mother. As a child, she experienced music-making and dancing as part of everyday life. Her hobby of Indian classical dance and Middle Eastern dancing became her profession, by destiny. Parallel to dancing she developed her spiritual interests and studied several religions in depth. Currently, she is one of the most well-known oriental dancers in Europe, living in Germany and teaching and performing in 27 countries. She combines dance and spirituality in her workshop and performances, speaks at least 8 languages fluently and is a qualified yoga teacher as well. She received a "Halima" prize for her pioneering activities in Middle-Eastern dance in Germany in 2003 and for the work with her dance troupe in 2008.

CHAPTER FIFTEEN

Transcendental Healing Dance

Iris J. Stewart

TRANSCENDENTAL DANCES have been known to almost every culture that has existed. One of the purposes of these dances was for general release or the curing of a particular illness. Since entrance into the ecstatic state happens spontaneously, one is said to be seized or taken over by these powers. The knowledge of healing was once said to be possessed by the priestesses or holy women. Supplications to the Goddess were accompanied by various ceremonies, such as laying on of hands; incantations or prayers; the application of amulets, talismans, rings, or gemstones; concentration on relics and images; and through dancing. Drawings or statues of dancers have been found in the inner sanctum of temples representing the priestess transcending the reality of her body as she takes on archetypal dimension, thereby replicating an inner condition through the psyche and the soul for transmission to participants. The rituals involved some form of *liminality* (relating to sensory threshold) or evocation of the boundaries of the material state.

The dance of healing belongs to the oldest form of combined medicine and psychotherapy in which focused exaltation and the release of tensions transformed physical and mental suffering into a new option on life. Rhythm and dance have a vitalizing effect, as does chanting and music. Movement, combined with rhythmic stimulation by drum or rattle, causes the body to temporarily undergo dramatic, neuro-physiological changes. The collective energies of people dancing or moving together amplifies and supports the individual's energy, aiding her ability to access heightened states of consciousness.

Dance, religion, music, and medicine were inseparable in the past. Special herbs were often used, as well as cleansing, fasting, and hypnotic suggestion. Yet, physiological changes alone cannot produce the spiritual experience. Focusing of accumulated energy or *mana* is the key factor that translates the physiological experience into healing. Focusing through ritual is embedded in all sacred traditions throughout history. The forms vary widely, some are simple, some are very elaborate, and some are carefully-guarded secrets.

According to the ancient tradition of Ayurveda, all creation rises from primordial vibrations or sounds of nature within an unseen universal field where matter and energy are united. However, there is an element with an infinite frequency that complements every specific vibration, from the subtle to the gross, that some call Bliss. This is accomplished by training the nervous system to alter its functioning through breathing techniques, movement, and listening to rhythms. The impulses that eventually diversify into a manifest form—such as a seed or a person—originate in this state of unity known in the Ayurveda tradition as *samhita*. Bliss, ecstasy, and trance are the attainment of a state of liberation from the senses, temporarily emptying the vessel for what we might call reprogramming or recharging. By the same process, healing occurs when the mind and body are reconnected, or rather, when the memory of the connectedness is restored, when the individual body regains the cosmic body. It is Bliss that is the messenger. The psyche put into motion begins to heal itself. Movement releases emotions that are blocked, long-buried, and forgotten. The dance draws on energies not accessible by other means, and when such emotions are released and expressed, healing begins.

When I experienced the pure qualities of dance in my life, I had no way of knowing what it meant or that it happened to other people. Now I know that it was no coincidence that the overwhelming health problems I was experiencing at the time preceded a transformation precipitated and aided by dance. Years later, I came to understand that it is all part of the process. In many traditions, to become a medium, a person must be called by the spirit through a direct disturbance in her life. This could include a serious illness or near-death experience; a major upheaval within a family, relationship, or career; or the loss of a loved one. It does not always have to be a traumatic experience, however. A gradual awakening can come about as we learn to comprehend the meanings of natural life changes such as reaching menopause, watching our grown-up children leaving home, and observing ourselves growing into our own power as vanity drops and ego subsides.

The aim and focus is to surrender one's personality or ego sense and become receptive to a higher power. The significance lies in how one reconnects to the universal power source through the repetition of movement and rhythm. Dances of exorcism are aimed at ridding the participant of a negative spirit, which is actually far more likely to be our own negative attitude. (The word "spirit" could be seen as another way of dealing with what we would now call blocked energy patterns, psychological problems, or our "dark side," but not the totality of our self.)

In the healing process, dance aims to heal—filling the now empty-vessel—thus becoming a balanced exchange of energy. For example, if you are depressed and dancing lifts the depression (which it inevitably will), you have also been filled with another energy: peace, calmness, even joy. Like acupuncture, it releases the blocked energy so that it is available to be drawn upon. Because modern, urban people have such minimal energy exchange with the natural environment and with other people, we have become "disrhythmic," out of sync, the rhythmic flow is blocked, the sense of order and harmony is missing. The effect of dance is to reconnect with one's center, that spark of light within. It is unfortunate that we in the West are missing the trained guide—the priestess—to guide us through our transformations.

It is also possible to access expanded states of consciousness, described as ecstatic, transcendent, or cosmic, through meditation, yoga, breathwork, chanting, prayer, and movement. By contrast, contracted states of consciousness result from addictions, eating disorders, workaholism, violence, sexual compulsions, and excessive consumption.

Our modern, western culture has become so control-oriented that we have forgotten what it is like to allow life to move us, to "Let go and Let God." We are so busy identifying, finding solutions, and accomplishing goals that we have forgotten that there may be another agenda operating on a larger scale. We try so hard to fit our lives into the boxes we ourselves create, forcing the natural channels of energy in our bodies and our manifested lives into channels too narrow and straight to fit.

To achieve ecstasy is not to escape; one needs to be conscious to experience the Divine. Consciousness is more than just a chemical phenomenon in the brain; there is a vast difference between dance ecstasy and "tripping out" on drugs, which can actually develop into paranoia or psychosis. In traditional societies where herbs may sometimes be used, there is a knowledge, discipline, and guidance that is lacking in our society.

Transcendental Dance in Traditional Cultures

Possession or transcendental dances have been known to almost every culture that has existed. It may be done alone or with others, and generally is for one's own release, or maybe to cure a particular illness. Drugs are not needed to induce trance, nor are masks employed to hide the identity of the participants. The dance relies on rhythms, clapping, breathing, and physical movement to achieve transcendence. Such forms of dance are not merely a free form or an explosive release. Though they may sometimes seem to be wild or irrational in our perception, their significance lies in how one reconnects to the universal power source through the repetition of the ritual. Healing involves the total group and as the group heals, so too does each individual, through the disciplined ceremony of the collective.

There is a healing dance in Egypt which has attracted the attention of historians, anthropologists, dance researchers, etymologists, reformers, and governmental bureaucrats. It is called the *Zar*, which means circle. (*Tsar* means leader of the circle.) The women's *Zar* is both a dance and a private ceremony. It is unknown where this dance came from or how and when it came to Egypt. Ceremonies similar to the *Zar* can be found in many places in Africa, including Tunisia (called *Stambali*) and Nigeria, as well as amongst the Christian Ethiopians and the Azande of Sudan.

The *Zar* has also been practiced in Morocco, Yemen, Turkey, Saudi Arabia, and southern Iran. Wherever it originated, there are two things that are clear: it emanates from ancient times, prior to the advent of the Judaic-Christian-Moslem religions and it is a woman's healing ritual. Briefly described, the *Zar* rituals include dance, invocations or prayers, incense, and incantations. The ceremony may last from one to several days. Quite often the patient asks for the ceremony because she feels she has developed a troubling malady caused by an "evil spirit." In today's psychological terms, we would probably call her depressed.

With drums and musical instruments, the *sheika* or *shayka* (priestess), also known as the *kodia*, will lead the patient or participant in a dance. When the patient is able to identify the spirit (which is sometimes helped by the wearing of different costumes), it is drawn into dialogue. Perfume or incense provides an ambience that is soothing to the participants as well as the spirit. The purpose of the ritual is not to "cast out" but to reconcile the patient with the visiting or "possessing" spirit through supplication and placation. The use of repetition and the constant crescendo of both music and movements create a hypnotic effect on both the dancer and spectator. The dancer's movements synchronize with the drumbeats. Shuffling and stomping, perhaps a hopping step on either foot done in combination with a step-slide, either forward, to the side, backwards, or whirling, they steadily increase in intensity. Arch-and-contractions of the ribcage and/or abdomen seemingly take hold of the dancer. Kneeling, the head and shoulders loosely hanging forward, the participant may create a larger arch and contraction involving the entire upper torso, bending from the waist, letting the head hang forward loosely and then slinging it from side to side in a semi-circle or a circle.

As the dancer becomes more intense, or as a guest indicates reaction to a song, the *kodia* and her assistants stand directly over her, drumming and singing, encouraging maximum participation in the dance, intensifying the charged, festive atmosphere, and assuring the success of the *Zar*. Eventually the dancer collapses in a trance and is later revived. In a safe atmosphere of supportive women and through the disciplined, focused ceremony of the group, there is a healing of both the individual and the group.

Unfortunately, the *Zar* has suffered from a bad reputation. The women of the *Zar* were labeled *magzoub* in Arabic. The meaning is similar to what the Greeks would call *maenads* or "mad women." The medical professions labeled the women as neurotic. Theologians, of course, condemned it as akin to devil worship or worse. Islam has felt a certain embarrassment about the whole affair and governments have tried for several hundred years to suppress or outlaw it. Still, it persists underground and in the privacy of homes.

Psychiatrists, sociologists and anthropologists have studied the different aspects of trance inducement from their own specialized perspectives. While the purpose of movements such as whirling, called *gurri*, is ostensibly to induce complete exhaustion or catharsis, our Western verbiage may interject erroneous meanings here. It is more likely that the result is to confuse the linear mind long enough to "unplug" the stream of consciousness that overtakes all of us from time to time… to empty the mind, the vessel, and bring peace.

The first time I saw a *Zar,* I had a feeling I'd seen something like it before. It took me some time to recall just where and when. Although nowhere as elaborate or ceremonious, still I was reminded of my childhood encounters with Pentecostal church services. I had no way of knowing that what I was witnessing then was a link connecting me to ancient expressions of dances from other countries.

Like Arabic and African music, gospel singing is alive, and it is more than just something to hear. It impels response and participation. The gospel service is theater. In this atmosphere, there is total involvement and surrender, a good example of the "supportive audience." In the gospel service there is no passive listening; as the ear hears, the body must move.

The Pentecostal belief is based on the Bible's account of the Pentecost, when the Holy Spirit settled on the heads of the faithful and everyone present was filled with the Holy Spirit and began speaking "with other tongues," definitely the stuff of trance. Cretans, who have been identified with transcendental dance, were said to have been at the feast of Pentecost. St. Peter prophesied additional ecstatic happenings, "On that day, the Spirit will be poured out on all flesh and your sons and your daughters shall prophesy."[128] It is not insignificant that the words "and daughters" appear here indicating the presence of female prophets in the early days of Christianity.

Old Testament prophets were oracles who did ecstatic dancing. In biblical images, the Spirit can be the power that emanates from God, or it is depicted as a member of the Trinity, the Holy Spirit. The living spirit connotes images of breath, wind, invisible power, and action, the Greek *pneuma*. As in the Goddess religion, it was often represented as a bird in flight, a dove, as well as flames—all feminine images.

The way the spirit becomes manifest on earth is to "work" through people. The work, or service, is seen in the word, "liturgy" from the Greek *leitourgia,* translated as work or service for the people, and for the spirit, forming a reciprocal relationship between community and spirit. One of the ways the presence of spirit is expressed is through communal prayer, invocation, music, and movement.

Many other cultural traditions practice ecstatic dance rituals. For example, the Berbers, the original inhabitants of Morocco, practice a dance called the *guedra,* its name deriving from the drum used for the cadence of the beat (the heartbeat rhythm). The aim of the *guedra* is to envelop all present with good energy, peace, and spiritual love.[129] For the Chleuh people, this is a solo dance performed by a woman, while women and men, arranged in a circle, chant and sing, clapping their hands to the *guedra* rhythm. The main focus of the dance is the hypnotic hand and finger movements, whose meanings have significance.[130] Chants and hand claps aid the dancer in attaining the trance state. The claps are similar to Flamenco in being counter to the drumbeats (ahead of or off-beat). Longer chants are used at the beginning while the dance ends with the sharper, shorter chants, the tempo remaining constant. Drummer and chanter synchronize with the dancer to change at the appropriate moment and in unison.[131]

Toward the end, the dancer bends backward until her head touches the ground and then slowly straightens up. Arching and contracting of the chest, swaying the head in a semi-circle to the cadence, her hair freed, its many long plaits whipping around her face as the controlled intensity of the drums, clapping, and calls of encouragement from the audience rise to a crescendo. As the rhythm intensifies, the dancer grows increasingly animated. In exhilaration, she throws all of her remaining energy into a final effort, which brings on an ecstatic state as the dancer collapses to the ground. The use of repetition of rhythm patterns, vocals, hand clapping from the audience, and movements all create a hypnotic effect on the spectators as well as the dancer, gradually hypnotizing them into participation of their own. Leaning forward, they follow similar motions quite involuntarily along with the dancer.

What all these dances have in common is the swinging of the head from side to side and around in a circle, arch and contraction of the torso, centering on the energies flowing along the spine and clearing this powerful pathway. Unfortunately, most of what we know about dance we call trance or possession is limited because it comes to us from outsiders. Inquiry into the practice is most often motivated by external interests. A few outsiders, though, have been motivated by the desire for deeper understanding.

Unfortunately, some onlookers and historians have mislabeled women in trance dancing as "orgiastic," implying sexual misconduct, which is nothing more than ignorance or misunderstanding at the least, and at the most, it is gross propaganda. A specific example of this misperception would be in the dance of the *guedra*. The dancer begins on her knees, completely covered with one or two black veils. She slowly and progressively emerges as she extends her arms forward.[132] This unveiling is often erroneously interpreted by Western writers as a strip tease.

Like the kundalini energy rising up the spine, the breathing and arching movements of ecstatic dance could be seen as an "ethereal orgasm." As explained by one modern-day participant in an African American congregation, "You don't lose control of your mind, you are aware of what is happening, but you are suddenly not in control. When the spirit comes in, it takes over, and you can't stop dancing until it releases you."

The Old Testament tells of similar rituals in the Israelite spiritual community. Saul, the first king, was also initiated in this manner. The prophet Samuel anointed him saying, "You will meet a band of prophets coming down the hill playing a psaltery, a timbrel, a flute, and a harp, and prophesying as they come. At that time, the Spirit of the Lord will come mightily upon you and you will prophesy with them and you will feel and act like a different person. From that time on, your decisions should be based on whatever seems best under the circumstances, for the Lord will guide you."[133]

Contrary to its black-magic reputation, the deeply pluralistic religion of voodoo is about healing, aimed at the relations between peoples, between the living and the spirits, the visible and the unseen worlds, not on individuals or their acts. The spirits become available to the participant through the priestess' possession-performances. Her role as *chwal* (horse or carrier of the spirits) is understood as a passive one. Extensive training is needed to learn how to summon the spirits, how to enter trance, and thus surrender ego control to the spirits more easily, and how to prevent trance when necessary. One advanced priestess explained that she corresponds with the Spirits, or powers of the universe, by way of body movement, just as one corresponds through language by moving one's hand with pen on paper. She corresponds with the movement of her feet—how high she steps, and in what direction, forms the language.

Healing Dance and the Modern World

Our bodies carry within a history of all of our life experiences and our responses to those experiences. Our bodies also have the power to reveal, express, and heal. From my own experience with depression, I found that rhythm and dance have a vitalizing effect. Physical movement somehow enhances the emotions and magnifies the flow of life. The brain also releases endorphins, which give a natural high and energize certain immune cells. Writing for the *American Journal of Dance Therapy*, Guindy & Schmais talk about participating and observing a *Zar* in Cairo. In recommending that dance/

movement therapists in the hospital setting could benefit from the type of healing process available in the *Zar*, they say,

> When we examine the **Zar** and other healing dances, we find there is much to learn from this ancient approach to healing. By stimulating the auditory, visual, olfactory, taste, as well as the kinesthetic sense, the **Zar** provides a multi-sensory experience for its participants. These sensory inputs in a familiar context are retained by the body/mind memory and create a sense of continuity for the individual and the group. By adapting rituals and practices from earlier cultures, such as the **Zar**, dance/movement therapy can become a more effective and inspiring experience.[134]

Dance is a powerful tool; it has profound implications for healing, psychotherapy, spiritual growth, and the full unfolding of human potential. When you can "Let go and let life," the natural flow of energy dances you, opens up the channels of the body to clear away old emotional blockages and outdated belief systems and memories that the body has held onto long after their usefulness. We must allow life to dance us again.

• • • •

IRIS J. STEWART has taught dance and lectured on women's subjects for over twenty years. She is the author of *Sacred Woman, Sacred Dance: Awakening Spirituality through Movement and Ritual* (Rochester, Vermont: Inner Traditions, 2000). Ms. Stewart lives in North Bay in the San Francisco Bay Area. Her website address is *www.sacreddancer.com*.

SM
2010

Notes

———

CHAPTER 1 - **Johanna Leseho**

1 Anahata Iradah, *The Gods have Meant That I Should Dance,* "Eternal Ecstasy of Being," Whidbey Island, WA, USA: The Sound Trap CD 8637.

2 Gabrielle Roth, *Dances of Ecstasy.* West Long Branch, NJ: Kultur Films Inc. Audio/visual recording, 2003.

3 Miriam Greenspan, *Healing Through the Dark Emotions: The Wisdom of Grief, Fear and Despair* (Boston: Shambhala, 2004), xiii.

4 Ibid., xii.

5 Marion Woodman, *The Owl was a Baker's Daughter: Obesity, Anorexia Nervosa and the Repressed Feminine* (Toronto: Inner City, 1980).

6 Mary Ann Matoon, *Jungian Psychology in Perspective* (New York: Free Press, 1981).

7 Wikipedia. http://en.wikipedia.org/wiki/Dances_of_Universal_Peace. 10 June 2008.

8 David G. Benner, *Psychotherapy and the Spiritual Quest* (Grand Rapids, MI: Bakeron, 1988).

9 Stanley Krippner, and Patrick Welch, *Spiritual Dimensions of Healing* (New York: Irvington, 1992.), 6.

10 David Elkins, "On Being Spiritual Without Necessarily Being Religious," *Association for Humanistic Psychology Perspective* (1990): 4.

11 Elaine Hopkins, et al., *Working with Groups on Spiritual Themes: Structured Exercises in Healing,* Vol. 2. (Duluth, Minnesota: Whole Person, 1995), 4.

12 Donald R. Dyer, *Jung's Thoughts on God: Religious Depths of the Psyche* (York Beach, Main: Nicolas-Hays, 2000), xi-xii.

CHAPTER 2 - **Jolie Pate**

13 Steve Christiansen. *Magnesium,* Video. (Northampton, MA: Videoda/Contact collaborations, Inc. 1972).

CHAPTER 3 - **Bonney Meyer**

14 Lydia was not my student. She is the college friend of Chelsea, Andraya, and Karina, who created the documentary on belly dance. Her mother encouraged her to belly dance when she was a teenager.

CHAPTER 4 - **Kathryn Mihelick**

15 Reverend Father Robert VerEecke, "Shall We Dance?" (*America,* March 2002): 13.

16 Ibid., 14.

17 Herbert Benson, MD, *Timeless Healing: The Power and Biology of Belief* (New York: Scribner, 1996), 287, 305.

18 Anthony DeMello, *Sadhana: A Way to God* (New York: Doubleday Religious Publishing Group, 1984), 16, 40.

19   Matthew 13:33
20   Isaiah 11:1-10
21   Lois A. Cheney, *God is No Fool* (New York: Abingdon Press, 1969), 64-65.
22   Psalm 150:4

CHAPTER 6 - **Sharon Took-Zozaya**
23   Sharon Took-Zozaya, *Intimate Distance*, unpublished data.
24   Wilder Penfield, *The Mystery of the Mind: A Critical Study of Consciousness and the Human Brain*, (Princeton UP, 1975).

CHAPTER 7 - **Opeyemi Parham**
25   Gabrielle Roth, *Maps to Ecstasy: A Healing Journey for the Untamed Spirit*, 2nd ed. (Novato, CA: New World Library, 1998).
26   Hans Christian Andersen, "The Red Shoes," in *The Complete Hans Christian Andersen Fairy Tales*, ed. Lily Owens, (New York, NY: Gramercy, 1993), 450-453.

CHAPTER 9 - **Rhavina Schertenleib**
27   Maria Alba Santos, *Avoz Does Quatro Elementos* (Ed Kalango, 2008), 55.
28   Terra Mirim Statute
29   Gabriel Carrington, "Corpos del Fuego," *Revista Performce, Cultura e Espetacularidade* (2000): 72-73.
30   *Candomble* is an Afro-Brazilian religion based on the cult of the Orixa, deities related to nature's forces and phenomena.

CHAPTER 10 - **Barbara Waterfall**
31   Barbara Waterfall, "Native Peoples and Child Welfare Practices: Implicating Social Work Education," in *Canadian Social Policy: Issues and Perspectives*, 4th ed., ed. Anne Westhues, (Waterloo, ON: Wilfrid Laurier Press, 2006.), 223-244.
32   Leilani Holmes, "Heart Knowledge, Blood Memory, and the Voice of the Land: Implications of Research Among Hawaiian Elders," in *Indigenous Knowledges in Global Contexts: Multiple Readings of Our World*, ed. George J. S. Dei, Budd L. Hall, and Dorothy G. Rosenberg (Toronto: University of Toronto Press, 2000). 37-53.
33   See Taiaiake Alfred, *Wasase: Indigenous Pathways to Action and Freedom* (Toronto: Broadview Press, 2005), 20.
34   James Maffie, "In the end, we have the Gatling gun, and they have not: Future Prospects of Indigenous Knowledges," *Futures* 41, no. 1 (2009): 53.
35   George J.S. Dei, "Towards an Anti-Racist Discursive Framework," in *Power, Knowledge and Anti-Racism Education: A Critical Reader*, ed. George J. S. Dei and Agnes Calliste, chapter 2 (Halifax, NS: Fernwood, 2000): 23-24.
36   Georg J.S. Dei, *Schooling and Education in Africa: The Case of Ghana* (Trenton, NJ: Africa World Press, 2004): 260.
37   George J. S. Dei, and Asgharzadeh Asgharzadeh, "The Power of Social Theory: The Anti-Colonial Discursive Framework," *Journal of Educational Thought* 35, no. 3 (2001): 300-301; Barbara Waterfall, "Native Peoples and Child Welfare Practices: Implicating Social Work Education," in *Canadian Social Policy: Issues and Perspectives*, 4th ed., ed. Anne Westhues, (Waterloo, ON: Wilfrid Laurier Press, 2006), 223-244.
38   George J.S. Dei, Budd L. Hall, and Dorothy G. Rosenburg, eds., *Indigenous Knowledges in Global Contexts: Multiple Readings of Our World* (Toronto: University of Toronto Press, 2000), 6.

39   Marie Battiste, "You Can't be the Doctor if you're the Colonial Disease," in *Teaching as Activism: Equity Meets Environmentalism*, ed. Peggy Tripp and Linda Muzzin, (Montreal: McGill-Queen's University Press, 2005), 121-133, at 132.

40   Wub-E-Ke-Niew, *We have the Right to Exist: A Translation of Aboriginal Indigenous Thought – The First Book Ever Published from an Anishinahbaeojibway Perspective* (New York: Black Thistle Press, 1995), 1-6.

41   It is noted that this author employs his Anishnabe name, Wub-e-ke-niew, and as such does not have a first and last name.

42   Royal Commission on Aboriginal Peoples, "Looking Forward Looking Back," *Report of the Royal Commission on Aboriginal Peoples* (Ottawa: Ministry of Supply and Services Canada, 1996), 148.

43   Carol Schaefer, *Grandmothers Counsel the World: Women Elders Offer Their Vision of Our Planet* (Boston: Trumpeter Books, 2006), 7.

44   Robert Antone, Diane Miller, and Brian Myers, *The Power Within People: A Community Organizing Perspective* (Deseronto, ON: Peace Tree Technologies, 1986), 23.

45   Paula Gunn Allen, *Off the Reservation: Reflections on Boundary-busting, Border Crossing, Loose Cannons* (Boston: Beacon Press, 1998), 42.

46   Oh Shinnah Fast Wolf, "Odyssey of a Warrior Woman," in *Profiles in Wisdom: Native Elders Speak About the Earth,* ed. Steven McFadden, (Santa Fe, NM: Bear & Company, 1991), 144-164, at 162.

47   I respectfully acknowledge other spiritual activities that are taking place around the world today which are also greatly assisting the earth and her elemental forces.

48   Ibid.

49   William Commanda, "Seven Prophet, Seven Fires," in *Profiles in Wisdom: Native Elders Speak About the Earth*, ed. Steven McFadden, (Santa Fe, NM: Bear & Company, 1991), 37-47, at 46.

50   Edward Benton-Benai, *The Mishomis Book: The Voice of the Ojibway* (Hayward, WI: Indian Country Communications, 1988), 93.

51   Schaefer, *Grandmothers Counsel*

52   Stan Louttit, and Elaine Keillor, "Dancing of the Anishnaabe: Traditional Dances," *http://nativedance.ca/index.php/Anishnaabe/Traditional_Dances*, 1-4 (accessed January 14, 2009), 1.

53   Ibid.

54   Royal Commission on Aboriginal Peoples, "Looking Forward Looking Back," *Report of the Royal Commission on Aboriginal Peoples* (Ottawa: Ministry of Supply and Services Canada, 1996), 291-293.

55   Stan Louttit, and Elaine Keillor. "Dancing of the Anishnaabe: Traditional Dances." at http://nativedance.ca/index.php/Anishnaabe/Traditional_Dances, 1-4 (accessed January 14, 2009), 1.

56   Howard Adams, *Tortured People: The Politics of Colonization* (Penticton, BC: Theytus, 1999), 53.

57   Taiaiake Alfred, *Wasase: Indigenous Pathways to Action and Freedom* (Toronto: Broadview, 2005), 24.

58   Eduardo D. Duran, Bonnie Duran, Maria Yellow Horse-Brave Heart, and Susan Yellow Horse-Davis, "Healing the American Indian Soul Wound," in *International Handbook of Multigenerational Legacies of Trauma*, ed. by Yael Daniel, (New York: Plenum Press, 1998), 350-351.

59   The piercing ritual is a very misunderstood practice by many outside observers, as it can appear to constitute as mutilation, invoking much physical pain. Yet, this is far from the

truth. From an Anishnabec standpoint, there is no greater commitment that you can give the Creator than to offer a piece of your own flesh. In many Anishnabec Sun Dances, the dancers have an opportunity to be physically pierced and tied to the Tree of Life, thereby adding to the power of the prayer requests being offered. While it can appear to an outsider that this is a very painful process, in reality, this ritual is virtually painless. If approached in an appropriately humble and respectful way, this practice can open up the Sun Dancer to mystical experiences, where one is oblivious to the physical realm.

60   The sweat lodge, also referred to as a purification lodge, is a place to pray. The sweat lodge is an enclosed space, similar to a sauna where water is poured over hot rocks. Participants pray in the sweat lodge for their People and for their own healing.

61   Anne Bishop, *Becoming an Ally: Breaking the Cycle of Oppression* (Halifax, NS: Fernwood, 2002), 111.

62   Linda McQuaig, *It's the Crude, Dude: War, Big Oil and the Fight for the Planet* (Toronto: Doubleday Canada, 2005), 41.

CHAPTER 11 - **Laura Shannon**

63   Women's worship in ancient Greece typically incorporated ritual dance and song, along with libation and offering. See Kaltsas, Nikolaos and Shapiro, Alan, eds. *Worshiping Women: Ritual and Reality in Classical Athens* (New York and Athens: Onassis Foundation, 2008); Lillian B. Lawler, *The Dance in Ancient Greece* (Middletown, CT: Wesleyan University Press, 1964); Marianne Parca and Angeliki Tzanetou, eds. *Finding Persephone: Women's Rituals in the Ancient Mediterranean* (Bloomington, Indiana: Indiana University Press, 2007); Joan Breton Connelly, *Portrait of a Priestess: Women and Ritual in Ancient Greece* (Princeton, NJ: Princeton University Press, 2007).

64   Yosef Garfinkel, *Dancing at the Dawn of Agriculture* (Austin: University of Texas Press, 2003).

65   Layne Redmond, *When the Drummers Were Women: A Spiritual History of Rhythm* (New York: Three Rivers Press, 1997). For links between ancient and contemporary Balkan dance forms, see Dora Stratou, *The Greek Dances: Our Living Link With Antiquity* (Athens: Dora Stratou Dance Theatre, 1966); also Maria-Gabriele Wosien, *Griechenland Tanz und Mythos* (Kindhausen, Switzerland: Metanoia Verlag, 2004).

66   Marija Gimbutas, *The Language of the Goddess* (San Francisco: HarperCollins, 1989). See also idem in *The Civilization of the Goddess*, ed. Joan Marler (San Francisco: HarperCollins, 1991).

67   For maps of Old Europe, see Gimbutas, *The Goddesses and Gods of Old Europe: Myths and Cult Images* (Berkeley, CA: University of California Press,1982), 16-35. I first explored the connection between circle dances and goddess artifacts found in the Balkans in Laura Shannon, 'Dances of the Great Mother: Three-Measure Dances and the Tree of Life', *A Great Circle Internet Journal of Sacred/ Circle Dance*, 1999.

68   Gimbutas, *The Goddesses and Gods of Old Europe*, 152.

69   "Why Women Need the Goddess," in Carol P. Christ and Judith Plaskow, eds., *Womanspirit Rising: A Feminist Reader on Religion* (San Francisco: Harper & Row, 1979), 273-287.

70   Circle dancing has been part of every culture in a vast area covering Europe and the Near East, from Russia in the north, south to the Levant and North Africa, east to Iran and India, and in Western and Northern Europe as far as Brittany, Scandinavia and the Faeroe Islands. The dances in my repertoire come from Central and Eastern Europe, Asia Minor and the Caucasus, specifically the southern Balkan countries of Bulgaria, Macedonia, Albania and Greece, as well as Armenia, Turkey and Kurdistan. I have been fortunate to travel to these places and witness their dance traditions on many research trips since the late 1980s. There are also many dances, such as *karsilamas, mandilatos, syngathistos,*

rachenitsa, and tsifteteli, which are danced in free form without a handhold, but my focus in this chapter is on women's dances in circle or open circle formation.

71 Mercia MacDermott, *Bulgarian Folk Customs* (London: Jessica Kingsley Publishers,1988) on the rain rituals of 'Gherman' and 'Peperouda'.

72 In this chapter, I refer to village traditions mainly in the present tense. Folk costume remained in general use in many parts of the Balkans up until WWII, and can still be seen, along with related customs, in isolated spots such as the Greek island of Karpathos, or on occasion in rural places such as Pentalofos where organisations of local residents aim to keep their heritage alive.

73 Mirella Decheva, *Gypsy / Roma Dress in Bulgaria* (Sofia: Roma Culture Initiative/Open Society Institute, 2004).

74 Riane Eisler, *The Chalice and the Blade: Our History, Our Future* (San Francisco: Harper & Row, 1988); Carol Lee Flinders, *Rebalancing the World: Why Women Belong and Men Compete and How to Restore the Ancient Equilibrium* (New York: HarperCollins, 2002), 71; Gimbutas, *The Goddesses and Gods*, 9. I find it of particular interest that Gimbutas describes Old European culture as 'art-loving' and Indo-European culture as 'indifferent to art.' Marija Gimbutas, "Women and Culture in Goddess-Oriented Old Europe" in Judith Plaskow and Carol P. Christ, eds., *Weaving the Visions* (San Francisco: Harper & Row, 1989), 63.

75 See Maria-Gabriele Wosien, Bernhard Wosien: *Der Weg Des Tänzers.* (Linz: Veritas, 1988); Wosien, *Sakraler Tanz: Der Reigen im Jahreskreis.* (Munich: Koesel, 1993). The term 'Sacred Dance' is not connected with the Sacred Dance Guild founded by Ruth St Denis in 1956, nor with the Liturgical Dance movement connected with church groups in the USA and UK. This way of dancing has spread all over the world where it is also known as circle dance or sacred circle dance. It is still used in the Findhorn community as a means to encourage group connection and awareness; I trained there as a facilitator of Sacred Dance with Anna Barton and others beginning in 1987. I also trained in Dance Movement Therapy with Dr Marcia B Leventhal and others, in Authentic Movement with Janet Adler, and with the ecstatic dancer Zuleikha, who taught me to approach indigenous dance forms as doorways to the wisdom of the earth. These experiences, together with many years of practicing yoga, qi gong and other body-based mindfulness practices, served to deepen my love and understanding of traditional circle dances.

76 Laura Shannon, "Meine Initiation in die Welt der Frauentänze," *Kreise Ziehen* 4/03 (Germany, 2003).

77 Lubow Wolynetz, *Rushnyky, Ukrainian Ritual Cloths* (New York: Ukrainian Museum catalog, 1981), quoted in Mary B. Kelly, *Goddess Embroideries of the Balkan Lands and the Greek Islands* (McLean, NY: StudioBooks, 1999), 159. See also Kelly in Linda Welters, *Folk Dress in Europe* and *Anatolia: Beliefs About Protection and Fertility* (Oxford, UK; New York: Berg, 1999), 161.

78 Anna Ilieva and Anna Shturbanova, "Some Zoomorphic Images in Bulgarian Women's Ritual Dances in the Context of Old European Symbolism," *From the Realm of the Ancestors: An Anthology in Honor of Marija Gimbutas,* ed. Joan Marler (Manchester, CT, USA: Knowledge, Ideas & Trends, Inc., 1997), 309-321.

79 Inayat Khan, Hazrat, *The Sufi Message: The Unity of Religious Ideals,* (New Delhi: Mortilal Banarsidass, 2003), 213-221.

80 Jean Shinoda Bolen, *The Millionth Circle: How to Change Ourselves and the World* (Boston: Conari Press, 1999), 7.

81 Marion Woodman, *Conscious Femininity, Interviews with Marion Woodman* (Toronto: Inner City Books, 1993), 37.

82 In dances such as Govand, Issos and Syrtos, for example.

83   Marija Gimbutas, *The Language of the Goddess*, and *The Goddesses and Gods of Old Europe*, 112-131. In keeping with its connotations of flowing water, the zigzag features most prominently in ancient art from the driest areas of the southern Balkans.

84   Goddess figures with typical symbolic decorations date back to the 7th millennium BCE in the Vinca culture of Old Europe and at Catal Huyuk in Anatolia, and the 5th millennium BCE in the Cucuteni culture of what is now Romania, as well as in Mesopotamia, Egypt and Crete. See Gimbutas, *Language of the Goddess*, and *The Goddesses and Gods of Old Europe*.

85   Patricia Williams in Linda Welters, *Folk Dress in Europe*.

86   Elizabeth Wayland Barber, *Women's Work, The First 20,000 Years: Women, Cloth and Society in Early Times* (New York: W. W. Norton & Co, 1994) for a discussion of research methods in the absence of tangible artifacts.

87   Carol P. Christ, *Laughter of Aphrodite*. (New York: Harper & Row, 1987). See also Flinders, *Rebalancing the World*.

88   Cloth does not survive the passage of time as other artifacts do. Extant examples of Neolithic string skirts date back only to the 2nd millennium BCE, but the same garments, which were worn to both emphasize and protect women's life force and fertility, have been found carved or painted on goddess figures going back at least 20,000 years. Red-dyed Neolithic string skirts survive to this day as essential components of many Eastern European women's folk costumes, in long red fringes on aprons and sash ends, sometimes worked in techniques known to have been used in the Bronze Age. See Wayland Barber, 56, 63.

89   Gimbutas, *The Goddesses and Gods of Old Europe*, 186. See also Buffie Johnson, *Lady of the Beasts: Ancient Images of the Goddess and Her Sacred Animals* (San Francisco: Harper & Row, 1988).

90   Angeliki Hatzimichali, *The Greek Folk Costume vol. 2*. (Athens: Melissa Publishing & Benaki Museum, 1984), 342.

91   Masha Zavialova, "A Homespun Life: Textiles of Old Russia." (Minneapolis, Minnesota: TMORA The Museum of Russian Art), 2010.

92   Kelly, *Goddess Embroideries of the Balkan Lands*, and Linda Welters, "Gilding the Lily: Dress and Women's Reproductive Role in the Greek Village, 1850-1950" in Welters, *Folk Dress*, 93.

93   Mary B. Kelly, *Goddess Embroideries of Eastern Europe* (Winona, MN, USA: StudioBooks, 1989) idem, *Goddess Embroideries of the Balkan lands*. Further examples may be found in Helene Cincebeaux, *Treasures of Slovakia* (New York: StudioBooks, 1996); Sheila Paine, *Embroidered Textiles*. (London: Rizzoli International Publications, 1990); Hatzimichali, *Greek Folk Costume* and many other resources.

94   James Mellaart, *Çatal Hüyük: A Neolithic Town in Anatolia* (London: Thames and Hudson, 1967).

95   In, for example, Sarakatsani women's sleeve ends from Thessaly and Thrace, and Chiprovtsi carpets from Bulgaria.

96   Kelly, (*Goddess Embroideries of the Balkan Lands*, 166). In the 21st century, the Birth Goddess image is still in use. Magdalena Stoyanova Karzhanova in Panagyurishte, Bulgaria, the last weaver in a town famous in Ottoman times for its weavers, features it in her woven carpets, one of which (with the ancient design of dancing goddesses in the *horo* pattern) appears in Iris J. Stewart, *Sacred Woman, Sacred Dance: Awakening Spirituality Through Movement and Ritual* (Rochester, VT: Inner Traditions, 2000).

97   Christ, 1987, *Laughter of Aphrodite*, 167.

98   Williams in Welters, *Folk Dress in Europe*, Gimbutas, 1982, *Gods and Goddesses*.

99   Gimbutas, 1982, *Gods and Goddesses*, 9.

100 Paine, *Embroidered Textiles*, quoted by Kelly in Welters, *Gods and Goddesses*, 160.

101 Stewart, *Sacred Woman*, 38.

102 Kelly in Welters, *Gods and Goddesses*,164; MacDermott, *Bulgarian Folk Customs*, 161.

103 These traditions view the sun as feminine, an embodiment of the Goddess as source of life, indicating a pre-Indo-European derivation of this body of folk symbols. See Lucy Goodison, *Death, Women and the Sun: Symbolism of Regeneration in Early Aegean Religion*. Bulletin Supplement 53 (Institute of Classical Studies: London, 1989) and Janet McCrickard, *Eclipse of the Sun: An Investigation into Sun and Moon Myths* (Glastonbury: Gothic Image Publications, 1990).

104 See Gimbutas in Plaskow and Christ, *Weaving the Visions*. Many thanks to Carol P. Christ for fruitful conversation on the theme of women's leadership in dance vs. hierarchical, male-dominated systems of meditation.

105 Martha Forsyth and Linka Gekova Gergova, *Listen, Daughter, and Remember Well* (Sofia: St Kliment Ohridski University Press, 1996).

106 See, for example, the dances Mairam Govand from Armenia, Meryem Ana from Turkey and the many Greek dance-songs such as 'Yiala' and 'O Sigane mou potame' which appeal to the *Panayia*, the Virgin Mary (lit. 'All-Holy').

107 I call such songs 'earth hymns' and believe they may be remnants of ancient song or poetic texts, such as the Homeric Hymn to Demeter and the poetry of Sappho, which lovingly honour the earth as a Goddess. They commonly accompany simple ritual dances such as Govand, Issos or Syrtos, for example.

108 The Tree of Life is also a universal symbol found all over the world. See Roger Cook, *The Tree of Life* (London: Thames & Hudson, 1974). For textile images see Paine, *Embroidered Textiles*, Kelly, *Goddess Embroideries of Eastern Europe*, and Kelly, *Goddess Embroideries of the Balkan Lands*.

109 MacDermott, *Bulgarian Folk Customs*.

110 Woodman, *Conscious Femininity*, 87.

111 Variations on this simple sequence (step, step, step, lift, step, lift) appear in every place where these dances are still alive. By far the most popular dance form throughout Eastern Europe and the Near East – it is the national dance in Bulgaria (Pravo Horo), Macedonia (Pravo Oro) and Albania (Valle) – it has many names and forms, and is particularly common on ritual occasions. In my original interpretation, the three measures of the dance pattern correspond to the three elements of the Tree of Life in its basic form: the two steps going forward are equivalent to the central trunk of the Tree, growing upwards, and the two steps mirrored to either side resemble the two symmetrical branches of the Tree. See Laura Shannon, 'Simple Dances: Where do they come from, where do they lead?,' in Judy King, ed., *The Dancing Circle*, vol. 3 (Winchester, England: Sarsen Press, 2001), 43-50. Also Laura Shannon, 1999, "Dances of the Great Mother."

112 Folk dancer and mathematician Bob Liebman has shown that three-measure dances ordinarily make up approximately 50% of the dances performed in Macedonian villages; when the dancing serves a ritual purpose, however, for instance at an engagement, wedding, or seasonal festival, the proportion of three-measure dances in the celebration rises to more than 80%. Robert Liebman, "*Dancing Bears and Purple Transformations: the Structure of Dance in the Balkans*," (Ph.D. Diss, 1992). In my own research, I have observed a similar increase in the proportion of Tree of Life images on ritual clothing such as wedding costumes.

113 Beginning in the period 4500-2500 BCE, Indo-European culture began replacing ancient Goddesses with male deities; in the early Christian period, for instance under the 4th-century reign of Roman Emperor Theodosius I, many Greek temples were destroyed or

converted into churches. I suggest that the women's dance circle, wherever it appears, can serve as an invisible and portable place of worship where familiar rituals can take place even when the sites once provided for them may no longer be accessed or no longer exist.

114 Louann Brizendine, *The Female Brain* (New York: Broadway Books, 2006), 122.

115 Giacomo Rizzolatti, Leonardo Fogassi and Vittorio Gallese "Mirror Neurons," *Scientific American* (November 2006), 56-61.

116 Woodman, ibid, 73.

117 Laura Shannon, "Living Ritual Dance for Women: Journey out of Ancient Times." *American Dance Therapy Association 27th Annual Proceedings* (Columbia, Maryland 1992).

118 I owe the development of this distinction between objective and subjective in my way of working to my seven-year training in Authentic Movement with Janet Adler, and its focus on differentiating, without interpretation, the perceptions of mover and witness.

119 In my research trips to Balkan villages, I seek out the older women whenever I can. Those in their 60s and 70s today were raised by mothers and grandmothers who had learned in their girlhood things they expected to pass on forever to future generations; they did not foresee that their way of life would vanish so quickly and this wisdom would lose its value so completely in the modern world. The rhythms of work and rest they learned from their elders are exactly the rhythms lost in the frantic pace of modern women's lives, and something we can still learn from the older women while they are still with us.

120 Barbara Ehrenreich, *Dancing in the Streets: A History of Collective Joy* (New York: Metropolitan Books, 2007).

CHAPTER 13 - **Māhealani Uchiyama**

121 Traditional 'Olelo No'eau Hawaiian wisdom saying. Hawaiian proverbs are sayings handed down from the ancestors through oral tradition to offer wisdom and appreciation for the natural world around us. Many of those included in this chapter were gathered and translated by Mary Kawena Puku'i. Her collection, "Olelo No'eau" is published by the Bishop Museum.

122 An important rule in hula.

123 Wisdom saying meaning, "Take the time to enjoy the beauty all around you. Be at peace with the world."

124 Kumu Edith Kanaka'ole. "E Ho Mai." Kamehameha Scholars. http://apps.ksbe.edu/kscholars/oli/ehomai.

125 Wisdom saying meaning, "Having a positive and humbling attitude will bring positive results."

126 Wisdom saying meaning, "Never give up. Believe you can make a difference."

127 Wisdom saying meaning, "Listen to your dreams. Look for signs in nature. Connect with the spirit world."

CHAPTER 15 - **Iris J. Stewart**

128 Acts 2:11

129 I.M. Lewis, *Ecstatic Religion*, (London: Routledge, 1989).

130 Carolina Varga Dinicu, "Dance as community identity among selected Berber nations of Morocco," (Joint conference of the Congress on Research in Dance and The Society of Dance History Scholars, New York City, June 11, 1993).

131 Ibrahim Farrah, "Dance Encyclopedia: The Guedra," *Arabesque Magazine,* July/August, 1978.

132 El Masri, "The Zar: A Psychological Anthropological Study," *Arabesque Magazine*, 1975.

133   1 Samuel 10:5-7

134   Howaida El Guindy and Claire Schmais, "The Zar: An Ancient Dance of Healing,"
       American Journal of Dance Therapy, Fall/Winter 1994.

Bibliography

—

CHAPTER 1 - Johanna Leseho

Benner, David, G. *Psychotherapy and the Spiritual Quest.* Grand Rapids, MI: Bakeron, 1988.

Dyer, Donald R. *Jung's Thoughts on God: Religious Depths of the Psyche.* York Beach, Main: Nicolas-Hays, 2000.

Elkins, David. "On Being Spiritual Without Necessarily Being Religious." *Association for Humanistic Psychology Perspective* (June 1990): 4-5.

Greenspan, Miriam. *Healing through the Dark Emotions: The Wisdom of Grief, Fear and Despair.* Boston: Shambhala, 2004.

Krippner, Stanley and Patrick Welch, *Spiritual Dimensions of Healing.* New York: Irvington, 1992.

Hopkins, Elaine, Zo Woods, Russell Kelley, Katrina Bentley & James Murphy. *Working with Groups on Spiritual Themes: Structured Exercises in Healing,* Vol. 2. Duluth, Minnesota: Whole Person, 1995.

Mattoon, Mary Ann. *Jungian Psychology in Perspective.* New York: Free Press, 1981.

Richards, Mary Caroline. *Centering in Pottery, Poetry and the Person.* Middletown, Connecticut: Wesleyan UP, 1989.

Roth, Gabrielle. *Dances of Ecstasy,* West Long Branch, NJ: Kultur Films, Inc. 2003. Audio/visual recording, 4 hours.

Weinman, J., M. Ebrecht, S. Scott, J. Walburn, & M. Dyson. "Enhanced Wound Healing after Emotional Disclosure Intervention." *British Journal of Health Psychology* 13.1 (2008): 95-102.

Wikipedia: The Free Encyclopedia. http://en.wikipedia.org/wiki/Dances_of_Universal_Peace. 10 June 2008.

Woodman, Marion. *The Owl was a Baker's Daughter: Obesity, Anorexia Nervosa and the Repressed Feminine.* Toronto, Canada: Inner City, 1980.

CHAPTER 2 - Jolie Pate

Christiansen, Steve. *Magnesium,* Video. Northampton, MA: Videoda/Contact Collaborations, Inc. 1972.

CHAPTER 4 - Kathryn Mihelick

Benson, Herbert. *Timeless Healing: The Power and Biology of Belief.* New York: Scribner, 1996.

Cheney, Lois A. *God is No Fool.* New York: Abingdon Press, 1969.

DeMello, Anthony. *Sadhana: A Way to God.* New York: Doubleday Religious Publishing Group, 1984.

VerEecke, Reverend Father Robert. "Shall We Dance?" *America* (2002): 13.

CHAPTER 6 - Sharon Took-Zozaya

Penfield, Wilder. *The Mystery of the Mind: A Critical Study of Consciousness and the Human Brain.* Princeton: Princeton University Press, 1975.

CHAPTER 7 - **Opeyemi Parham**
Anderson, Hans Christian. "The Red Shoes." in *The Complete Hans Christian Andersen Fairy Tales*, edited by Lily Owens, 450-453. New York, NY: Gramercy, 1993.
Roth, Gabrielle. *Maps to Ecstasy: A Healing Journey for the Untamed Spirit.* Novato, CA: New World Library, 1998.

CHAPTER 9 - **Rhavina Schertenleib**
Biao, Armindo (Org.) Anais do V colóquio Internacional de Etnocenologia. PPGAC. 2007.
Carrington, Gabriel. "Corpos del Fuego." *Revista Performce, Cultura e Espetacularidade* (2000): 72-73.
Chaves, Virgínia M. Rocha. "DANÇA: uma estratégia para revelação e reelaboração do corpo." Dissertação para obtenção do título de Mestre. Programa de Pós-Graduação em Artes-Cênicas da Universidade Federal da Bahia. PPGAC-UFBA. Salvador, 2002.
Cohen, Renato. "Xamanismo e Performace." *Revista Repertório,* ano 4 nö 5 2201.
Damasio, Antonio. "O Mistério da Consciência. ED. Companhia das Letras." 1999.
Damasio, Antonio. "O Erro de Descartes: emoção razão e o cérebro humano." Portugal: Companhia das Letras, 1996.
Fernandes, Reis (orgs.). "Estudos en Movimento 2: Corpo, Criação e Análise." Cadernos do Jipe-Cit. PPGAC, 2008.
Freire, Paulo. "Pedagogia da Autonomia." ED. Paz e Terra, 1996.
Katz, Helena. "A dança é um pensamento do Corpo." FID, Ed. Helena Katz, 2005.
Lewis, Samuel. *Foundation Dances and Walks: Dances of Universal Peace.* Peace Works International, 2001.
Morin, E. A, Cabeça Bem-Feita. *Repensar a Reforma, Reformar o Pensamento.* Rio de Janeiro: Bertrand Brasil, 2000.
Santos, Maria Alba. *A Voz dos Quatro Elementos.* ed. Kalango, 2008.
Santos, Severiano, Joseh: "Limites da Modernidade: Atualidade do Saber/Fazer tradicional." Dissertação para obtenção do título de mestre. Programa de Pós – Graduação da Universidade Federal do Rio de Janeiro em março de 2000.
Zabala, Antonio. "A prática Educativa-Como ensinar." Porto Alegre, ed. Artmed.

CHAPTER 10 - **Barbara Waterfall**
Adams, Howard. *Tortured People: The Politics of Colonization.* Penticton, BC: Theytus, 1999.
Alfred, Taiaiake. *Wasase: Indigenous Pathways to Action and Freedom.* Toronto: Broadview Press, 2005.
Allen, Paula Gunn. *Off the Reservation: Reflections on Boundary-busting, Border Crossing, Loose Cannons.* Boston: Beacon Press, 1998.
Antone, Robert, Diane Miller, and Brian Myers. *The Power Within People: A Community Organizing Perspective.* Deseronto, ON: Peace Tree Technologies, 1986.
Battiste, Marie. "You can't be the doctor if you're the colonial disease," in *Teaching as Activism: Equity Meets Environmentalism*, edited by Peggy Tripp and Linda Muzzin, 121-133. Montreal: McGill-Queen's University Press, 2005.
Benton-Benai, Edward. *The Mishomis Book: The Voice of the Ojibway.* Hayward, WI: Indian Country Communications, 1988.
Bishop, Anne. *Becoming an Ally: Breaking the Cycle of Oppression.* Halifax, NS: Fernwood, 2002.
Commanda, William. "Seven Prophet, Seven Fires," in *Profiles in Wisdom: Native Elders Speak About the Earth*, edited by Steven McFadden, 34-47. Santa Fe, NM: Bear & Company, 1991.
Dei, George J. S. *Schooling and Education in Africa: The Case of Ghana.* Trenton, NJ: Africa World Press, 2004.
Dei, George J. S. "Towards an Anti-Racist Discursive Framework," in *Power, Knowledge and Anti-Racism Education: A Critical Reader*, edited by George J. S. Dei and Agnes Calliste, chapter 2. Halifax, NS: Fernwood, 2000.

Dei, George J. S., and Asgharzadeh Asgharzadeh. "The Power of Social Theory: The Anti-Colonial Discursive Framework." *Journal of Educational Thought* 35, no. 3 (2001): 297-323.

Dei, George J. S., Budd L. Hall, and Dorothy G. Rosenburg, eds. *Indigenous Knowledges in Global Contexts: Multiple Readings of Our World.* Toronto: University of Toronto Press, 2000.

Duran, Eduardo. D., Bonnie Duran, Maria Yellow Horse-Brave Heart, and Susan Yellow Horse-Davis. "Healing the American Indian Soul Wound," in *International Handbook of Multigenerational Legacies of Trauma*, edited by Yael Daniel, 341-354. New York: Plenum Press, 1998.

Fast Wolf, Oh Shinnah. "Odyssey of a Warrior Woman," in *Profiles in Wisdom: Native Elders Speak About the Earth*, edited by Steven McFadden, 144-164. Santa Fe, NM: Bear & Company, 1991.

Holmes, Leilani. "Heart Knowledge, Blood Memory, and the Voice of the Land: Implications of Research Among Hawaiian Elders," in *Indigenous Knowledges in Global Contexts: Multiple Readings of Our World*, edited by George J. S. Dei, Budd L. Hall, and Dorothy G. Rosenberg, 37-53. Toronto: University of Toronto Press, 2000.

Louttit, Stan, and Elaine Keillor. "Dancing of the Anishnaabe: Traditional Dances." http://nativedance.ca/index.php/Anishnaabe/Traditional_Dances, 1-4 (accessed January 14, 2009).

Maffie, James. "In the end, we have the Gatling gun, and they have not: Future Prospects of Indigenous Knowledges." *Futures* 41, no. 1 (2009): 53-65.

McQuaig, Linda. *It's the Crude, Dude: War, Big Oil and the Fight for the Planet.* Toronto: Doubleday Canada, 2005.

Royal Commission on Aboriginal Peoples. "Looking Forward Looking Back." *Report of the Royal Commission on Aboriginal Peoples.* Ottawa: Ministry of Supply and Services Canada, 1996.

Schaefer, Carol. *Grandmothers Counsel the World: Women Elders Offer Their Vision of our Planet.* Boston: Trumpeter Books, 2006.

Waterfall, Barbara. "Native Peoples and Child Welfare Practices: Implicating Social Work Education," in *Canadian Social Policy: Issues and Perspectives.* 4th ed., edited by Anne Westhues, 223-244. Waterloo, ON: Wilfrid Laurier Press, 2006.

Waterfall, Barbara. "Reclaiming Identity: Native Wombmyn's Reflections on Womb-based Knowledges and Spirituality," in *Back to the Drawing Board: African Canadian Women and Feminisms*, edited by Nnoki N. Wane, Katerina Deliovsky, and Erica Lawson, 292-308. Toronto: Sumach Press, 2002.

Wub-E-Ke-Niew. *We have the Right to Exist: A Translation of Aboriginal Indigenous Thought – The First Book Ever Published from an Anishinahbaeojibway Perspective.* New York: Black Thistle Press, 1995.

CHAPTER 11 - **Laura Shannon**

Bolen, Jean Shinoda. *The Millionth Circle: How to Change Ourselves and the World.* Boston: Conari Press, 1999.

Brizendine, Louann. *The Female Brain.* New York: Broadway Books, 2006.

Christ, Carol P. *Laughter of Aphrodite.* New York: Harper & Row, 1987.

Christ, Carol P. "Why Women Need the Goddess" in Carol P. Christ and Judith Plaskow, eds., *Womenspirit Rising: A Feminist Reader on Religion* (San Francisco: Harper & Row, 1979).

Cincebeaux, Helene. *Treasures of Slovakia.* New York: Studio Books, 1996.

Connelly, Joan Breton. *Portrait of a Priestess: Women and Ritual in Ancient Greece.* Princeton, NJ: Princeton University Press, 2007.

Cook, Roger. *The Tree of Life.* London: Thames & Hudson, 1974.

Decheva, Mirella. *Gypsy / Roma dress in Bulgaria.* Sofia: Roma Culture Initiative/Open Society Institute, 2004.

Ehrenreich, Barbara. *Dancing in the Streets: A History of Collective Joy.* New York: Metropolitan Books, 2007.

Eisler, Riane. *The Chalice and the Blade: Our History, Our Future.* San Francisco: Harper & Row, 1988.

Flinders, Carol Lee. *Rebalancing the World: Why Women Belong and Men Compete and How to Restore the Ancient Equilibrium.* New York: HarperCollins, 2002.

Forsyth, Martha and Linka Gekova Gergova. *Listen, Daughter, and Remember Well*. Sofia: St Kliment Ohridski University Press, 1996.

Garfinkel, Yosef. *Dancing at the Dawn of Agriculture*. Austin: University of Texas Press, 2003.

Gimbutas, Marija *The Goddesses and Gods of Old Europe: Myths and Cult Images*. Berkeley, CA: University of California Press, 1982.

——. *The Language of the Goddess*. San Francisco: HarperCollins, 1989.

——. "Women and Culture in Goddess-Oriented Old Europe" in Judith Plaskow and Carol P. Christ, eds., *Weaving the Visions* (San Francisco: Harper & Row, 1989.

Gimbutas, Marija, ed. Joan Marler. *The Civilization of the Goddess*. San Francisco: HarperCollins, 1991.

Goodison, Lucy. *Death, Women and the Sun: Symbolism of Regeneration in Early Aegean Religion*. Bulletin Supplement 53. London: Institute of Classical Studies, 1989.

Hatzimichali, Angeliki. *The Greek Folk Costume vol. 2*. Athens: Melissa Publishing & Benaki Museum, 1984.

Ilieva, Anna and Anna Shturbanova. "Some Zoomorphic Images in Bulgarian Women's Ritual Dances in the Context of Old European Symbolism." *From the Realm of the Ancestors: An Anthology in Honor of Marija Gimbutas*, ed. Joan Marler. Manchester, CT, USA: Knowledge, Ideas & Trends, Inc., 1997.

Inayat Khan, Hazrat. *The Sufi Message: The Unity of Religious Ideals*. New Delhi: Motilan Banarsidass, 2003.

Johnson, Buffie. *Lady of the Beasts: Ancient Images of the Goddess and Her Sacred Animals*. San Francisco: Harper & Row, 1988.

Johnson, Susan. *A Homespun Life: Textiles of Old Russia*. Minneapolis, Minnesota: TMORA (The Museum of Russian Art), no date.

Kaltsas, Nikolaos and Alan Shapiro, eds. *Worshiping Women: Ritual and Reality in Classical Athens*. New York and Athens: Onassis Foundation, 2008.

Kelly, Mary B. *Goddess Embroideries of Eastern Europe*. Winona, MN, USA: StudioBooks, 1989.

——. *Goddess Embroideries of the Balkan Lands and the Greek Islands*. McLean, NY: StudioBooks, 1999.

Lawler, Lillian B. *The Dance in Ancient Greece*. Middletown, CT: Wesleyan University Press, 1964.

MacDermott, Mercia. *Bulgarian Folk Customs*. London: Jessica Kingsley Publishers, 1988.

McCrickard, Janet. *Eclipse of the Sun: An Investigation into Sun and Moon Myths*. Glastonbury: Gothic Image Publications, 1990.

Mellaart, James. *Çatal Hüyük: A Neolithic Town in Anatolia*. London: Thames and Hudson, 1967.

Paine, Sheila. *Embroidered Textiles*. London: Rizzoli International Publications, 1990.

Parca, Marianne and Angeliki Tzanetou, eds. *Finding Persephone: Women's Rituals in the Ancient Mediterranean*. Bloomington, Indiana: Indiana University Press, 2007.

Redmond, Layne. *When the Drummers Were Women: A Spiritual History of Rhythm*. New York: Three Rivers Press, 1997.

Rizzolatti, Giacomo, Leonardo Fogassi and Vittorio Gallese. "Mirror Neurons." *Scientific American*, (November 2006): 56-61.

Shannon, Laura. "Dances of the Great Mother: Three-Measure Dances and the Tree of Life," *A Great Circle Internet Journal of Sacred/ Circle Dance*, 1999.

——. "Living Ritual Dance for Women: Journey out of Ancient Times." Columbia, Maryland: American Dance Therapy Association 27th Annual Proceedings, 1992.

——. "Meine Initiation in die Welt der Frauentänze," *Kreise Ziehen Heft* 4/03. Germany, 2003.

——. "Simple Dances: Where do they come from, where do they lead?" in King, Judy (ed.) *The Dancing Circle* vol. 3. Winchester, England: Sarsen Press, 2001.

Stewart, Iris J. *Sacred Woman, Sacred Dance: Awakening Spirituality Through Movement and Ritual*. Rochester, VT: Inner Traditions, 2000.

Stratou, Dora. *The Greek Dances: Our Living Link With Antiquity*. Athens: Dora Stratou Dance Theatre, 1966.

Wayland Barber, Elizabeth. *Women's Work, The First 20,000 Years: Women, Cloth and Society in Early Times.* New York: W. W. Norton & Co, 1994.

Welters, Linda. "Gilding the Lily: Dress and Women's Reproductive Role in the Greek Village, 1850-1950." in idem, *Folk Dress in Europe and Anatolia: Beliefs About Protection and Fertility.* Oxford, UK; New York: Berg, 1999.

Williams, Patricia and Linda Welters. *Folk Dress in Europe and Anatolia: Beliefs About Protection and Fertility.* Oxford, UK; New York: Berg, 1999.

Wolynetz, Lubow. *Rushnyky, Ukrainian Ritual Cloths.* New York: Ukrainian Museum catalog, 1981, quoted in Kelly, Mary B. *Goddess Embroideries of the Balkan Lands and the Greek Islands.* McLean, NY: StudioBooks, 1999.

Woodman, Marion. *Conscious Femininity, Interviews with Marion Woodman.* Toronto: Inner City Books, 1993.

Wosien, Maria-Gabriele. *Bernhard Wosien: Der Weg Des Tänzers.* Linz: Veritas, 1988.

——. *Griechenland Tanz und Mythos.* Kindhausen, Switzerland: Metanoia Verlag, 2004.

——. *Sakraler Tanz: Der Reigen im Jahreskreis.* Munich: Koesel, 1993.

CHAPTER 15 - Iris J. Stewart

Dinicu, Carolina Varga. "Dance as community identity among selected Berber nations of Morocco: From the ethereal and sublime to the erotic and sexual." Joint conference of The Congress on Research in Dance and The Society of Dance History Scholars, New York City, June 11, 1993.

El Guindy, Howaida, and Claire Schmais. "The Zar: An Ancient Dance of Healing." *American Journal of Dance Therapy* (Fall/Winter 1994).

El Masri, F. "The Zar: A Psychological Anthropological Study." *Arabesque Magazine* (1975).

Farrah, Ibrahim. "Dance Encyclopedia: The Guedra." *Arabesque Magazine* (July/August 1978).

Lewis, I.M. *Ecstatic Religion.* London: Rutledge, 1989.

Thanks

—

The Authors wish to thank the following for the use of pictures:

Bartholomaei, Dieter	p.156
DiBartolomeo, Steve	p. 83, 90
Elbing, André	p. 183, 192
Froehlich, Thomas	p. 53, 59
Fuerst, Sonja	p. 154
Iradah, Anahata	p. 116, 119
Iraklion Museum, Crete	p. 151
Jain, Manoj	p. 163, 165
Marcus, Jana	p. 92
Muna, RJ	p. 179
Mysore, Dr. Suresh	p. 191
Osgood, Larry	p. 27, 29
Schnetlage, Tom	p. 177
Zeis-Loi, Antje	p. 187

F I N D H O R N   P R E S S

Life Changing Books

For a complete catalogue,
please contact:

Findhorn Press Ltd
117-121 High Street,
Forres IV36 1AB,
Scotland, UK

t +44 (0)1309 690582
f +44 (0)131 777 2711
e info@findhornpress.com

or consult our catalogue online
(with secure order facility) on
www.findhornpress.com

For information on the Findhorn Foundation:
www.findhorn.org